By Cheyenne Campfires

PRIEST SMOKING.

By Cheyenne Campfires

George Bird Grinnell

With Photographs by Elizabeth C. Grinnell

UNIVERSITY OF NEBRASKA PRESS · LINCOLN

International Standard Book Number 0–8032–5746–5

Library of Congress Catalog Card Number 79-158083

First Bison Book printing: October 1971

Bison Book edition published by arrangement with
Yale University Press

Manufactured in the United States of America

FOREWORD

by Omer C. Stewart

GEORGE BIRD GRINNELL might be characterized as an ideal American example of the great gentleman naturalists of Europe of the nineteenth century. Equally at home in the drawing rooms of intellectual Boston and New York and in the teepees of the Cheyenne, he maintained practical business activities concurrently with scientific exploration and, at the same time, kept a dedicated sportsman's enthusiasm for hunting and fishing. His Americanism manifested itself in his popular as well as authoritive writing about Indians, in his nation-wide appeals for public support for wild life conservation, as well as in his work for the establishment of National Parks and National Forests for the pleasure of the general public.

Born in Brooklyn September 20, 1849, Grinnell had the good fortune to be moved as an infant to Audubon Park, which lay between the present 155th Street and 158th Street and Hudson River in New York City. There he was a close neighbor to the widow and sons of the famous naturalist-artist John James Audubon, and there Madame Lucy Audubon conducted a school for small children which Grinnell attended. Close association with the Audubon family seems to have instilled in him a profound interest in bird lore. In 1886, for example, he founded the Audubon Society, and financed and publicized it by his own magazine, *Forest and Stream*.

Grinnell came to own a large portion of the old Audubon

estate and in 1905 aided in the establishment there of the Hispanic Society of America. Later, under his incentive, the headquarters for the American Geographical Society, the American Numismatic Society, and the American Academy of Arts and Letters were built nearby. The history of Audubon Park is contained in a pamphlet published by Grinnell in 1927 for the Hispanic Society.

This ardent naturalist campaigned to protect birds from commercial slaughter for decorations on women's hats, and later became a fighter for conservation of all types of wild life. He was one of a small band of far-sighted men who forecast the droughts, dust storms, and stream pollutions which have later occurred. The development of National Parks he encouraged as game preserves as well as places of scenic beauty. Moreover, he acted upon his conviction, finding the time and energy to be an official for many years in the National Park Association.

Like the great naturalists of Europe of his time—Darwin, von Humboldt, Nordenskiold, and Burton—Grinnell had received a sound academic training. With an A.B. degree from Yale in 1870, he began the exploring expeditions which became almost annual scientific pilgrimages. During his first trip of six months to the "unmapped West," he collected vertebrate fossils under the direction of Professor O. C. Marsh. After establishing himself in business in New York City, he returned to Yale to work as a graduate assistant in osteology in the Peabody Museum while completing his studies and research for the Ph.D. in zoology. His dissertation was entitled "The Osteology of *Geococcyx Californianus* [Road-Runner]."

Although Grinnell was on the staff of Yale University only from 1874 to 1880, he served as a voluntary collector for the Peabody Museum while on many extended expeditions as well as while engaging in personal trips for hunting and study. In 1874 he was naturalist with the General Custer Expedition to the Black Hills; in 1875 he held the same position with the General Ludlow Expedition to Yellowstone Park. In 1899 he was a member of the Harriman Alaska Expedition.

Grinnell wanted to share his love of nature with everyone— his scientific colleagues, interested amateurs, and laymen. The New York Zoological Society and the American Ornithologists Union profited by his enthusiastic support over the decades. The Hispanic Society of America, the Explorers Club, and the Boone and Crockett Club are other societies he joined.

Grinnell's American democratic urge to share as widely as possible his pleasure in the out-of-doors is seen in his long association with the popular sportsmen's weekly *Forest and Stream* (later *Field and Stream*) and in his many articles in other popular magazines. Beginning as natural history editor in 1876, he became president of the Forest and Stream Publishing Company in 1880, a position he held until 1911. From 1892 to 1925 he contributed popular scientific articles to *Scribner's, Harper's, Atlantic, Review of Reviews, Outing, Mentor,* and *Century. Bird-lore* and *Science* published his scholarly papers in natural science.

Grinnell's ability to enjoy close companionship with Indian guides, half-breed canoe men, and fellow hunters while sharing the chores and discomforts of camp life was equaled by his skill in association with the nation's leaders in business and government. He was a close friend of President Theodore Roosevelt and was named to the Honorary Advisory Council of the Roosevelt Wild Life Station when it was established in 1919 under the New York State College of Forestry, in Syracuse. With Grinnell were three members of the Roosevelt family and Gifford Pinchot, Chauncey J. Hamlin, George Shias III, Frank M. Chapman, Viscount Grey, Viscount Bryce, and Sir Harry H. Johnston. In the first number of the *Roosevelt Wild Life Bulletin* (December 1921) there is a portrait of Grinnell, and the foreword is written by him. After expressing his own support of the Wild Life Experimental Station and that of Roosevelt's friends in the Boone and Crockett Club of New York, he wrote:

> The average field-naturalist tends to become a collector of specimens rather than an investigator of the ways of animal life. . . . he neglects the opportunity to observe it in life and to learn something about its habits and its ways. . . . No one more than Theodore Roosevelt appreciated the value of the work done by the field-naturalist.

In the same *Bulletin* Dr. Charles C. Adams, Director of the Field Station, said:

> Dr. George Bird Grinnell, the Nestor of American sportsman-naturalists, and a life-long friend and co-worker of Roosevelt, wrote, May 19, 1919: ". . . Mr. Roosevelt would have felt an interest far keener [in the Wild Life Station] than in the various monuments. . . . My long friendship with Theodore Roosevelt gives me a peculiar interest in this Station on sentimental grounds."

This is the man who developed deep and lasting friendships within the various tribes of Plains Indians, started during his first trip to the West in 1870 and renewed and strengthened by repeated return visits.

Since Grinnell was professionally trained in zoology yet became best known as a newspaperman, businessman, and publicist, it was not improper for him to be linked with George Catlin (1796-1872) and Lewis Henry Morgan (1818-81) as the "Dedicated Amateurs" in the recent volume *The Golden Age of American Anthropology*, edited by Margaret Mead and Ruth L. Bunzel (New York, Braziller, 1960).

Bunzel wrote of Grinnell, in part, as follows:

He knew and loved the prairie when the buffalo ran, before it had been torn up by plows and railroads. He loved the people of the prairie, too. And of all the tribes he knew, it was the Cheyenne he loved best. . . . He first met the Cheyenne, he writes, in 1890, and for the next forty years no summer passed that he did not visit them. After forty years of living with them as friend and brother, he was ready to write of the things he had learned sitting around their campfires. Of all the books written about Indians, none comes closer to their everyday life than Grinnell's classic monograph on the Cheyenne. Reading it, one can smell the buffalo grass and the wood fires, feel the heavy morning dew on the prairie.

Grinnell's thoroughness is especially appreciated today when so many professional ethnographies, based on only a few months' field work, appear thin where his accounts are so rich and strong.

In 1950 Dr. Joseph Jablow, in his Ph.D. thesis "The Cheyenne in Plains Indian Trade Relations 1795-1840," further complimented Grinnell: "The early history of the Cheyenne has been dealt with by Mooney, Dorsey, Will, Clark, and especially Grinnell whose various works on that group make one of the finest tributes ever accorded the American aborigine."

Notwithstanding the sympathetic knowledge apparent in his writings on the Cheyenne, Grinnell had established himself as friend and interpreter of the Indians long before he published his Cheyenne ethnographies. His intimate knowledge of the Blackfoot tribe and his records of their history and folklore resulted in a half-dozen scientific articles in the *American Anthropologist* (Journal of the American Anthropological Association) and in the *Journal of American Folklore,* as well as in two books on Blackfoot oral literature. Of more practical importance for his Blackfoot Indian friends and hunting companions was his appointment in 1895 to the Fort Belknap Blackfoot Treaty Commission to arrange for the purchase at a fair price of surplus Blackfoot lands.

The Pawnee were also early friends of Grinnell, who published a book (417 pages) of their "hero stories" as a commercial venture in 1889 and contributed several articles about the Pawnee to the anthropological journals before 1900.

In many ways Grinnell recorded and then published factual accounts of the lives of the Plains Indians in a manner similar to his natural history descriptions of the ways of water fowl or Plains antelope. He sought to understand, and finally achieved a profound respect for, the game animals and the aborigines who jointly occupied the Plains he loved. He succeeded to a remarkable degree in placing himself, by proxy and imagination, in the role of the Indians. Reliving the lives of the Indians in the stories they told, he was able to report, from an Indian point of view and without personal bias, a great number of historical and mythical events remembered and enjoyed by the Indians themselves.

Being a practical business man as well as a scientist, Grinnell tried in many ways to share with the general public his own sympathy and concern. His popular books, *The Story of the Indians* (1895) and *The Indians of Today* (1900, new editions 1911, 1915, 1921), were designed to make readily available the basic facts about the condition of the Indians, so that popular indignation would facilitate reforms. A visit to the large encampment of the Indian Congress of tribes from all parts of the United States, held in conjunction with the Omaha Exposition of September 1898, stimulated the first edition of *The Indians of Today*. Through this book he hoped to continue and further the mutual respect and understanding initiated at Omaha. The book supplied a complete summary of official statistics about American Indians in addition to other useful information.

After 1890 always foremost in his affection and attention

were the Cheyenne Indians. The Cheyenne had been shamefully massacred by Colonel Chivington and the Colorado Volunteers at Sand Creek, and had been settled in country they disliked in Oklahoma. A part of the tribe had made an epic march to Montana against odds so great it is a wonder a single Northern Cheyenne survived.

After his marriage to Elizabeth Curtis Williams in New York City in 1902, when Grinnell was 53 years old, his wife accompanied him on his annual visits to the Cheyenne and became his official photographer, assisted by Mrs. J. E. Tuell. In the preface to his most comprehensive work, *The Cheyenne Indians, Their History and Ways of Life* (Yale University Press, 1923), Grinnell wrote: "I have never been able to regard the Indian as a mere object for study—a museum specimen. A half-century spent in rubbing shoulders with them during which I have had a share in almost every phase of their old-time life forbids me to think of them except as acquaintances, comrades, and friends."

Usually Grinnell appears to be describing and explaining his friends on the Plains to his acquaintances in New York, and along the eastern seaboard. In most instances, as in the present book, Grinnell lets the Indians speak for themselves. Reading the legends and myths of the Cheyenne in their own words, one becomes more fully immersed in the knowledge, feelings, and values of the people. This was often Grinnell's method.

The life of a Cheyenne youth from infancy to marriage as told in the words of an old Cheyenne is the small volume *When Buffalo Ran,* first printed by the Yale University Press in 1920 and reprinted four times by 1940. This delightful story is further enhanced by Mrs. Grinnell's photographs of Indian children and adults in native costume engaged in homely everyday activities.

Many of Mrs. Grinnell's photographs are in the present volume, showing Indians at work and play in their native environment. In this volume are found folk tales of the Cheyenne, historical events, ethical values, and oral history. Grinnell published the stories as he recorded them, without evaluating or criticizing them on aesthetic or moral grounds. As with the earlier books on the Pawnee and the Blackfoot in which the Indians speak eloquently for themselves, the Cheyenne tell with simple dignity of their wars, of their heroes, and of their relationships with supernatural powers. The value of *By Cheyenne Campfires* resides in its being an anthology of separate, discrete stories about many different subjects, in approximately the form in which they were told during winter months in a Cheyenne teepee.

The journal of the scientific American Anthropological Association published eight of Grinnell's articles on the Cheyenne and the journal of the scholarly American Folklore Society published four of Grinnell's articles on the Cheyenne during the years he was producing commercially the five volumes on the same tribe.

Judging from the excellence of his published materials dealing with the American Indians—a dozen books and two dozen scholarly articles, as well as a dozen popular articles—it is difficult to justify his being classified as an "amateur anthropologist," except on the grounds that he received his graduate degree in something else—zoology—and earned his living as a publisher and as president of Bosworth Machine Company, and that he wrote as many books and articles on hunting, exploring, and frontier life as on anthropology.

He was a specialist in many things: in ethnography, in ornithology, in zoology, in hunting and fishing, in conservation, in publishing, in business, in manufacturing, and in literature—all of which he did with distinction. In 1921 Yale University awarded George Bird Grinnell the honorary degree of Litt.D.,

FOREWORD

and the citation read at that time may serve well as a concise
summary of his life:

> *Assistant in the Peabody Museum in 1874—closely con-*
> *nected with Professor Marsh. George Bird Grinnell has*
> *lived up to his middle name, many of his publications*
> *dealing with fowls of the air. He has been on good terms*
> *with wild animals and wilder men; he is one of the lead-*
> *ing authorities on the North American Indian, being*
> *naturalist with General Custer's expedition to the Black*
> *Hills in 1874. He has written books which have inter-*
> *ested many readers, for his experience and knowledge*
> *are mingled with sympathy and humour. A useful*
> *American.*

BOULDER, COLORADO
JANUARY 1962

Contents

	Page
Foreword by Omer C. Stewart	v
Introduction: The Cheyennes and Their Stories	xix

War Stories

The Medicine Arrows and the Sacred Hat	3
The White Horse	6
The Brave Ree	8
Bear's Foot and Big Foot	10
Rope Earrings' Arrow-Point	13
Many Crow Horses	15
Big Head's Return to Life	21
When the Cheyennes Were Driven	27
Where Medicine Snake Was Pictured	31
Wolf Road, the Runner	34
Lone Wolf's Last War Trips	38
A Storm Eagle	51
Starving and Killing Fat Meat	56
The Prophecy of Bear Man	59
A Hard Warpath	64
The Speech of the Wolves	69
A Fight with the Pawnees	74
White Bull's Scouts	77

Stories of Mystery

Sees in the Night	83
The Buffalo Wife	87
Black Wolf and His Fathers	104
The Bear Helper	115
Sand Crane	121
The Stolen Girl	129
An Eagle's Teaching	131
A War Party of Seven	134
How the Turtle Went to War	136

CONTENTS

Page

The Mouse's Children 138
The Woodpecker's Mother-in-Law 141
The Four Servants 146
The Wolf Helper 149
The Under-Water Man 154
The Little Girl and the Ghost 157
The Turtle Man 161
The Stone Buffalo Horn 167
The Power of Stands in the Timber 171

Hero Myths
Hero Myths 177
Stone and His Uncles 178
Falling Star 182
The Bad Hearted Man 193
The Red Eagles 200
Bow Fast to His Body 206
The Red Duck 211
Makos' Story 216
Possible Sack and Her Brothers 220
Found in the Grass 232

The Earliest Stories
The Very Earliest Stories 241
Creation Tale 242
E hyoph sta 244
The Race 252

Culture Hero Stories
Old Woman's Water and the Buffalo Cap 257
Sweet Medicine and the Arrows 263

Wihio Stories
Tales of Wihio 281
He Loses His Hair 281
Plums in the Water 282
A Medicine Man's Arrows 283
The Woman's Camp 284
Wihio and Coyote 286

CONTENTS

	Page
Where the Mice Danced	291
The Back Scraper	292
The Lost Eyes	294
He Catches Fish	296
A Scabby Bull	298
How He Got Tongue	299
The Turning Stones	301
The Wonderful Sack	302

Illustrations

Priest Smoking	*frontispiece*
Pawnee Warrior Leader	*facing page* 54
A Pause in the March	120
Watching the Return	150
A Sweat Lodge	160
The Sacred Buffalo Skull	160
Woman's Work	182
The Stick Game	248
The Ceremonial Fire	276

THE CHEYENNES AND THEIR STORIES

THE Cheyennes* are a tribe of buffalo-hunting Indians well known in the early days of western travel and settlement on the plains. The tribe belongs to the Algonquian linguistic stock, and is one of three usually spoken of as the western Algonquians, the other two being the Arapahoes and the Blackfeet.

We commonly think of the Indians as mounted nomads following the buffalo over the plains. Yet, since there were no horses in America at the time of the discovery, the Indians were then foot travelers. Many of them lived in permanent settlements, which they left at certain seasons to go on their hunting expeditions to secure the animals which furnished them their flesh food. In those days, when they moved, they carried all their possessions on their backs, except so far as they were helped by the dogs, their only domestic animals. These dogs usually carried small packs on their backs, and also hauled travois on which too loads were placed. The travois was of two poles, the smaller ends of which were tied together over the dog's shoulders. The poles ran back on either side of the dog and dragged on the ground, and on them rested a light load. This was the Indian's cart—his vehicle. When the Indians secured horses they adapted the travois to the larger animal.

The Cheyennes have always cultivated the ground, raising crops of corn, beans, and squash. They also gathered wild fruits and roots, and these vegetables constituted a good portion of their support. They ate most birds and all small animals, and, of course, the large game, also, when they could

* Compare *The Cheyenne Indians*, Yale University Press, New Haven, Conn., 1923.

INTRODUCTION

get it. When they first reached the plains they made foot surrounds of buffalo, and when possible drove the large animals into snowdrifts. The meat not needed for immediate use was preserved by drying.

From among their brave wise men, chiefs were chosen to advise the tribe how it ought to act in cases of doubt or difficulty, and often the orders or instructions of these chiefs were enforced or carried out by "soldiers," who were bands of brave young men organized to act as the police of the camp.

The social life of the people was friendly and agreeable. As a rule, husbands and wives were devoted to one another, and parents loved their children tenderly. The training of the little ones began in infancy, the first lessons being that they should always be good-natured and never quarrel with their fellows.

The skins of the wild animals which they killed for food gave the Cheyennes the material for their clothing. These skins were skillfully tanned so that they were soft, and they were warm and durable. Buffalo skins tanned with the hair on served for warmth and for bedding. It is probable that in early days, when the Cheyennes lived far to the east of their present homes, their movable lodges or tents may have been covered with birch bark, as were those of some of the canoe Indians of the forest, but after they reached the plains the lodge coverings were always of tanned buffalo skin.

Their tools and implements in primitive times were of bone, wood, horn, or stone, and the bones, sinew, and hide of the buffalo furnished much of this equipment.

Like all other people, the Cheyennes had their amusements. The little children played games suited to their years, while those older competed in contests of skill, the boys in wrestling, shooting, the stick game, or throwing arrows, and the girls in games with balls or throwing-sticks over the ice or crusted snow.

INTRODUCTION

The Cheyenne tribe is made up of two closely related groups, the Cheyennes, or Tsistsistas, and the Suhtai—now united into one. In the days of Lewis and Clark these two were separate tribes, but a little later they came together and the Suhtai were gradually absorbed in the Cheyenne. Even the Suhtai dialect—for their speech differed somewhat from that of the Cheyennes—has now been lost.

Lewis and Clark spoke of the Suhtai as Staetan, which, as elsewhere pointed out, was probably a mishearing of the reply of some man who, when asked who he was, replied *Suh tai he-tan*, "I am a Suhtai man." They were referred to by Lewis and Clark as Kites or Kite Indians, from the fact that they were constantly on the move—flying.

The Cheyennes have been traced in a westerly direction from Lake Superior across Minnesota and the Dakotas to the Missouri River, on whose banks they had their villages for a long time. Then, by little groups, they began to move westward until they reached the Black Hills, about which they lived for generations. Many of the Cheyennes were there when Lewis and Clark crossed the continent, but others still lived on the Missouri River. It was while they were living about the Black Hills, and in the first half of the last century, that the Suhtai and the Cheyennes became united to form a single tribe.

In ancient days the Cheyennes lived in permanent houses somewhat like the earth lodges formerly occupied by the Pawnees, the Mandans, and the Arikara. Some of the old village sites with remains of the earth lodge circles have been identified in recent years.

The Cheyennes were a warlike tribe and almost the first lesson taught a growing boy was that he must be brave. He was told that success in war would cause him to be respected and praised by all the people, and was reminded that the most important men of the tribe had reached their distinction through their bravery and triumphs in war. If he wished to become the equal of those men, to be talked about and respected by the people, and at last to become a brave and a chief, he too must display courage and do his best in war. The Indian is eager for the approval and praise of his tribes fellows, and such advice stimulated a boy's ambition and gave him a strong motive to do his best in warlike pursuits. The Cheyennes were brave warriors, and on many occasions made strong and even successful fights against white troops.

In early days, although actively at war with many of their neighbors, the Cheyennes were on friendly terms with the first white people that they met, and it was not until 1856 that, through a misunderstanding, they began depredations on settlers and emigrants. The so-called Sand Creek Massacre in 1864 set on foot an Indian war which, with occasional intermissions, lasted until after the battle on the Little Big Horn in June, 1876, when the Seventh Cavalry was defeated and General Custer was killed. About 1877 a part of the Northern Cheyennes surrendered to General Miles,* and thereafter served effectively as scouts in the wars against the Sioux and those of their own people who still were hostile. The wars practically ended in the year 1880, and since then there has been no trouble with these Indians.

For many years the Cheyennes have been separated into two groups known as Northern and Southern Cheyennes, the latter those in Oklahoma. These are merely two divisions of the same people, and the separation took place less than one hundred years ago. There is nothing permanent about it. Some people go to the south, live there for a few years or a generation, and then come back to the north; or, in some cases, one part of a family may live in the south and another part in the

* *The Fighting Cheyennes*, p. 369, Chas. Scribner's Sons, New York, 1915.

north. In the old days before the coming of the railroads there was frequent passing back and forth between Northern and Southern Cheyennes.

Since the Indians had no books and none of the usual forms of civilized diversions, their entertainment was derived largely from social intercourse, such as conversation, story telling, and speech making. They were great visitors and spent much of their time either in discussing the news of the camp or in talking of the events that had happened in the past.

Since they had no written characters their history was wholly traditional, handed down from one generation to another by word of mouth. The elder, who transmitted these accounts to younger people, solemnly impressed upon his hearers the importance of repeating the story just as it had been told to them.

Story telling was a favorite form of entertainment, and it was a common practice for hosts at feasts to invite some story teller to be a guest, and then, after all had eaten, to relate his stories. Men known as good story tellers were in demand, and were popular. The learning of these stories must have been a fine training for the memory of the young, who were frequently examined by their elders to see how completely they had assimilated the tales so often repeated to them.

Some of the stories were short, others were long, sometimes told in great detail, and even in sections. A short story might be told, and when it was finished the narrator stopped, and, after a pause, said, "I will tie another one to it." Then there was a long pause; the pipe was perhaps lighted and smoked, and a little conversation had; then the story teller began again and told another section of the tale, ending as before. Such stories were often told in groups of four or six, and might last all night. At formal gatherings a man might tell a story and when it was finished might say: "The story is ended. Can anyone tie another to it?" Another man might then relate one, ending it with the same words, and so stories might be told all about the lodge. Or a story might end with the words, "This cuts it off."

Of the tales of the past, those narrating the events of the warpath were perhaps the most popular; by listening to them a fairly clear notion may be had of the methods by which the tribal wars were carried on. Yet mystery, magic, and the performances of doctors and priests—men who possessed spiritual power—had their part, often an important part, in the narratives related by the older men. Sacred stories were told reverently, and with some ceremony. After the people had assembled in the lodge the door was closed and tied down and all sat still; there was no conversation; no one might go in or out; no noise might be made in or near the lodge during the telling of the story, lest the lack of reverence should bring misfortune. These sacred stories were to be told only at night. If related in the daytime the narrator might become hunchbacked.

The oral literature of the Cheyennes is extensive and the tales vary greatly in character. Some of them are well worth listening to, and others seem more or less trivial. Of the older stories there are many variants. Some of the stories contain the same incidents, and it is not easy to separate them into groups. Many are very old, while, on the other hand, some of the war stories deal with matters of but a generation or two ago, and in certain cases the precise year is given.

The stories which the Indians narrate, covering a wide field of subjects, furnish to us concrete examples of their ways of thought. Besides their inherent interest, many of them have a direct relation to the early history of our country, and some tell of events happening on ground now occupied by great numbers of white people.

WAR STORIES

THE MEDICINE ARROWS AND THE
SACRED HAT

IN the different war stories frequent mention is made of the medicine arrows and buffalo hat,* two protective mysteries long possessed and greatly reverenced by the Cheyennes. These were brought to them by the culture heroes of the two tribes, sent by the Great Power to insure to the people health, long life, and abundance in time of peace, and protection, strength, and victory over their enemies in war.

The medicine arrows were brought to the Tsistsistas by Sweet Medicine, and the buffalo hat to the Suhtai by Standing on the Ground. The arrows were four in number, with stone points as in the ancient times, and the sacred hat is a cap or bonnet made of the skin of the buffalo cow's head, ornamented by a pair of buffalo horns shaved down, flattened, and decorated.

The arrows were in charge of a special man, who, when he supposed he was about to die, handed them over to be cared for by some man of his family—his younger brother, or his son, or perhaps his nephew. The arrow keepers were men of wisdom and of power, and were respected advisers in the tribal affairs. In the same way the sacred hat was in charge of a chosen man, from whom it passed on to another, usually a relative, and from him to another.

From time to time occasions arose when it was necessary to renew the arrows, by which was meant taking the four arrows from their bundle, perhaps removing the stone points from the shafts, replacing them with fresh winding of sinew, and putting new feathers on the shafts. There were various reasons for this renewing the arrows; sometimes it was performed as a sacrifice

* For details concerning these sacred objects see *American Anthropologist,* N.S., vol. 12, p. 542, Oct.-Dec., 1910.

or an atonement for a wrong done; sometimes to ward off a feared misfortune; sometimes to end an existing evil; and sometimes as the payment of a vow. Some man must have pledged himself to do this renewing, and it was a difficult and a costly sacrifice to make. If in the camp an individual killed one of his tribesmen by accident or design, the arrows must be renewed. If inspected after such an event the arrows all showed little specks of blood on the heads. Sometimes such marks on the arrows were seen when no one had been killed, and in that case it was thought either that someone was about to be killed, or else that a great sickness threatened the camp.

When the arrows were to be renewed all the divisions of the tribe, which might be scattered out in many different groups and places, were summoned to come into the main camp, and there to remain during the four days that were occupied in the ceremony. All the people were usually glad to come, for they would be benefited by the ceremony, the good influences of which were helpful to all in the camp.

Sometimes, in order to be revenged for injuries inflicted by enemies, the whole tribe, men, women, and children, set off to war, and on such an occasion took with them the medicine arrows and buffalo hat. To insure the success of such a war journey it was necessary that these sacred objects should be treated in a special ceremonial fashion. If not so treated, their protective help was lost. So long as proper reverence was paid to them, and the ceremonies performed which the culture heroes had prescribed, it was believed that these mysteries would protect the tribe from harm.

It was the law that when these two sacred objects were taken to war by the tribe as a whole, a certain ceremony must be performed before the enemy was attacked. Before this, two young men were chosen to carry these things into battle, one to carry the arrows and the other the sacred hat. Before they were given to these men the ceremony which was part of the ritual of these

4

objects was performed. It was intended to confuse and to alarm the enemy. Before the attack was to be made the arrow keeper took in his mouth a bit of the root that is always tied up with the arrows, chewed it fine, and then blew it from his mouth first toward the four points of the compass, and finally toward the enemy. This blowing toward the enemy was believed to make them blind.

After this had been done, the arrow keeper took the arrows in his hand and danced, pointing them toward the enemy and thrusting them forward in time to his dancing. Drawn up in line behind the arrow keeper stood all the men of the tribe, each one standing as the arrow keeper stood, with the left foot forward, dancing as he danced, and making with their lances, arrows, or whatever weapons they might hold, the same motions toward the enemy that the arrow keeper made with the medicine arrows. The arrow keeper thrust the arrows four times in the direction of the enemy, and a fifth time he directed them toward the ground. After he had gone through this ceremony and sung the songs which go with it, the man chosen to carry the arrows into the battle went to the arrow keeper, who tied the bundle of arrows to the young man's lance. He who was to wear the sacred hat took that up from the ground and put it on his head, securing it there by means of a string which passed under his chin. The two men then mounted their specially chosen swift horses and rushed toward the enemy, riding ahead of the line of fighting men. When the two had come close to the enemy, each turned toward the other, and they crossed each other in front of the charging line, and then passed around behind it. This method of riding was supposed to blind, confuse, and frighten the enemy.

All these operations should be performed before any attack was made on the enemy; yet it frequently happened that young men, eager to gain personal glory for themselves, did not wait for these ceremonies to be completed, but stole off to attack the enemy independently. If this attack was made before the ceremonies were completed, the act took away the power of the arrows and of the hat, their spiritual power was neutralized, and the Cheyennes were very likely to be defeated. This explanation seems necessary, in view of various allusions made to the arrows and the hat in the war stories here given.

Long ago, in the year 1830, the Cheyennes and the Skidi Pawnees had a great battle on the head of the South Loup River in Nebraska, and in this battle the Cheyennes lost their medicine arrows, which were captured from them by the Pawnees. At a much later date there was a dispute in the tribe over the guardianship of the sacred hat, and a lack of reverence was shown the object by Broken Dish, who had it in his possession, and by his wife, who removed and kept in her possession one of the horns attached to it. The capture of the arrows by the Pawnees and the failure to treat the sacred hat with respect are supposed to have brought to the Cheyennes many of the misfortunes which came to them in the latter half of the last century.

It is not known that any white man has ever seen the medicine arrows or the complete sacred hat. With the passing of the older generations the importance of these objects has grown much less.

THE WHITE HORSE

A CHEYENNE war party started off against the Crows. This was after the Cheyennes had crossed the Missouri.

Before starting, the chief, he who was to carry the pipe, went to Old Lodge, a medicine man, and asked him to sing and pray for them that night. Old Lodge owned a *hōhk tsĭm'* —a lance with a hoop on it. The leader asked Old Lodge if he would lend him this *hōhk tsĭm'* to take with them. Old Lodge replied that he would let him take it, and added: "At sundown all who are going on the party may come to my lodge. I will sing and call in the spirits." They all went there.

Old Lodge called the spirits, and when he had finished talking with them, he said: "Your party shall take many horses from the Crows. In the herd that you will take there is one horse that is pure white and its tail is cut short. That horse you must bring back to me. You will not know until the next morning which one of you has it in the bunch he has taken, but the man who has it must say, so that all may hear, 'That is your horse, Old Lodge,' and must bring it back to me. It is a very fine horse and the man who has captured it will not like to give it up, but if you should refuse to promise it to me, be careful, for the spirits I have called have given it to me. If you promise that this white horse shall be mine, all will be well and the enemy will not overtake you."

Next morning the war party started, and after traveling many days, stopped near a big creek to eat. While they were eating a large village of Crows camped on the river near by, but below them, so that they did not see the Cheyennes. The war party hid in the stream bottom until the sun went down and at night entered the Crow village and drove off many horses. At daylight next morning, all saw the short-tailed white horse in the herd. Everyone advised the man who had taken this horse to call out "Old Lodge, here is your horse," but it was such a fine-looking animal that the man who had taken it did not want to give it up.

When he refused to offer the horse to Old Lodge, five of the party left the others, wishing to travel by themselves, for they feared that something bad might happen. The party with the white horse traveled all that day and night.

The next day at noon they came to a herd of buffalo, and the leader said to his men, "We are now far enough from the Crows, and we are hungry; let us hunt buffalo and get some meat." All mounted their best horses, and the man who had captured the white horse mounted him to run buffalo on. While they were cutting up the meat, the pursuing Crows saw them and circled out beyond them, so they would suspect nothing. Then the Crows charged and killed every one of them. The Crows drove back their horses and captured the *hōhk tsĭm'*. The five who had left the main party escaped, for they were not seen by the Crows.

When the owner of the lance and the rest of the people in the village had finished mourning for the dead, Old Lodge began to sing in his lodge. He called the spirits, and when they came they told him that the Crow women and children were abusing the lance, and that it wanted to come back to him. He declared that he would call it back.

Old Lodge had it cried through the village that everybody must go to one end of the camp and stand there in a line facing the east. All must go, men, women, and children. They did so and Old Lodge, wearing his robe hair side out, walked up and down the line singing. Soon after he began singing, while all were looking toward the east, they saw coming a little whirlwind of dust. Old Lodge dropped his robe and stood in the path of the whirlwind with his hands stretched out. It came toward him and as it passed he reached out his hands and picked out of it the *hōhk tsĭm'*. All crowded round him to look at it. Many of the feathers were gone, for it had been badly used. Everyone gave something to be used in renewing it, and their offerings were piled around it.

THE BRAVE REE

ABOUT the year 1825 the Cheyennes heard that a party of Mandans and Rees were coming to visit them to make a peace. The news caused much excitement in the Cheyenne camp, and for some time there was a difference of opinion as to what should be done. At last the Cheyennes determined that they would go out and meet the visitors in a friendly manner, and invite them to the camp, and that when they had reached it and were separated, after having been invited to visit at the different lodges, they would fall on them and kill them all.

When the Rees and the Mandans approached the camp, therefore, a large party of Cheyennes met them cordially, and shook hands with them. The visitors were marching on foot, and each Cheyenne motioned to one of them to mount behind him and ride, saying to the Rees and Mandans: "Friends, you must be tired. Get on our horses behind us, and come on to the village, and there we will give you something to eat, and you can rest."

The leader of the approaching party was a Ree—a brave man. He advised his people not to do what the Cheyennes asked. He said: "Do not get on behind these men; keep going on foot. We do not know how they are going to treat us. We will go right straight to their camp; if they want to fight us it will be well for us to be there. They cannot take away their women and children. We will kill many of them if they try to fight us. We do not know what they intend to do."

Not heeding this warning, three of the young men mounted behind three of the Cheyennes, and went on toward the village, which was now in sight. The Ree leader pulled out from his bundle a long strip of red cloth, like a dog rope, ornamented with feathers, and put it over his shoulder, and drew his bow and strung it. All the time he was walking toward the Cheyenne camp.

When the Cheyennes saw that he was going straight to their camp, they tried to get in front of him and stop him, but he kept on. At last one of the Cheyennes came too close to him, and the Ree drew his bow and shot down the Cheyenne's horse, which fell on the rider, breaking his leg. The Ree sprang on the fallen man in an instant, and dashed his brains out with

9

the butt of his gun. Another man ran up to him, and the Ree drew an arrow and shot the Cheyenne through the body, and he fell from his horse. After this the Ree counted coup on the second man, and then shot the horse, which was tied to the rider's belt. The Ree leader would not get on the horse and leave his people.

All the Cheyennes were now frightened, for they saw that these people were brave, and were going straight ahead toward the camp. They set off running to the village, in order to look out for their women and children, and save them. Between the Rees and the Cheyenne village there was a stream, on which timber grew. The Rees and the Mandans stopped in this timber, and were not molested by the Cheyennes. However, the Cheyennes killed those whom they had taken on to the camp on their horses. Later, the Cheyennes made peace with the Rees and Mandans, and then they told each other the story. The Ree told the Cheyennes what he had said, and that it was his purpose to get into the camp and to kill all the people he could.

After this, that Ree was given a Cheyenne name, Red Dog-Rope, *Mă he hsĭt' ū ă mă.*

BEAR'S FOOT AND BIG FOOT

ABOUT 1830 or 1835 Bear's Foot, then a brave, invited three of his special friends to go with him on a war journey. One of these was Big Foot. They decided to go to war against the Utes, and as their purpose was to take horses, they went on foot.

They traveled along for some time, and at length came upon the trail of lodge poles, where a camp had been moving. They followed it. Big Foot said to the others: "We ought not to follow this trail; we ought to travel along off to one side of it. If any of these people should turn back to look for anything they have lost, they may discover us."

"Oh," said Bear's Foot, "if they should come back, there would be only one or two of them, and we are four, and can easily overcome them."

They went on, and that day came to where a camp had been. All the signs were fresh. It seemed as if the Utes must have gone on that same morning. They looked about, and found where the Utes had been cutting up meat to dry it, and here there was still much meat left on the bones, and some pieces that had been thrown away. For several days the party had had hardly anything to eat, and the leader said to Big Foot, who was the youngest of them, "Do you stay here and roast some of this meat for us, and we will go up on that high point and look off over the trail, to see whether we can see anything."

Big Foot went down into the bed of the stream and built a fire and began to roast the meat, while the others went up on the hill to look. Big Foot had roasted some of the meat when suddenly he heard a shot in the direction in which his people had gone, and then another. He gathered up the meat that he had roasted, and put it in a fold of his robe, and started off; not toward the shots where his friends were, but down the stream, keeping in the timber until he had climbed a hill covered with pines, from which he could see his friends fighting the Utes.

The Cheyennes were surrounded, but were fighting bravely. One of them had been killed, and Big Foot, who was so near that he could see all that was going on, saw three Utes carried off dead or badly wounded. At last, the two Cheyennes who were alive made a rush for a little patch of plum bushes, and hid among them. The Utes stayed about them all day, shooting into the brush, but when night fell they returned to their camp.

Then Big Foot left his place and went over to the other hill, and crept near the plum brush, and called out, "Are you yet alive?"

At first Bear's Foot thought that this was a Ute, but when he recognized Big Foot's voice, he called to him, saying: "I am alive, but our friend is dead. He has been shot in the forehead." Big Foot crept into the brush, and there found Bear's Foot and the dead. They were very sorrowful.

Bear's Foot said, "Now our friend will not know of it, and will not be harmed, so I shall take his coat." He took his coat and his ammunition, and the two men went away leaving the dead man there. They returned to the hill where Big Foot had been, and there hid among the pines.

The next morning the Utes returned, and after shooting into the brush, and charging about it, one of them—a brave man— crept into the brush, and at length called out, and all the Utes rushed in. They brought out the Cheyenne and scalped him, and then went back to their camp. The two Cheyennes remained on the hill.

When this day had partly passed, Bear's Foot said to Big Foot: "My friend, I wish we had something to eat. Before this I have not felt like eating, but now I am hungry."

This made Big Foot think of the meat in his robe, and he said, "Friend, I have plenty of food here, that I cooked two days ago; I had forgotten it until now." He took out the meat from his robe, and they ate.

The next night they went on toward the Ute camp. When they reached it, Bear's Foot said to his friend, "Friend, you wait here, and I will go into the camp and see how things are, and perhaps cut loose some horses and bring them back to you here." Big Foot waited.

After a time, Bear's Foot came to him again, leading three horses. "Here, my friend," he said, "is a horse for you; take one of these. I have been all through the camp. All the Ute men are gathered in a big lodge—they are talking about the fight; for as I looked in the lodge I saw a big Roman-nosed Ute say in signs, 'I was the first one to strike the last man that we killed.' Now I am going down there to the camp, and up to that lodge to shoot that man."

"No," said Big Foot, "do not do that; it is dangerous—you may be killed."

"Well," said Bear's Foot, "then I will go into the camp and cut loose all the horses I can, and turn them down the creek, and we will get around them and drive them off."

"That will be good," said Big Foot. Bear's Foot went into the camp and did as he had said, Big Foot remaining outside. the camp and holding the three horses. Bear's Foot cut loose all the horses he could, and drove them down the stream, and when they were out of the camp, he caught one, and, Big Foot joining him, they drove the herd off. This was Big Foot's first war journey. Bear's Foot was a great warrior and had many adventures—many of them with Big Foot.

Big Foot died in 1905, then regarded as the oldest man in the tribe, perhaps ninety-five years of age.

ROPE EARRINGS' ARROW-POINT

LONG, long ago, a war party of about thirty men set out from the Missouri River against the Crows. All were on foot. They had a dog, on which they packed their moccasins. They went north along the foot of the mountains, toward the Crow country.

The leader of the party was Rope Earrings, an oldish man, of forty or fifty years. Tied to his scalp lock he always wore one of the old-time flint arrow-points. Perhaps his dream had told him to wear this; or it may have come down to him from long ago.

They traveled on day after day without seeing enemies until they came to the head of the Rosebud River. There they stopped all night.

At daylight next morning the leader sent one of his young men up on a high hill not far off to see whether he could discover anything. The young man went up on the hill, and saw, a long way off, a man coming toward him. He watched to see which way the man would go, and at last the stranger had come so near to him that the young man could see that he was an enemy. The young man was just about to run down to the camp to tell the leader that an enemy was coming, when the dog, which was loose and had been out on the prairie, ran toward the stranger and began to bark at him. The young man called down to those in camp, "Hurry this way; the dog has barked at an enemy, and he is running away." Just where the dog had barked at him the Crow had dropped his blanket and had run off as fast as he could go. He ran for the hills, and all the Cheyennes ran after him.

Rope Earrings, who wore the stone arrow-point, was a good runner and passed all the others, and got a long way ahead of them, but the enemy also was swift of foot, and the Cheyennes began to grow tired and kept dropping back, far behind.

They followed the enemy for a long time, and at last Rope Earrings, though he was getting near to the Crow, was very tired and stopped. He untied the arrow-point from his head, placed it on the palm of his outstretched hand, and then shut his fingers on it. Then he held his hand up to the sky and sang a song, and motioned with his hand toward the Crow. He made the motion four times, and the fourth time he threw the arrow-point at the Crow, and the Crow fell forward to the ground on his face.

By this time many of the Cheyennes had overtaken Rope Earrings, and they charged on the Crow, came up with him, shot him, and scalped him. Then the old man began to look for his arrow-point and found it. It had gone into the Crow at his backbone, and had passed in between two of the joints and broken his back.

From here they went back to their home, leaving the arrow-point in the Crow's body.

A long time after that, a war party went against the Crows, and it chanced that one of the young men who was sent ahead as a scout was one of those who had been with the party when the Crow was killed by Rope Earrings. This party passed close to where that enemy had been killed, and the young man determined to go to the place to see if the bones were there, and if he could find the arrow-point. When he reached the place he found the white, bleached bones lying on the prairie. The backbone still held together, and when he looked at it he saw the arrow-point, still sticking in the joint. He took the point home and gave it to Rope Earrings.

MANY CROW HORSES

A GOOD many years ago Lame Medicine owned a protective weapon called *hōhk tsĭm'*—a wheel lance. This was the same Lame Medicine who some years afterward—in 1838—was the keeper of the medicine arrows.

One night Lame Medicine dreamed that he went with a war party to the Crow Country on the Big Horn River, and that there they took many Crow horses, and in his dream he carried his *hōhk tsĭm'* with him on his journey. The next morning he called High Wolf to his lodge and told him about his dream. In those days, when a medicine man dreamed anything like this, the people believed that the dream would come true. So when Lame Medicine told his friend, High Wolf, what he had seen in his sleep, High Wolf said to him, "*Ha ho', ha ho'*, thank you, thank you," repeating it twice. Then he said to Lame Medicine, "We will get up a party and start at once—as soon as the moccasins can be made."

High Wolf now went to some of his friends and told them

what Lame Medicine had dreamed, and said that they must make ready to start in a few days. They prepared everything, and before long a party of nine started for the Big Horn River, about which Lame Medicine had had the good dream. High Wolf and Lame Medicine were the leaders of the party and carried the pipes. One night when they stopped, the coyotes came close to their camp and howled. After they had stopped howling, Lame Medicine said to them, *"Ha ho', ha ho'*, thank you, thank you." He did not say what he had heard until High Wolf had filled the pipe and offered it to him to smoke; then he repeated what he had heard, that the coyotes had said that the party was on a good road, and would get many horses.

One day two scouts had been sent ahead to look for Crow signs, and after they had started the other seven also went on, High Wolf and Lame Medicine walking a little ahead. As they were going along, one of those behind called out, "Drop to the ground; a person on horseback is on a hill above us." They all fell to the ground, and from where they lay looked toward the hill and saw there a man riding a horse. The Cheyennes all crept to a hollow near by, and when they had hidden there High Wolf told the others to lie still, and raised his head to take another look. When he had looked, he told his friends that the hill ahead of them was covered with Crows, and when he looked again he said that the Crows had started down toward where they were lying. As the Cheyennes watched the people coming, they could tell that the Crows had not seen them. They were on the way to hunt buffalo. High Wolf told his party to lie close to the ground, and then he spoke to Lame Medicine, saying: "I have always believed you to be a strong medicine man; take pity on our men now and help us, so that the Crows shall not find us. As for me, when I get back to the village, I will wrap about the medicine arrows a fine blanket." Then, speaking to the arrows, he prayed: "Although you are a long way from us, we always believe, O arrows, that you listen

16

when anyone speaks anything toward you. I ask you to make these Crows blind, so that they may not see us." After he had made this prayer he stopped speaking.

As the Crows came toward the party, Lame Medicine crept along the ground a little way ahead of his men, and then he thrust the handle of the *hōhk tsĭm'* in the ground, and rising stood in plain view of the enemy. Then he began to sing a medicine song, using words which should blind the enemies and turn them away from the Cheyennes. The Crows passed near them and crossed the stream below. The Cheyennes could hear them laughing and talking. Lame Medicine continued to sing until all the Crows had gone by. The whole party afterward said that the Crows did not once look toward the place where they were lying.

After the Crows had passed out of sight, High Wolf went up on a high hill to watch them and to see which way they were going. When he had come back, he said that they were going toward herds of buffalo, and the Cheyennes went to a near-by stream and stayed there until the Crows had gone back to the place they had come from. Then the Cheyennes still waited for the return of the two scouts that had been sent out in the morning. Toward evening they were seen coming running, so that the Cheyennes knew they had news—that they had seen something. When they came up they said they had found the Crow village on the Big Horn River, and also had seen the same party of hunters that had passed the Cheyennes.

Now High Wolf and Lame Medicine decided that they should go to some good place to leave their things, and afterward should meet at that place with their horses. The scouts had said that they had seen many horses on both sides of the Big Horn River. They went to the place and left their things. Now the whole party began to make promises that if they returned home successful they would offer certain sacrifices. Some said that they would renew the arrows, and others that they would wrap the buffalo cap with fine blankets, and others still that they would paint white blankets with sacred paint, which the Cheyennes believed came from the same place from which the arrows came.

It was moonlight and they had a good chance to select good herds of horses. That night they did not go in pairs, as was the custom—two men together as partners and helpers, since two together could drive the horses more easily and better in that way. Often it was hard for a single man to drive the horses at night and do it quietly. But this party saw so many horses that all agreed that each one should take horses for himself. High Wolf and Lame Medicine thought that this was best, because there were plenty of horses for everyone, and each man could take as many as he wanted. All the members of this party had before been on horse-taking expeditions. There were no young men who needed advice as to how to take horses.

All agreed to meet and wait at the place where they had left their guns and other things, and where Lame Medicine left his *hōhk tsĭm'* thrust in the ground. They took with them only their bows and arrows, their lariats, and small twisted hair ropes for bridles. The lariats they would drag behind them as they rode, using them like long whips, and driving the herds faster by throwing forward the lariats and snapping them like a whip.

When the Cheyennes returned to their meeting place they found that Crooked Neck had taken the largest and finest bunch of horses of any of the men, but all had secured good horses. When Crooked Neck got back to the place where they had left their things, he did not wait for his party to come up. They found that he had been there and had taken his gun and other things and gone on; but when the others reached the place they waited until all had got there, and then started together. The members of a war party should not separate. All

18

are expected to remain together. If anyone is left behind the other members of the party would be criticised in the camp.

Crooked Neck got into the camp ahead of the others. The reason he gave for not waiting for the others to come up was that he had so many horses that he thought it best to go on; for if he stayed back with the others he might prevent the others from going fast. Crooked Neck said that between Powder River and Tongue River he had come to a lake where he had seen a great turtle standing on the edge of the lake. His horses seemed to fear the turtle, and although they were thirsty would not go near the water. The horses got the scent of this monster turtle and kept away from the water. The people felt that Crooked Neck would not tell a lie. He said that the turtle's back was all overgrown with moss. It must have been very old. Crooked Neck talked to the turtle and asked it to take pity on him, as he was very poor, and to help him with his herd of horses, so that he might get them safely home. He waited until the turtle had gone out of sight in deep water and then rode off after his horses. During the night, while driving his horses, he could still see this monster turtle before him. It is said that after this he made a shield with the turtle painted in the center, and he used to skin the tails of snapping turtles and roll them on his scalp lock. He made a turtle shield for his brother also. He always said that he would not die until his head was cut from his body. In his dream the turtle had given him this power.

The next day after Crooked Neck reached the camp, High Wolf and Lame Medicine came in with the rest of the party. They said that the Crows had followed them, as they could see the dust rising a long way off. They drove fast and always left one member of the party behind to keep a look-out on the back trail. They had agreed what they would do in case the Crows should overtake them. Each man would keep only three horses—the best horses. This would give them a better opportunity to get away, for if anyone found that the, horse he was riding was getting tired, he could change to another and let the tired one go.

After the Cheyennes had reached camp and all had rested, they made the sacrifices as they had pledged themselves. High Wolf took a fine blanket over to the Medicine Arrow Lodge where the arrows were hanging in front of the lodge. He was crying, and carrying in his arms the blanket he had promised. He stood in front of the lodge still crying, and then walked four paces toward the arrows and put the blanket around them. After this was done, he walked into the arrow lodge and smoked with the keeper of the arrows. He thanked the arrows and told their keeper to come over to his lodge with him. After food had been given this man, High Wolf said to him, "When you go home take with you that horse that is tied in front of the lodge." This was one of the Crow horses that High Wolf had taken.

Crooked Neck wrapped a blanket about the buffalo cap, as High Wolf had done with the arrows, wrapping the cap in the blanket. In olden times blankets and other property were given to the arrows, but this has not been done recently to the buffalo cap. It was done, however, among the Northern Cheyennes as lately as 1865.

Among the Cheyennes the buffalo cap was not looked upon as being so great as the medicine arrows, but a long time ago, when the Suhtai owned the hat, they considered it as great as the arrows. High Wolf was a great warrior. He was the man Catlin painted and called Highback Wolf. He met General Harney on the Missouri River when General Harney was a young lieutenant. General Harney told of this in 1867. High Wolf led many war parties and was a leader in the great fight when so many Crow prisoners were taken.* He died the year the stars fell—1833.

* *The Fighting Cheyennes,* p. 22, Chas. Scribner's Sons, New York, 1915.

BIG HEAD'S RETURN TO LIFE

BIG HEAD was the chief man of the Fox Soldiers' Society and a noted warrior. After High Wolf and his party had returned to the camp, Big Head called his friends to come into the lodge and told them that he was envious of High Wolf and Lame Medicine because they had brought in from the Crows so many fine horses, and he wished to start out to war against the Utes and Shoshoni. "And now, my friends," he said, "all of you that wish to go with me, make ready; get your moccasins; get some food and bring all the guns that you can get together, with plenty of powder and balls." In those days they used flintlock guns.

Now the Fox Soldier Society had a bow lance, shaped like a thunder bow. It had a bowstring but was not used as a bow. It was really a short lance and had a long steel head made from the blade of a knife. This bow lance Big Head carried.

Big Head and his party of men started for the mountains, on foot. Little Wolf ("Big Jake"), lately living at Colony, was one of the party. He was then very young, and his brother, Man Above, took him along as a servant. The party followed up the North Platte River to the mountains, and then turned north to Wind River, where they had heard the Shoshoni were camping. When they supposed they were near to the enemies' camp, they began to send out scouts to look for the enemy.

One evening, while they were roasting meat and eating, all at once they heard someone howl like a wolf, close to them. All sprang to their feet and exclaimed, "The scouts are coming." The leaders stood up in line and began to sing, and presently the three scouts came running toward them, and then they stopped and turned sideways, and the leader howled like a wolf. The other two followed him. As they came up, they stopped not far from the line of leaders, and Big Head went forward and took the leading scout by the hand and led him up to where the others were standing. Then he said to him: "Now, my friend, tell us what you have seen. You have come to us running, and we know that it is not for nothing that you came fast, but because you have something good to tell us."

The leader of the scouts was Stone Calf, then a young man. He said to Big Head, "Hand me the pipe." They had already filled the pipe and had it ready, as was the custom at such times, and they passed it to Stone Calf and he smoked, and the other two smoked, and then Stone Calf said to the two: "I want you to listen carefully and see that I tell truly what we have seen. I want you to correct me if I make any mistake, or tell anything that is not true." He turned to Big Head and the others and said: "As we were going along, we saw first the tracks of a horse, fresh, and we followed that a little way and presently the horse stopped and the rider dismounted. The tracks were made either by a Shoshoni or a Ute. The moccasins showed this. Now we ran to the top of a high mountain and looked down on the lower land, and there, in the valley, we saw everywhere people packing their horses with buffalo meat. The Shoshoni had been chasing buffalo and were just leaving the killing ground with their loads of meat. This was in the middle of the day."

Big Head said to the scouts, "Look at the sun, and see the way it stands in the sky now; is the distance too far for us to go there to-day to take horses?" The scouts said: "Yes, it is too far to do anything to-day. It will be better this evening to go a little closer to the enemy, and to send out two more scouts to locate their camp. We do not know just where the camp is. It is possible that these people may have come a long distance to chase buffalo."

"What you say is true," said Big Head; "I had not thought of that. We must find where the camp is situated before going any further." Stone Calf said, "I, for one, will go to look for this camp." Three or four others spoke up and said that they would go with him. Big Head said to Stone Calf, "I am glad that you want to go again; for you know just where to go to find the trail of these people." Stone Calf and two others started again. The other men followed them. Stone Calf told them where they had better stop, and said that he and his scouts would come back and meet them there. Big Head said to these young men: "If you come suddenly upon the camp, do not take any horses; that would spoil this trip. I depend upon you not to alarm these enemies."

Stone Calf and his scouts were gone all night, returning early next morning. They said that they had found a big camp, and the whole party remained hidden in the mountains until toward evening, and then set out for the camp. Stone Calf, because he knew the way to the camp, went ahead, and took them up into the high hills so that they could see the place where the camp was pitched at the foot of the mountain. As they were watching the camp they saw a man riding a white horse. Big Head said, "He is out hunting for deer." There was much talking going on between all the members of the war party.

At length Big Head said it was time to start; that all should get ready and go and take horses, but that they must keep away from the camp while driving off the horses. They must not go into the camp to cut loose the horses in front of the lodges. They all agreed to this and it was understood that they should meet again at this place.

At length everybody had returned with some horses except one man who had not appeared. His name was Walks Out. Pretty soon he came up leading four horses that he had taken from the camp. When the men learned that he had taken these horses from out of the camp, all said: "Now they will know at once that someone is taking horses, and will follow us the first thing in the morning. We must get away from here as fast as

23

we can." They started at once. Walks Out said that he had not found any horses away from the camp, and did not wish to come away without horses.

When they started to drive off their horses, they had a hard time. Some of the horses kept trying to run back; others kept running into the brush and into the timber, and they went but slowly. When day came they were still in the heart of the mountains. The trail that they left was plain, for they had many horses. All knew that before long they would be over- taken by the Shoshoni, and they kept looking back to see if they could see any signs of people following them.

Now when the Shoshoni missed the horses that had been tied in front of the lodges, the ones which Walks Out had taken, they knew that someone was stealing their horses. The horses taken showed that during the day they had been used for hunting buffalo and had come in just at night, for blood stains were seen on their sides, showing that they had been carrying meat to the camp.

The Cheyennes could not see far around them on account of the mountains and hills, but before they had gone very far, and after the sun rose, they could see dust rising behind them. The Shoshoni were coming. The Cheyennes were trying to get to the mountains ahead of the Shoshoni, for they knew that there would be a good place to fight, but when almost at the foot of these mountains they heard the war whoop in front of them, and before they could catch good horses the Shoshoni had charged them, and were riding upon them shooting at them. A Shoshoni on a white horse with a brass shield rode right through the Cheyennes.

Big Head told his men to dismount and fight on foot. Most of them had guns, and they dismounted and let the horses go, and made for the rocky hills to take their stand there and fight. The Cheyennes fought their way toward these mountains. They fought in pairs, and as one would shoot, the other would aim his loaded gun and threaten to shoot. This he did while the one who had shot was loading his gun. After it was loaded his friend had a chance to shoot. In this way they kept the Shoshoni from coming close to them. This was the old style in which the trappers used to fight the Indians.

The Shoshoni with the brass shield was brave. He charged with the lance in his hand, up to where Sitting Bear and Lone Bear were standing. As this Shoshoni rode at them, Sitting Bear told Lone Bear not to shoot, but to hold his load, for he (Sitting Bear) would do the shooting and would give Lone Bear the chance to count the coup on the Shoshoni. Sitting Bear was one of the best shots in the party. When the Shoshoni came close enough, Sitting Bear aimed at him carefully, and shot him and he fell from his horse. Lone Bear ran up and struck him on the head with the butt of his gun. When the man fell, the Shoshoni tried to close in upon them, and here in this close fight Big Head was wounded. The Cheyennes wounded several of the Shoshoni and killed three horses. After this charge the Shoshoni fell back and the Cheyennes made for the rocky place. Big Head was badly wounded and was using his gun for a cane. Stone Calf took the bow lance and told him to try to reach a rocky hill. The Shoshoni came at them again, but the Cheyennes reached the hill and found it to be a good place to fight, because there were great stones to fight behind. When the Shoshoni found that the Cheyennes were in this good place, they gave up the battle.

Now the Shoshoni got all their wounded together and cried over them, and also mourned over the death of the man with the brass shield. The Cheyennes did not have time to scalp this man, but they counted three coups on him. The first coup was counted by Lone Bear, the second by Heap of Birds (Many Magpies?), and the third by Iron Crow. Three coups may be counted. Sitting Bear had the honor of shooting him, and that counted the same as a coup.

By this time Big Head was dying from the loss of blood. They leaned him up against a large stone, and Stone Calf placed the bow lance near his head. As soon as the Shoshoni left them, those who had blankets wrapped them about the dead man. The party then left for their village, which was on the North Platte River—a regular camping ground in those days. When they reached the village they told how Big Head had been killed by the Shoshoni, and all his relations and the Fox Soldiers mourned for him. The Fox Soldiers held a council and at last they decided that they would go and see their leader and wrap his body with good blankets. They were intending to start in a few days.

Big Head's party had not been long in the village when some men who had been chasing buffalo came running into the village and said, "Big Head is coming, riding behind one of the hunters." Big Head's relations had already mourned for him, and had had their hair cut off, and had killed his best war horse, as was the custom then. The whole camp ran out to see Big Head, who had been left for dead. They did not doubt that Big Head had been dead and had now become alive.

It was not long before Big Head appeared, riding behind one of the hunters. When he came up, all his friends hugged him and kissed him, for it was formerly the custom for men to hug and kiss those who had been lost for a long time, and who had come back to the camp. Big Head said that toward night he became conscious, and was suffering much for want of water. He started in the direction he thought his party had taken and took his bow lance with him. He walked all night, very slowly, using his bow lance to lean upon. The next morning he came to some water and stayed there for a long time, bathing his wound and washing away the blood. After he had taken that bath he felt very well. The next thing he thought of was something to eat. He had no knife, but he used the steel point of his bow lance to dig some roots.

26

A little later, as he was sitting resting near a small stream, he saw an old buffalo bull come down to the water. Big Head made up his mind that he would see whether it would be possible for him to kill this bull with his lance. Afterward he said that the Great Spirits took pity on him. The bull lay down near the bank of the stream with his back toward the creek. Big Head crept along under the bank until close to the bull. The point of his bow lance was of steel and was very sharp, and when he had come right close to the bull, Big Head thrust the lance right into its side. The bull jumped up and ran a short distance, and then stopped. The blood was running from its mouth and nostrils. Big Head stood behind the bank and waited for him to fall over, as he knew that he had struck him in the right place. When the bull fell over Big Head began to have life in him and ran toward the carcass. He thrust his lance into it near the kidneys, and cut the bull open and took out the kidneys and ate them. After eating what he wished, he took what he could carry with him, to eat on the road. After he had eaten he was all right, and walked without using his bow lance for a cane. On the way back he stopped only to eat, and to drink when he came to water.

NOTE. Big Head died in 1857. He was several times shot by the soldiers at Fort Kearny, but always recovered.

WHEN THE CHEYENNES WERE DRIVEN

ONCE a large party of the Cheyennes started from the South Platte River to search for the Pawnee camp. Only a few of the war party took horses with them, most of them going on foot. The horses were not ridden; they led them. They were to be used to charge the Pawnee camp. When the Pawnees came out to fight, those who had made the charge would run away and so lead the Pawnees away from their camp, to try to bring them to where the other Cheyennes were hidden—into a trap. It was easier for the Cheyennes to fight the Pawnees outside of their village.

The Cheyennes had with them their medicine charms, and Wolf Pipe carried a *hōhk tsĭm'*—a wheel lance owned by Bear.

In those days the Pawnees used to go west to the headwaters of the Republican River and to the head of Smoky Hill River. This was then their hunting grounds. The Cheyennes used to say that in these old times there were so many of the Pawnees that whenever they attacked a camp, the Pawnees came out of the lodges like a swarm of bees.

The Cheyennes selected eight fast runners to go ahead of the party as scouts, to learn where the Pawnee camp was. These scouts did not come back, so other scouts were sent out, to try to find out what had become of the first eight, but the last ones could find no traces of the first scouts, and returned to the camp. The war party did not know what to think about this. They knew that the eight scouts could not have been lost, for they had been told where to go to meet the party and make their report. The war party waited for them for three days at the appointed place.

At length High Wolf, the leader of the war party, filled a pipe and took it to Bear, who owned the *hōhk tsĭm'*, and asked him that night to call on the spirits (*Măĭ yūn'*), and to ask them what had become of the eight scouts sent out some days before—to learn if they were still alive. To have asked if they were dead would have been an unlucky question, likely to have a bad answer. It was for the spirits to say this—to tell if they had been killed.

When Bear asked the spirits this question, they said that the scouts were still out looking for the Pawnees, and did not wish to return until they had found the enemy. The leaders all said that this was good, and the war party started down the Smoky Hill River. Two scouts who were ahead of the war party had not gone very far when they saw wolves running up out of a hollow, and one of the wolves was dragging something. When they came close to the hollow where the wolves were feeding, they saw entrails scattered all about where the wolves had been dragging this thing, and lying in the hollow were the bodies of the eight missing scouts. They had been killed by the Pawnees. The Cheyennes saw tracks where many people—men, women, and children—had been at the place after the killing.

Of the two scouts who found the bodies one was Man on the Hill, who was born about the year 1800. He used to tell about it.

The two scouts ran back on a hill in sight of the party, and signaled with their buffalo robes. Man on the Hill walked twenty steps away from Hawk, the other scout, and then the two spread out their robes on the ground eight times. Each held up his robe and then dropped it on the ground eight times; this sign meaning that eight had been killed. When the men in the camp saw these signs, they all began to run toward them. The two scouts waited until the whole party had come up, and then all ran down to the place where the scouts had been killed. When they reached this place, they all cried for their friends who had been killed.

They all thought that the Pawnee camp must have been at this place, and that the scouts must have gone into the Pawnee camp before they saw it. They remembered now that there had been a heavy fog the next day after the scouts had started. The Cheyennes always believed that except for this it would have been impossible to get so near the Pawnee camp without seeing someone. The trail showed that, after killing the eight scouts, the Pawnees had moved across the Smoky Hill River. The Cheyennes who had horses were told to mount and follow the trail to see where it led. The war party placed the bones of the eight scouts in a hole in the river bank. When they found the bodies, the wolves had eaten all the flesh from the bones.

Meanwhile the big party left behind them everything that was heavy, for they felt certain that the Pawnees were not very far away. At that time Indians were all very swift and very enduring, for they were all the time moving about on foot. They could run fast and travel far. After those who were on horses had gone on, the others did not feel as if they could wait —they were all so angry at finding the bodies of their friends —and the footmen started on after the horsemen. They called to those who were on horseback to attack the Pawnees whenever they found them, and then to run back to the main party. Those on horses had not gone very far when they saw two persons sitting on a hill, and, in order to keep out of sight, they followed up a little ravine toward where the two Pawnees were sitting and charged on them. Black Wolf, who had the fastest horse of the Cheyennes, was in the lead. When the Cheyennes charged on them, one of the Pawnees ran and one stood his ground. This one had a gun in his hand.

The stream on which the Pawnees were camping was close to the hill on which the two men were sitting. Black Wolf charged the Pawnee to strike him, and when he struck him with the medicine stick he had in his hand, the Pawnee shot Black Wolf in the breast. The Cheyennes killed the Pawnee who shot Black Wolf. Black Wolf did not at once fall from his horse. His party held him on his horse while they were running back to the main war party.

It was not long before the Pawnees came out from the creek in great numbers. Many of them were on foot, but many were mounted. There they had a fight.

This was one of the greatest battles ever had between the Cheyennes and Pawnees. The Pawnees drove the Cheyennes up the stream on the south side of Smoky Hill River, called by the Cheyennes from that time Driven River, because the Cheyennes were driven up the stream.*

While they were running, Bear, who owned the *hōhk tsĭm'*, declared that he was going to hold his ground. In one hand he grasped the *hōhk tsĭm'*, and in the other his rattle. He stopped, but High Wolf ran up to him and struck him with his bow, and made him go on with the party. The Cheyennes declared that this was the biggest body of Pawnees they had ever seen. They said they looked like ants rushing from their camp. Several Cheyennes were killed, and a good many wounded. Black Wolf did not die until after they had reached the village.

The place where the Pawnees were camped at that time is called by the Cheyennes "Where the Scouts are lying." After this the Cheyennes never camped on this spot. To them it is like a grave. This happened in the year 1836.

WHERE MEDICINE SNAKE WAS PICTURED

THE killing in the year 1838 of a war party of five Cheyennes led by Medicine Snake gave the name to a place on the Solomon River, in Kansas, which the Cheyennes still call "Where Medicine Snake Was Pictured."

Some time after the fight between the Cheyennes and Pawnees on Driven River, Medicine Snake, the father of old Whirlwind, with four other men, set out in winter, going toward the Solomon River to look for the Pawnee camp. They wished to take horses from the Pawnees. This party of five was not again heard from. No one knew what had become of them.

The Cheyennes sometimes requested a man who possessed unusual spiritual power to ask the spirits for information as to events of which nothing was known. The man who was to communicate with the spirits was tied hand and foot, so that

* This stream was called by the whites Punished Woman's Fork. Its map name now is White Woman Creek.

31

he could not move, was placed in a little shelter by himself, the fire was put out, and people awaited the coming of the spirits. This was done now.

When Medicine Snake's party did not return, the chiefs carried a pipe to Elk River, who was then the keeper of the medicine arrows, to ask him to call up the spirits and inquire what had become of the missing men. As the chiefs approached the arrow keeper's lodge they cried and mourned as was the custom. They walked side by side, the one who carried the pipe walking in the middle. Elk River accepted the pipe, and by doing so agreed to comply with their request.

That night the chiefs tied Elk River with a bowstring, tying his toes and fingers and his arms and legs together, and placed him inside the small lodge, which was made of hide and stood in the middle of a big lodge. Lying on the ground a little way from the small lodge was a bone whistle. The large lodge was full and many were gathered outside, who had come to learn what the spirits would say. Whatever they might tell in this lodge would be true, for hanging in the lodge were the medicine arrows to hear what was said.

When all was ready the fire was put out, and as soon as it became dark the bone whistle began to sound. When the whistle stopped sounding, one of the spirits, called by the medicine man Sun Flower, came down from the top of the lodge. Perhaps he came through the smoke hole. He first spoke while he was up where the lodge poles were tied together, and said he was coming down to learn what they wished. They could hear him coming down. When he touched the ground it shook. The chief who had taken the pipe to Elk River was standing below. He asked the spirit, Sun Flower, to take pity on the chiefs for one of their fellow chiefs, with his party, was missing and they wished to find out about him and his men; their relations were anxious about them, for they had now been gone one winter. The spirit, Sun Flower, told them plainly that these men had been killed long ago by the Pawnees on one of the streams that run into the Solomon River. The chiefs were all very sad, and mourned and cried for their dead.

Some little time after this, a small war party of Sioux who were looking for Pawnees came into the village, and told the Cheyennes that on their war journey they had come to an old Pawnee camp ground on the Solomon River, and had seen there, on a big white log, pictures made in charcoal, showing that the Pawnees had killed five persons, and there was a finger drawn pointing down the river. The Sioux did not go down the river to see what had happened. The Cheyennes said that they believed that this was the party of Medicine Snake.

Standing On The Hill made up a party to go and see where these people had been killed. As the wolves and coyotes were very many, they thought that now they would find only bones. The war party of Sioux told them just where to go, and described the old camping ground where the Pawnees had been camped for a long time, and where the log was that had the drawing on it.

Standing On The Hill and his party started for the Solomon River. They were several days on the way before they found the place, for in those days this was a strange country to the Cheyennes, and they were on the Pawnee hunting grounds. They found the big white log, and saw on it just what the Sioux had described. The drawing showed that five people had been killed. The foot tracks sketched showed that the five persons had come close to the Pawnee camp, and then the foot tracks turned back. This was well drawn on the log. Whoever made these drawings took pains to make them easy to be understood.

A Pawnee man and his wife who had been getting wood had seen these people. In the drawing the man had an axe in his hand, and a woman had wood in her arms, and they were running back to the camp. Pawnee tracks showed that they had come back, and then many tracks going out were shown. There were horse tracks and foot tracks. Medicine Snake's party had gone down the river and then had run up a small creek, where the Pawnees overtook them, and here they made a stand and fought. The Pawnees had taken pains to mark with small piles of stones the places where they had killed these men, who had made their stand on the side of a rocky bluff. Medicine Snake must have charged the Pawnees as they came up to it, for one pile of stones had been set up, and foot tracks marked by small stones showed where the man had come toward the Pawnees. The Cheyennes could not be sure that it was Medicine Snake, but they think it must have been he, for he was a brave man.

It was the custom that the leader of a war party should fight for his men in case they got into great danger. He was looked upon as the one who should die first. It is commonly felt that a leader must fight for and defend his men. He might say to his enemies, "When you have killed me, then you can kill my men."

Standing On The Hill could find only a few scattered bones. These few they gathered up and wrapped in a blanket and placed in a hole. The place was afterward called by the Cheyennes, "Where Medicine Snake Is Pictured," because the Pawnees made pictures of him and his party.

Soon after this a Pawnee girl was captured by Young Whirlwind. She told the Cheyennes that Medicine Snake and his party had come up close to the camp while it was snowing, so that they did not see the camp until they suddenly came on a Pawnee and his wife. This chief man, she was told, had killed one Pawnee, and this was the reason that they had pictured him.

WOLF ROAD, THE RUNNER

ABOUT the year 1839 ten or twelve men, under Standing On The Hill as the leader, set out on the warpath from the camp on the South Platte River. They went south and on the way stopped at Bent's Old Fort on the Arkansas, and there obtained guns, ammunition, blankets, and new knives. Colonel Bent usually gave the Cheyennes these things on credit. He did not know all the Indians, but he knew the chiefs, and the leader of any war party commonly vouched for the men with him, giving Colonel Bent the names of the relatives of the different men and saying that if the men were killed these relations would pay their debts. As a matter of fact, they always did pay.

This party crossed the Arkansas and the Cimarron and when they reached Wolf Creek turned off a little toward the east. While crossing the divide between the Arkansas and the Cimarron rivers they lived altogether on horseflesh, for on the divide wild horses were everywhere. Standing On The Hill, a man of great experience, told his young men that before they went into an enemy's camp to capture horses they should wash themselves thoroughly and scour themselves with mud, in order to rid themselves of the odor of the horseflesh that they had been using. Horses greatly feared this smell, and if the men entered the camp smelling of horseflesh, the horses would be afraid of them and would be hard to catch.

After they had crossed Wolf Creek, they saw signs where people had been traveling, but they could not be sure who the people were or where they were going. To find out about this they sent out scouts—Wolf Road, Sun Maker, and Walking Coyote. The main party stopped above the Antelope Hills on the divide between the North and South Canadian, and the scouts set out before daylight. They were told to cross the South Canadian and go to the west of the Antelope Hills and to look over the Washita, following up a tributary of the South Canadian and, as usual, traveling in ravines and low places.

As they were traveling up this tributary stream they saw some people come up over a hill. Buffalo were everywhere on the plain. The people who had come in sight rode toward the scouts and began to chase a large herd of buffalo that was not far away. The scouts ran up to the head of the ravine and there hid in a little hollow. Buffalo were falling all about them.

As the scouts lay there watching, one of them looked down the ravine and saw a Kiowa riding across the stream they had followed up. Suddenly the man stopped and turned up the stream in the direction they had come, riding slowly, looking at the ground, and evidently following the tracks they had made. He kept on up the stream and just before he reached the place where they lay hidden he turned off their trail and rode up on a side hill to look. The scouts had determined that as soon as he was near enough they must kill him, but that it would not do to kill him with a gun, for those who were running buffalo would be sure to hear the shot.

When the Kiowa turned off the trail, the scouts crept up a little side ravine and under a bank over which the Kiowa would be likely to come. Presently they saw him approaching. He was looking all over the country, far off, trying to see people, and rode within twenty or thirty feet of them without seeing the scouts. All three shot at him with arrows. Walking Coyote shot his horse, Wolf Road's arrow stuck in the pommel of the saddle, and Sun Maker's passed through the Kiowa's heart under his arm. The horse gave a great plunge, the man fell off, and the three scouts rushed forward to count coup. Wolf Road reached him first, and then Sun Maker, who also received the credit for knocking him from his horse. They dragged the man into the ravine, got his horse and led it down there. There they scalped the man and shot the horse again.

The Kiowa was wearing silver hair plates and the horse a good bridle. The scouts recovered their arrows and taking these things started down the creek as they had come. When they had come to the flat they looked back and could see some Kiowas still cutting up animals, and a few buffalo running. When they reached an open place which they were obliged to cross they got close together one behind the other, stooped down and hung a blanket over themselves and walked across the flat, looking like a buffalo. When they again came to the brush they ran on as fast as they could.

They reached the stream where their party was and found everyone asleep, except one man, who was watching on the hill. They reported what they had done, and Standing On The Hill said to Wolf Road: "Now, my friend, you are the fastest runner; you must stop behind and watch the trail and we will go back. These people will look for the man who is dead and may find our tracks. It will be too dangerous to go on further." They started back.

Wolf Road waited until the party had disappeared over the farthest hill and then, seeing nothing, he ran on and at length overtook his people. They ran all that night, slept a little in the morning, and then ran on until late that night, when they rested for a short time.

When they reached the Arkansas River they met a war party going south and talked for some time with their friends, learning that the main camp was near by, on the north side of the river. For a little while they said nothing about what they had done, but at length Standing On The Hill drew out the scalp and said: "Friends, here is what we have done. If you will come back with us, we will have a dance." As he said this, Wolf Road snatched the scalp out of his hand and ran toward the main camp, and the others of the party ran after him. No one could overtake him, for he was the swiftest of all. He ran about the camp circle singing, and then, going to the lodge where the medicine arrows were kept, he hung the scalp on the bundle as an offering.

BY CHEYENNE CAMPFIRES

LONE WOLF'S LAST WAR TRIPS

LONE WOLF had asked the proper persons to make him a thunder bow (*hōh nŭhk a wō'?*). It was made on the head of the Smoky Hill River.

A thunder bow is an implement of mysterious power. It protects its owner from the power of the thunder, and, besides that, almost always brings him good luck. No man who owned one has ever been struck by lightning. The thunder bow looks something like a common bow, strung, but it has a lance-head on one end, and is ornamented with portions of various birds and animals which possess spiritual power. To it may be tied the feathers of a swift hawk, to give dash and courage in attack; the feathers of an owl, so that one may go silently through the night; some portion of a bear, so that the owner may have power to cure himself if he should be wounded.

The owner of a thunder bow carries it with him wherever he goes. It is light and is carried in the hollow of the left arm, the point up. When he has the thunder bow with him the owner of a thunder bow never carries a bow and arrows. Except when out running buffalo, he leaves his bow and arrows in the camp. At night the thunder bow is hung up on a bush or tree or is placed on something to keep it off the ground. If the owner wishes to hunt, he may let one of his party carry the thunder bow in the same way that he does. A man who owns one of these bows believes that he cannot be hit by bullet or arrow, and this is one reason that he carries it wherever he goes.

When a man has counted coup with the thunder bow, its wrapping is painted with Indian red paint, but until he has counted a coup with it, it is left unpainted. It used to cost much to have a thunder bow made, and few men had them. The more presents the thunder bow owner gave to those who were making it, the better it was made, and the stronger its power.

38

At last Lone Wolf's thunder bow was finished, and the night after it was given to him he had a dream. His dream told him to take six men on a war party to the country of the Utes and there to take from the Utes many horses. Lone Wolf kept this dream to himself, but he went to each man that he wished to have go with him, to tell him what he purposed and that in a few days—as soon as their moccasins could be made—he intended to start on this journey. When they went on foot to take horses, they always took many pairs of moccasins, for moccasins soon wear out.

It was best that these trips to take horses should be made by a few men only. If too many went, things did not always turn out well. Some might wish to go one way and some to go another, and there were different opinions. A small party had the best chance of success. If, however, they were setting out to fight and kill enemies, the parties might be much larger. It was in the middle of the night that Lone Wolf and his party set out from the village, and no one knew of their starting except the families of the men who went with him.

Lone Wolf was a brave warrior who had been in many battles, but of his party four were young men, without much experience in going after horses. Wolf Face, who died only a few years ago, was with the party. He was one of the youngest men. They all had great faith in Lone Wolf's success, because he had just had his thunder bow made, and this was certain to give them good fortune. It would protect them wherever they might go. Besides his thunder bow Lone Wolf carried also a gun the barrel and stock of which had been cut off. It was so small he carried it in his belt.

Not very long after they had gone into the mountains they came to a place which the Utes had just left. There had been eight lodges of Utes, and they had camped at this place for a long time, hunting elk, deer, antelope, and bear. On the ground just outside of the camp were piles of bones of different kinds—

even some buffalo bones! The trail of the people who had left the camp was two days old. In those days the Indians by looking at a trail could tell just how much time had passed since it had been made.

After the trail had gone a little way, it came to a stream and went into the water and did not come out on the other side. Not a track was to be seen. Lone Wolf had seen Ute trails before this, and he told his party how cunning the Utes were about hiding their trail. He told one of his men to walk on down the creek and to look for a trail on the other side, and said that he would go up the stream and look for the trail there. The four younger men he told to go up on a hill, to wait until he returned from his scouting. Lone Wolf went a long way up the stream before he found the place where the trail came out of the water. When he found it, he came back running; and the other scout had come back just before, without finding a trail. The Cheyennes were carrying with them some dried buffalo meat and before starting they ate. Since the Utes had gone so far up the stream, Lone Wolf went far ahead of the party toward the trail, on a trot, and told the others to follow him at a distance, saying that if he saw anything he would throw himself on the ground, and that they must do the same thing, and creep to the nearest brush to hide.

The Utes moved a long way before they camped again, and the Cheyennes did not overtake them that night. Early next morning they again started on the trail. Soon it began to snow, and Lone Wolf had to go fast to follow the trail before it should be covered with snow. They were now close to the backbone of the mountain. That night they stopped and built a great fire of pine wood. Lone Wolf had with him a large dog. Their food had given out, and they were hungry.

The next morning he told his young men that he would go out and look about and that while he was gone, they should kill his dog and roast it. Lone Wolf was gone for a long time, nearly all the morning, but at length he came back and told them that he had found the Ute camp and had seen the ponies all around it. From a bluff, he had counted eight lodges of Utes. "We will take all their ponies," Lone Wolf continued. "Then they will have nothing to ride to follow us, and there will be nothing for us to fear. I have chosen the way to go to the camp. We need not follow the trail. I know where the camp is, and just how to get to it." The snow was melting fast.

They started to go to the Ute camp and went slowly, wishing to reach it a little while before the sun went down, so that they might look about and locate the herds of horses, and could thus go directly to the herds without searching for them in the dark.

When they had come to a high hill, Lone Wolf said, "This is our lookout place." On the hill there were many cedar trees, and many big rocks which would keep them from being seen by the Utes in the camp. He took the members of his party up on the hill to look down in the valley, where the camp was, so that they could not say later that Lone Wolf had not been willing to have them see the camp and the horses. From this hill they could see only the tops of the lodges, and the smoke rising; the horses feeding, down below them and beyond the camp. Wolf Face told me that it was a pleasant view that they had from the top of this high hill.

After they had gone back from the top of the hill where they had been looking, they began to stretch and soften their rawhide ropes, pulling them back and forth around trees and rocks, so that they should be pliable and could be easily thrown on the horses. Lone Wolf advised them to tie about their waists the small, short, twisted hair ropes that they used for bridles. These were light and easy to put in a horse's mouth, and would untie more easily and quickly than a rawhide rope, after it had become wet in the horse's mouth. At this place, too, they put on new moccasins, and hung up on the trees their robes, and anything that was heavy. They left here two guns that they had. They wished to go as light and to be as free as possible.

Since there were six of them, Lone Wolf advised them to go in pairs, for in this rough mountain country, two persons could drive the horses more easily and quickly than one. Another thing he said to them was this, "If you meet do not speak, but whistle to each other." If any man should come out from the Ute camp and meet someone, he would be sure to speak and to ask, "Who are you?" as was the custom of all Indians, if they saw anyone among their herds. If the person did not reply, it was known that some stranger had come to take horses. Men who went off to take horses whistled to one another, and this was always understood. Lone Wolf said also: "If you come upon a herd of horses, do not wait for one another, but drive them away as soon as you can. While doing this make no noise, but take them back to where we left our things, and wait there for the others of our party. Wait until all have got there, so that we can all start together." He did not wish to leave any-one behind him, for the leader felt responsible for the members of his party, and if he lost anyone, or even left him behind, all the people in the camp would talk about it when he reached home.

While they were at work on their ropes, Lone Wolf continued to talk to and advise them. He said: "We shall do well to wait until all the Utes are sleeping, and by that time the moon will be up. We should not leave behind us any horses, so that they may follow us, or may go and tell their friends, if any Utes are camped near here. We must try to take all their horses." The young men said they would try to do this.

Lone Wolf encouraged them, and said: "Now what you are going to do is a very creditable thing. There are few things more honorable than to take horses from our enemies, and all the families and sweethearts of you young men will be glad to see you coming back, driving before you the horses of our enemies." When Lone Wolf talked to them like this it gave them courage; and they needed this, for in the strange country, far from their home, and with high mountains all about them, some of the young men felt lonely and frightened. Yet they felt sure that Lone Wolf knew how all things should be done, for before this he had been on many journeys to take horses from the enemy, and they knew they could trust him.

When the moon was up, and the time to go down into the camp had come, they went down the hill toward the camp and passed around it, not going through it, lest the dogs should bark at them. Snow was lying on the ground in only a few places.

When they had come near to where the horses were, they separated, going by twos. Wolf Face and his friend went down toward where they saw something moving, and when they got close to the animals they stood still for a time, so that the horses should not be frightened and run away from them. While they were there, someone came down from a bluff and whistled, so that they felt sure that it was one of their party, and they whistled back again. It was Lone Wolf. He directed them to drive the horses they had on to the place where they were to come together. Lone Wolf said he had found only eight horses and was looking for more.

While Wolf Face and his friend were driving these horses away, they saw another man riding toward them. The man whistled, so they knew it was one of their party. This was Island. He was the one who had gone with Lone Wolf. When he rode up, he told them that his herd was just over the hill, and that he was now looking for more horses, for he did not have as many as he wished. Wolf Face said to him: "I do not think that there are any more horses. Lone Wolf is out looking for more, and if there are any more he will get them." While they were talking there, the other two young men also rode up. They did not have many horses, but had brought along all that they had found. Now they all started for the place where they were to meet, to wait there for Lone Wolf.

Each pair of men agreed between themselves that they would divide up the horses in the morning, on the road, so that each man would recognize his horses. It was the custom to divide the horses before going into the village, and if anything happened to any one of the party before he reached the village, his family would then receive what he had taken. Sometimes an older man would take away horses from a young man, but when this was done, the brother or uncle or father of the young man whose horses had been taken would take these horses back again after the party reached home, and sometimes quarrels arose over these matters.

A short time after these young men had reached the meeting place, Lone Wolf came up with about fifteen head of horses. It is said that the Utes do not have very many horses, and few of those they have are good. Most of these horses had sore backs, and the reason for this is that the Utes travel in such a rough country. Lone Wolf said to the others: "I think we have taken all their horses, but none the less we must travel fast. There may be another Ute camp near by, and they may follow us. Now I will ride ahead and pick out the easiest trail, and you young men can follow me with the horses, and keep them up." It was about midnight when they started, and they could see that they had nearly 100 head of horses. When daylight came they were still in the mountain country—still in the enemy's land. Lone Wolf urged them to drive the herd fast. They had to go through some very bad places with their horses, but the Ute horses, which live always in the mountains, are used to roads of this kind. When they came to narrow paths the horses would fall in line, one behind another, as they had been accustomed to travel. Toward evening they got out into the open country.

Again Lone Wolf said, "Now let us push on with the horses, and make them go as fast as we can."

After they had gone out some distance on the prairie, Lone Wolf pointed out to the young men the direction to go, and said that he would stay behind and watch to see if the Utes were following them. If they were coming, he would see the dust rising from where they were riding. Lone Wolf stopped in the hills and looked back over the way they had come. After a time, when he saw nothing, he mounted his horse and rode on again, and overtook the young men, and then after a time stopped once more to let them get ahead. He told them that they must push hard all that day, and at night they could stop for a time. By this time all were tired; and beginning to be sore from riding bareback. They came to some water and let the horses drink all they wanted, and then they drove them on to another place, and stopped for a little while to let the horses graze. Meanwhile Lone Wolf was behind, watching the way they had come. They were now in the open country and could see all about them. At sundown, after watering the horses again, and themselves drinking all the water they could hold, they started on. Late in the night they came to a hollow place, and stopped there for the night.

Lone Wolf said to them, "Now, before you lie down let each one catch up the best horse he has, and tie him up." This advice was given so that in case of an alarm each one could jump on the fast horse and ride off. He started the herd in the direction they were going, and then left them alone, feeding. He said that the horses were tired and would not wander far.

Lone Wolf was a wonderful man. He did not seem to get tired or to get sleepy. He said to his men: "Lie down now and sleep well. As soon as the morning star rises, I will wake you." As soon as the young men lay down they went to sleep and knew nothing more.

Island was something like Lone Wolf. When they stopped that night he was as fresh as ever, and had the best horses and more of them than anyone in the party.

As soon as the morning star had risen, Lone Wolf called to them, "Get up now, and we will start." Island had been up for some time and had driven the horses together in a bunch, ready to start. He said: "We have all the horses that we brought here. Not one is missing." Lone Wolf and Island had been walking around them all through the night, while the other men were sleeping. As they were about to start, Lone Wolf said: "We will go slowly now, for we are out of danger. As soon as we get a little further away, I will kill an antelope."

When a person is tired out he does not feel like eating. They did not feel hungry, yet it was two days and two nights since they had eaten. Antelope were abundant all over the prairie, and just before they came to a stopping place, Lone Wolf killed one. They ate everything there was inside of the antelope without cooking it, liver, kidneys, tripe, and fat, and when they came to where there was some water, they stopped and built a fire of buffalo chips and had all they could eat. They remained here until sundown, and after it got dark went on to another place to stop for the night. There was no more danger now. They were now out of the Ute country—in their own.

Next morning they set out toward the Arkansas River, where they expected to find the Cheyenne village, for when they started out on this trip the Cheyennes were moving toward the Arkansas.

It took them five days to reach the Cheyenne camp with the horses they had taken. When they came in sight of the camp, and Lone Wolf saw it, he mounted his best Ute horse and rode ahead of his party and fired the short gun that he carried, to let the camp know they had done something. All the people ran out of the lodges to meet them, and when they saw Lone Wolf carrying his thunder bow they knew the party.

While the men in this war party were on the road returning, they had given away almost all their horses to their relatives and friends. Lone Wolf had talked to them about this, and had said that it was greatly to a man's credit to give to relations and friends horses that had belonged to the enemy, and it was still more creditable to give them to a man whose daughter one wished to marry.

"Now is the time to marry a wife," he said, "if any young men in this party wish to take a wife." They all declared that at this time they did not care to get married.

"That is good," said Lone Wolf. "The longer you remain single the better it will be. I have no wife, and I do not intend to marry for some time yet."

When Lone Wolf got back from this war trip—the first trip he had made with this thunder bow—he presented a horse to each of his thunder bow makers. It was a great credit to the makers that Lone Wolf had had such good luck. He gave away all the horses that he had taken. While they were on their way back from this trip Lone Wolf had told his party that as soon as he reached the village, he intended to start back against the Utes, and that if any of them wished to go with him they might do so.

Lone Wolf was the chief of the Fox Soldiers. He had been in camp only a few days, when he chose six young men from the Fox Soldiers band to go with him to war. This made seven* persons in his party, and he told them to make ready to start before long. Some old men heard that he intended to go back again, and told him he must be careful. It was too soon for him to go again, just after he had had such good luck; that it would be better for him to wait until spring. One of them said to him: "If you go now the luck will turn against you. This has always happened even if the returning war party had brought back many scalps. If the same party has started again at once, someone is pretty certain to be killed on the next trip."

Old men talked about this in the village, but Lone Wolf had

* A war party of seven is deemed very unlucky by the Cheyennes.

made up his mind to go and he did go. He started in the day-time. He alone knew the young men he had selected to go. The young men left the village separately.

The second leader of this war party, after Lone Wolf, told Lone Wolf that they ought to stop somewhere and kill buffalo, and dry the meat to take with them, for in the mountains it was hard to get anything to eat, and it would not do to fire guns while in the Ute country. Lone Wolf agreed to this, for Long Back was an old warrior who had been out on the warpath many times, and was a good adviser.

Two days after leaving the village they came to a place where there were plenty of animals. They had three guns in the party, and they stopped here and killed some fat cows, and cut up and dried plenty of meat, and killed also some antelope and half dressed the hides, to make sacks in which to carry the buffalo meat. For three or four days they stopped here, and then packed their dried meat in their antelope hide sacks, and started for the Ute country. Lone Wolf said he knew a place which the Cheyennes call Open Park, and that this was a great hunting place for the Utes. It was here that he was going. After several days they reached the mountains, and here they began to look out for people who were their enemies. These were the Utes, the Pueblos, and the Mountain Apaches.

Now when they were in camp they made very little fire, for pine or cedar makes much smoke, and this smoke might be seen by enemies.

One day a young man named Hawk was sent on ahead as scout, and presently he came running to the camp, and said that he had heard two shots fired up the stream, not very far off. When they heard this they started. Long Back and Lone Wolf advised them to take all their things along with them. If they did not find a camp of the enemy, they would go on fur-ther, and would not come back this way. The young men hurried up the creek, walking very fast, and had not gone very far when they came upon a pony track, and this track they followed right up to the camping place from which the Utes had just gone away. They had moved that morning. There were five lodges of them, and the camp showed that they had stopped here only one day. The trail was very fresh.

The two leaders were now ahead. Soon they stopped and told their men to leave their loads here on the limbs of the trees, at a little distance from the trail. The young men went into the timber, and hung up what they wanted to leave. The leaders advised each one to take along an extra pair of moccasins in case they should get lost from one another, for in this rough country it was easy to get lost. Meantime Lone Wolf had uncovered his thunder bow, for it was the custom to uncover a thunder bow before going into battle.

While Lone Wolf was uncovering his thunder bow, the other young men were getting ready for battle, and when all were ready Lone Wolf and Long Back said, "Since there are only five lodges of these Utes, we may as well attack them as soon as we find the camp." Those young men who had bows and arrows strung their bows and pulled on the strings to see that they were all right, and would not break. They took from the quivers four or five arrows and began to string them, and to smooth out the feathers and to fix the arrow-points. After hanging up their things they went forward at a trot.

Before they had gone very far they heard, not far ahead, the barking of a dog. They ran to a hill just ahead of them to take a look. They crept up the hill, and lay there at the top to look around and see what was the best place from which to charge on the camp. While they were looking, a shot was fired at them from behind, and a Ute rode by them, shouting to the camp. Long Back shot at the Ute as he rode by, but missed him, and the Cheyennes all charged on the camp. They could see the women and children run into the timber, which was on the hills back of the camp.

Lone Wolf was ahead, and Long Back called out to him to be careful, as there were Utes ahead, behind the trees, but Lone Wolf did not seem to hear him. Just then a Ute standing behind a tree fired and shot Lone Wolf in the breast and he fell. In his right hand Lone Wolf held his short gun, and in his left his thunder bow.

After firing the shot the Ute ran into the timber, and another Ute on horseback drove away all the horses. Lone Wolf died at once. His party carried his body to the stream near by and placed it on the rocks, and leaving it there started for home. It had turned out just as the old men in the village had said. Their leader had been killed. The thunder bow was left with Lone Wolf's body, for when the owner of a thunder bow is killed, or dies, no one else may use the bow and it is always left with the owner. The wrapping of the thunder bow was left hanging where Lone Wolf had placed it.

Long Back and his men returned to where they had left their loads, and took their moccasins and enough meat to carry them back home. They traveled night and day to reach the village, and were three days in getting home. Everyone mourned for Lone Wolf, for he came of a good family and was well thought of.

The Fox Soldier Society held a council. In old times when anyone was killed by enemies it was the custom for the soldier band to which he belonged to go to the place where his body was left, taking blankets to wrap about him.

The Fox Soldiers started to the place where Lone Wolf's body had been left. Long Back led the party. It was now late in the season and in the mountains the weather was beginning to be cold. When they reached the place where Lone Wolf's body lay, it was almost night. The next morning they carried the body to a good place, wrapped the blankets about it, and left it there. They went to the Ute camp, and there found the lodges standing just as the Utes had left them. They had not come back,

50

even to get their saddles. They must have been a long way from the main Ute village, or they would have returned to get their things. What they left behind showed that they were a hunting party. The lodges were very small, and there was nothing in them but the saddles, and a few sheepskins to sleep on.

After they had seen all this, the leaders of the Fox Soldiers said: "Now we have seen our friend, and have dressed him in good clothing, and wrapped him up well. It is useless to go further, for the Utes have had the alarm, and have gone off to their hiding places, and are on the watch. We will now start for home, and next summer will get up a large war party and come back here for revenge."

A STORM EAGLE

ONE winter—1854-1855—seventy-five Cheyennes, led by Little Wolf and Lean Bear, went down the Arkansas River as far as the Pawnee Fork, and from there north to the Smoky Hill River. After they had reached it New Dog went down the Smoky Hill River to see what he could discover. Buffalo were everywhere, as far as he could see, and all were feeding quietly except in one place where he saw buffalo moving. He had no field glasses but could see something going toward the timber on the river.

When he returned to the camp he told what he had seen and Lean Bear came out from his war lodge and told the young men to saddle up, and directed that what New Dog had seen should be cried out through the camp. They all made ready and set out, but it was late, nearly sundown, when they started for the place, and by the time they had reached there it was late at night and very dark, so they stopped and slept there.

Next morning at daylight someone went a little way down the river and there found a fire, still burning. Pawnees had

stopped there with a herd of ponies that they had taken from
the Arapahoes on Crooked Creek south of the Arkansas River.
The Cheyennes took the trail, which led north. After a time,
however, they lost the trail, because the buffalo were all over
the country and had run over it and trodden it out. The Cheyennes determined to go on north to the next river, thinking
that there, on the sandbars, they would see the trail where the
Pawnees had crossed. When they reached the river it was
nearly night. Some wanted to go down the river and some up.
As they could not decide what to do, they stopped for the night
on this stream, which the Cheyennes call Cedar River—the
Saline River.

Very early in the morning some started down the river and
some up, to look for the trail of the Pawnees. Little Wolf went
with the party which rode down the stream, and Lean Bear went
up the stream. Lean Bear's men found nothing, and at daylight
they went to the hills, and the older men dismounted and sat
down in a circle to smoke. The wind was blowing from the south
and they sat with their backs to the south. The young men who
did not smoke sat on their horses, leaning forward. Presently
those who were sitting on their horses heard someone singing.
The sound came from the river and the south. The young men
told those who were smoking that someone was singing, and
all stopped to listen. The older men said, "That is not a Cheyenne song." Then Lean Bear said: "Let no one move. Keep
still." All kept still and sat there.

Those who were on horseback could see further than those on
the ground, and presently they said that a man was coming,
leading a horse. He was coming closer still singing. He was singing a Pawnee song of thanksgiving. They sing this song when
horses are given them as presents. To this day, when anyone
gives them presents of horses, the Cheyennes and Arapahoes
too sing this song.

This Pawnee, when he saw horses standing there without

riders, must have thought he was overtaking his party. The Cheyennes who were on horseback were leaning forward on their horses' necks, and it may have looked to him as if these were all loose horses. When the Pawnee got close, he saw that he was walking up to his enemies. He had some buffalo meat on the horse he was leading, so he jumped off the one he was riding, threw the meat from the one he was leading and mounted it. It was a spotted horse. They think that if he had stayed on the horse he was riding he might have gotten away, for that was a fast Arapahoe horse, which the man had taken from the Arapahoes on Crooked Creek. The Pawnee started back the way he had come, to get to the river, where there was much brush and sunflower weeds. The Cheyennes followed him.

When he crossed the stream he left his horse and ran on foot so that he might hide, and the Cheyennes could not find him. They hunted for him in every direction. Three of them, Gentle Horse, Sand Hill, and Crazy Wolf, followed up a little stream to its head. Sand Hill had left them and had started across to look in another creek. Then Crazy Wolf shouted out, "There he is, in the weeds." Gentle Horse said to Crazy Wolf, "You are young and have never counted a coup; rush on the Pawnee and touch him." The enemy was still hidden in the weeds. Crazy Wolf charged on the Pawnee, but before he got near him, turned and ran back. Gentle Horse said to him, "You must not act in that way—like a coward." Gentle Horse went up alongside of Crazy Wolf and said to him, "Charge on him again." By this time the Pawnee was on his feet with bow and arrow in his hand, and this time again Crazy Wolf turned off and did not go near to the Pawnee.

Now Sand Hill was seen coming up on his black horse, which was one of the fastest horses in the Cheyenne tribe. Sand Hill counted the first coup on the Pawnee, then Crazy Wolf, and Gentle Horse the third coup. He also shot him with a gun. Gentle Horse took the scalp, and gave it to Lean Bear when he

53

came up, for it was the custom to give a scalp to the one who carried the pipe.

When the shot sounded, all the other Cheyennes came running to this place. After a time they all rode up on a hill to look for other enemies, when on another hill they saw Indians running toward the stream. Lean Bear cried out, "They have found the Pawnees," and all started for that creek. Lean Bear cautioned the young men, saying to them, "Go slowly, we will get there in time." When they rode up they saw three men sitting against a bank and before them stood some medicine men singing—doctoring them. These three had been wounded by Pawnees. The fight had been going on since early in the morning, but as the wind was blowing the other way, Lean Bear and his party could not hear the shots. Lean Bear cried out, telling his men to dismount and fight on foot. The Pawnees were in the stream bed and hidden among the dogwoods, so that the Cheyennes could not see them.

Lean Bear was an old brave man and had counted more coups than any of the Cheyennes. When he saw his men wounded he growled like a bear and cried out to them to be brave and to fight carefully, as he had fought in many battles. Because of the brush at the forks of the stream where they were hiding, the Cheyennes could not see the Pawnees and could not tell how many there were in this party. Two Pawnees were shooting from the forks, and two other Pawnees were shooting from another place further up the stream. Lean Bear and Little Wolf told those of their men who had guns to fire at these two places. So they kept loading their guns and firing together at these places. After they had fired many shots at these points, the fire from the Pawnees ceased. The Cheyennes began to draw in closer, but there were no more shots from the Pawnees.

Eagle Feather—the son of that Bull who had lost the medicine arrows when the Pawnees captured them—mounted his horse and said he intended to ride into the brush where the

PAWNEE WARRIOR LEADER.

*In Ceremonial Dress; buffalo robe, hair lariat, otter collar,
with ear of corn and storm eagle.*

Pawnees were, and everyone made ready to jump into the bushes as soon as Eagle Feather rode in. All the others were on foot, since they could run in better afoot. As soon as Eagle Feather rode into the brush they all whooped and ran in after him. They heard a shot. Eagle Feather had ridden on a wounded Pawnee who had a gun in his hand, and, as Eagle Feather struck him with the bowstring lance he was carrying, the Pawnee raised his gun and shot Eagle Feather between the eyes. Cheyennes on foot were coming behind Eagle Feather and they shot the Pawnee.

At the forks of the stream Lean Bear rushed into the brush, his son following close behind him. He saw a dead Pawnee lying on the other side of the stream and told his son to count coup on him. Man Above and some other young men rushed forward to count coup. Little Wolf picked up the Pawnee's gun. Under the man Lean Bear saw something and pulled it out. It was wrapped up in cloth and smelled like medicine roots. He carried it out and opened it. It was an eagle stuffed with all kinds of Pawnee medicine tied up in different pieces of buckskin. The Pawnees call this eagle a storm eagle. When the Pawnees used to go out on the warpath to take horses, they took this eagle with them to cause a storm to come up when they were taking horses, so that their trail would be washed out and could not be found.* The Cheyennes found that this was true, for when Lean Bear opened this eagle after the fight a big storm came up.

They counted nine dead Pawnees and found and counted ten buffalo robes, so one Pawnee must have escaped. They say that a warrior used to carry with him only a single buffalo robe, since two were too heavy a load to carry on foot.

When the party came in with these scalps, they did not mourn for Eagle Feather, because he was killed while counting

---

* The Crows are reported to have possessed a medicine object by means of which a storm might be called up by its owner where enemies were pursuing him. See Wildschut, *Indian Notes*, vol. 3, no. 2, p. 99, New York, April, 1926.

coup on his enemy. They brought the scalps in to Bent's Fort, on the Arkansas River, where the big village of Cheyennes was camped.

STARVING AND KILLING FAT MEAT

A GOOD many years ago a party of seventeen Cheyennes started from the camp on the Laramie River to go to war against the Utes. They traveled along, looking for enemies, and at length among the mountains they found a Ute camp. When they came in sight of the village, however, some of the Utes saw them and gave the alarm, and set out to attack them, and before they knew it the Utes were close to them. They ran away and the Utes chased them. The Utes kept after the Cheyennes and were so close to them that they scattered. By this means they got away from the Utes, and not one of them was killed or even wounded. Three of the young men kept together, Shell, Tangle Hair, and another. They had nothing to eat, and after a day or two they got hungry, and pretty soon they began to starve.

Tangle Hair had a gun, while the others carried bows, but Tangle Hair could not kill anything. There was game, but he could not hit it. It was in the spring of the year, the season when the birds were sitting on their eggs, and they used to look for birds' nests and gather the eggs. Sometimes there were young birds in the shells, but they did not mind that. They ate the eggs, birds, and all, for they were starving.

They traveled on, always hungry, until they reached the place where the Laramie River comes out of the mountains on to the Laramie plains. On this day two of them were riding along side by side, talking about what they were likely to get to eat that day. One of them said, "Perhaps we may find a duck's nest." "Yes," said the other, "perhaps we may kill the duck, too."

Shell was riding ahead, saying nothing, but he too was thinking about eating.

They went up the side of a little hill, and as Shell looked over the crest, he saw, a little way off on the other side of the hill, a big buffalo bull coming toward him. He dodged back and said to the others: "Here is a bull. Quick! let us strip off our saddles here and chase him and try to kill him."

Tangle Hair said: "No, no; I'll shoot him. I'll shoot him."

They had quite a little discussion as to what should be done, but the two who had bows pulled off their saddles and got ready to chase the bull, if Tangle Hair should not kill him.

Shell said: "All right, go ahead. You shoot, and if you do not kill him, we will chase him, and will try to get him in that way."

Tangle Hair crept up to the top of the hill, and the others were close behind him. The bull kept coming closer and closer. At last Tangle Hair shot, and the bull fell, and they were so glad they all laughed. The two who were on horseback started on the full run to go up to the bull, and Tangle Hair was only a little behind them. They all held up their hands to *He' ămmă wíhio,* and thanked him for having given them a bull to eat. The bull looked nice, and they were all in a hurry to begin to eat. They were excited.

After he had looked at the bull lying there, Shell rode off a little way and jumped off his horse and threw down his rein, and began to gather buffalo chips for a fire. Then he struck his flint and steel, and in a little while the fire was blazing nicely. He wanted to cook as soon as they had some meat cut off. After this he ran up again to look at the bull. Tangle Hair and the other man had pulled the bridles off their horses, and were at work gathering buffalo chips for the fire. After he had looked at the bull again, Shell ran back to his fire.

The bull was not quite dead; he could hear him breathing; and he called out to Tangle Hair: "He is not dead. You will

57

do well to shoot him again." Then he pulled the bridle off his horse, and piled some chips on the fire. He called out once more: "Shoot him again, and begin to cut some meat off." Then he piled some more chips on the fire and ran back to the bull.

He drew his knife out and thrust it into the bull just in front of the hip-bone, to see if it was fat. When he drew out his knife after doing this, a big piece of fat stuck out of the wound, and he tore off a piece of it. The bull was not yet quite dead, but still he did not move. Shell thought he would walk around to the bull's head and look at him; and he did so. He took an arrow from his quiver and poked the bull's nose with it, and just as he did so one of the other men stuck his knife in the bull's ribs.

As he felt the knife, the old bull bounced up to his feet—mad. There was a little pile of rocks a short distance in front of where it had been lying, and Shell ran for this to get on it. The other two ran for their horses, to get behind them, and the bull chased these two. As they dodged around behind their horses, the old bull caught one horse under the belly, and raised him on his horns and threw him over his back. The horses were frightened, and ran off in one direction as fast as they could, and the bull ran over a little hill another way, and disappeared.

The men followed their horses a long distance, but at last they got around them and caught them. They went back to look for the bull, for they expected to find him lying down or dead just beyond this little hill. They could not find him anywhere. After they had made up their minds that they could not find him, they went back to where he had lain, to get their saddles, and as they started on again, Shell looked at where his fire had been. It had burned out.

He said, "Now it is just white ashes, and I expected to roast fat meat on it."

They went on, and at last reached their village.

THE PROPHECY OF BEAR MAN

IN the winter of 1856-1857 a part of the Cheyennes were camped for the winter on Running Creek. Three bands of them were there, the *Wūh′ tā piu*, *O ī′vī mănăh′*, and *Hēv′ā-tăniu*. One day a medicine man called Bear Man, after coming out of a sweat house where many old men were taking a sweat, stopped by some men who were sitting smoking near the pile of earth where the buffalo skull faces the sweat house, and said to them, "While my friends there were all singing inside the sweat house, I saw something."

"What is it," said the others; "tell us about it."

"As we were sitting there," said Bear Man, "praying and sweating, it came into my mind strongly that it will be good for us to keep close and tie up all our gentle horses, for in my mind I saw coming toward our camp on foot a war party of Pawnees. The leader was carrying in his arms something wrapped up in a cloth."

When Bear Man had finished speaking, Bear Tongue rose to his feet and went through the camp, crying out and telling all the people what Bear Man had seen in his vision.

As the sun drew to the west all the people drove up their horses and all the gentle ones were tied up. Some young men went out a little way from the camp and watched during the night for the Pawnees. Two nights passed and nothing happened. On the third day people began to say that Bear Man must have been mistaken in his vision, and that night they did not tie up their horses, and on this third night everything was quiet. Nobody now thought anything of Bear Man's vision.

Early in the morning after the fourth night a young man came running into the camp, calling out that the Pawnees had stolen horses. He held in his hand a Pawnee arrow that had dropped out of a Pawnee quiver while its owner was getting on

a horse. The man's tracks showed where he had mounted a
Cheyenne horse. All the men now ran out to see if their horses
were taken. When the women went down to the stream for
water they found a blanket that a Pawnee had lost. Those who
were out hunting for their horses came to a place on the hill
below the camp where the Pawnees had sat in a row and made
prayers before taking the horses. On the ground they had
marked horse tracks leading toward the Pawnee country. They
had left their sacks just as they had set them in a row, with
corn and dried meat in the sacks and also some moccasins.
They had driven the horses by this place and taken a few of
their things, for their tracks showed where they had dismounted.

Thus it was seen that Bear Man's vision had come true. His
prophecy was fulfilled. The Cheyennes came back to the camp
and told what they had seen, and now men began to saddle up
their horses to follow the trail. As the men were beginning to
start, Bear Tongue cried out, "Follow them slowly, for the
Pawnees have not taken very many good horses." The best
horses were above the camp, but the Pawnees coming up the
stream had taken the horses below the camp and mainly from
the camp of the *Hēv'ātăniu.* The clans *Wŭh' tā piu* and *O ĭ'vĭ
mănăh* were camped further up the creek and their horses were
above the camp.

As fast as the men were saddled up they started on the trail.
It was very plain and led toward Solomon Forks. In the evening
the pursuers stopped on a small stream that runs into those
creeks. The trail was now very fresh.

Black Kettle had been chosen as the leader on this trip. He
was a young chief and had married into the *Wŭh' tā piu* group.
When they stopped that evening he said to the young men:
"Now we are getting close to the Pawnees. All those of you who
have good horses must saddle them and leave your poor horses
here. Those of you who are riding slow horses stay here with
these horses." A good many of the men were riding common

horses and leading their war horses, but some people whose good horses had been stolen were riding poor horses. Buffalo were all about them, and Black Kettle told those who were going to stay there not to go away from the place, but to go out and kill some fat cows, so that when his party returned they might have plenty to eat. He told them also to keep up a good fire during the night, for he and his party would come back as soon as they had overtaken the Pawnees.

Black Kettle and his party started on the trail and when they got near the Solomon River, Black Kettle told his men to form in line and all to get off their horses. They did so and all the men stood in line in front of their horses. Then Black Kettle took an arrow from his quiver and stepped ahead of his men and held the arrow as if he were going to shoot; then he drew the arrow back and came to his men and said to them: "Do you see the point of that hill over there? Right under it the Pawnees are resting and eating." All mounted their horses and charged for this point, and when they reached it they found that the Pawnees had just left it. The fire was still burning. They had killed a buffalo and had been roasting meat. The Cheyennes then started down the creek and had not gone very far when they saw the Pawnees rounding up the horses and trying to catch the fast horses to get away on. But the Cheyennes were all on good horses and they were too quick for the Pawnees. Two Pawnees caught fast horses, one a white horse that belonged to Thin Face and one a gray horse that belonged to Lump Nose. These two were noted horses. Thin Face and Lump Nose, who in their younger days had been great warriors, had stayed back with those that had the slow horses, as leaders of that party.

Five Pawnees ran to the timber near by and got among the willows and cottonwood trees, but the Cheyennes got all around them, and it did not take them long to kill all five. The two on fast horses got away. The Cheyennes knew that they could not catch them, so they let them go. Antelope was the first man to count a coup.

They had recovered all their horses except the two that the Pawnees had ridden off and nine more that were still missing. These nine were eight unbroken mares and a very old mule that had been broken to ride.

It was night when they turned back. On the way they stopped to rest, and early next day started on, though their horses were getting very tired. Black Kettle said, "Let us stop on the creek and dress the scalps," and they did so and rested for a time. They all said, "We must not show the scalps to the other party until we get near them and then we can shake the scalps in their faces." This was the custom in those days.

The party that had been left behind got up on the hill to watch those who were approaching to see whether anyone had been hurt or killed, but those who were coming made no signal. When Black Kettle and others got close to those who had stayed behind and were just about to shake the Pawnee scalps at them, Thin Face, who was Black Kettle's brother-in-law, ran up to Black Kettle and pulled out a scalp from under his robe and waved it in front of Black Kettle's face. Black Kettle and his party were surprised at this. Thin Face pointed down the creek and said to them, "You will find his carcass there." He meant that they had killed the Pawnee there.

When those that were left behind went out to kill buffalo, they saw a man driving eight head of horses and riding a mule. This Pawnee was unlucky. The horses he had taken were all unbroken mares. Only the old mule was gentle and could be ridden. In the darkness these wild mares looked fat to the Pawnee, and he thought he was getting a fine herd, but in the morning he found his mistake, for he had nothing to ride but this very old mule.

The Cheyennes say that this man must have been crazy. When they charged toward him he jumped off the mule and ran down the creek. He came to a coyote hole and spread his buffalo robe over the hole and pulled his moccasins off and placed them on the ground in such a way that it looked as if he were lying down there. At first the Cheyennes thought he was lying in the hole, and when they charged him the first man struck the robe with his bow and then saw that there was no Pawnee there. They ran further down the creek, searching everywhere, and at length found him hiding in the bed of the stream. When he saw that he was discovered, he jumped up, holding his bow and a handful of arrows. He pointed to the sun and made signs that he was like the sun and that it would be a great thing for them if they should kill him that day. The Cheyennes say that whether he was crazy or not he made a good fight. Twice he came very near catching Thin Face, and they say that if he had been on a horse he would have killed a number of them. Thin Face fought on foot and the Pawnee kept running after him. Big Nose had a gun and got off his horse to shoot at him, and when the Pawnee saw that Big Nose was off his horse he made a dash for him. Big Nose got behind his horse to shoot, but the Pawnee did not turn back but kept rushing toward him, and when he got very close, Big Nose shot him and he fell. For a long time the Cheyennes were afraid to go close to him. Once before he had lain on the ground and pretended that he was shot, and when they went near to him he had jumped up and run after them. They thought he was playing this trick again.

After loading his gun, Big Nose walked up to the Pawnee and he was dead. They say he was a fine-looking young man.

This time the Cheyennes got six scalps and got back all their horses except two that the Pawnees had ridden off. For the rest of the winter the Cheyennes held big scalp dances.

A HARD WARPATH

A PARTY of twenty-eight young men, all on foot, set out from the mouth of Lodge Pole Creek, on the South Platte River, going to take horses. White Bull was the leader. They went into the mountains, into the Ute country. It was in the autumn, when the leaves were beginning to fall, and in the mountains it had already begun to snow a little.

They went on up toward the heads of the South Platte and the Arkansas, following up between the mountains until they got into South Park. There they found where some Utes had camped lately, and it looked as if they had been gone only a couple of days. It had snowed a little in the morning, so that the ground was covered, and they built a war lodge. They looked about for a time to see if they could find any trail, and then came back and slept there.

The next day they scattered out to go to all the high points, to see what they could discover. Two of the men found the trail where the Ute lodges had moved along. They followed it on to the next creek, and found where the Utes had camped— two lodges. They had moved away that morning. They had been there the night that the Cheyennes had camped in the park. The two young men went back and reported. Now it began to snow.

When all had come in and had heard what these two had found, White Bull said to his young men, "I think we would better go on now to this Ute camp that we have found." They set out. Just a little way from the camp there was a projecting ledge of rock. It was still snowing hard, and they built a fire under this ledge and stayed there all night. It snowed all that night, and all the next day, and all the next night, but the third morning it cleared up. During this time, from the day when they had entered the park, they had had nothing to eat. They had been hungry for four days.

That morning White Bull took his gun and went out to try to kill something to eat, a deer or some other animal. The snow was so deep that he did not go very far. He found no game, and soon he went up on a hill and sat down there, and for some time he sang his war song, and then sang his medicine song, to try to bring something to help them. Nothing came, and he went back to the camp and went in under the rocks, where all were waiting for him. He said to them: "I can find nothing to kill, and it is my opinion that we would better try to go home. There is no game here, and we are likely to starve to death. If we go on further and find the camp of the enemy and take their horses, we cannot get home with them because the snow is so deep; therefore we had better try to go home now." All agreed to this, and they started on the trail back toward their home, leaving their camp about the middle of the day. They traveled on for about half the afternoon, but the snow was so deep and the men got so tired, that White Bull said to them: "Now we are all tired out, and we are all getting wet in the snow; let us turn around and go back to our old camp, and take the chances that some game may come to us." They did this, and spent the night at their old camp.

Early in the morning White Bull went out and found a place where many cherry bushes grew. He cut many limbs of these bushes and brought them into the camp. Then he sent some of his young men out to get snow and melt it by the fire, and told them that they must unplait their rawhide ropes; then he made a frame of the cherry brush, and with the strands of the lariat he made a snowshoe, and then they all made snowshoes, and on these they started home.

They walked easily with the snowshoes, but they could not go very far in a day. All they had to eat was the buds of the rose bushes sticking up through the snow along the creek. They went on for eighteen days, eating nothing but such buds as they could gather. On the eighteenth night they camped at a place where a big pine tree had fallen and its limbs had broken off, and they built a fire against the trunk of this tree. After the fire had heated the log, two rabbits came out of the hollow in it. They caught them, cut them up and divided them, and ate them up, flesh, entrails, hides, and all. From this time they went on for two days more without anything to eat. By this time they were out of the mountains and down close to the South Platte River. Here there was less snow than there had been higher up, and White Bull said to his young men: "Now we can walk better without these snowshoes. Let us throw them away." They threw away their snowshoes. Going on, the snow got less deep, and they made a camp early, for they were very weak and tired. Then White Bull said to his young men, "Now, my friends, the snow is less deep and we are about starving to death, let the stronger ones take their guns and go out and see if they cannot kill something to eat." He went out himself, and only those who were too weak to walk stayed in camp.

As White Bull was walking along, looking about to see what he could find, he heard something whistle. He looked about him, and presently he saw, not far off, one of his own men standing by a pine tree, and beckoning him to come to him. White Bull went over to where the man was, and there, up in the tree where he pointed, was a great big porcupine. It was too high up to be reached, and they did not like to shoot, because that day they had seen in the snow signs where people had passed, but the tracks were not very fresh, for snow had fallen or blown into them. Still, there was danger that if they shot they might alarm these people.

They finally made up their minds that they must shoot the animal, and they did so. He fell down, turning over and over, and they opened and skinned him, and then the two men sat down and devoured the entrails raw. They took the carcass into camp and cut it into pieces—a piece for each man, telling them that they could cook it or eat it raw. Some cooked it, and some ate it raw.

The next day they started on again toward their home. The snow was always less deep, and now they could walk easily. White Bull said to his young men, "Now, there is not much snow, so all of you scatter out and see what you can kill, and we will all meet to-night at an appointed place." When they reached camp at night, one man had a wildcat and two had turkeys. They skinned and ate these, and all felt better and as if they should get home. They were cheerful and told stories and acted as if they had never been starving.

Next morning all rose early to start, and one young man went out a little way from the camp, and soon those in the camp heard the report of a gun, and then the young man came in dragging a wolf behind him. This made them a breakfast. The wolf was following the trail where the wildcat had been dragged along the day before.

All that day they traveled, and killed nothing to eat. There was still a light snow on the ground, and they walked fast; but they got tired early and camped, and built a fire and lay down about it. Not far from the camp there was a little hill, and White Bull thought he would climb to the top of it and see if he could see anything. He climbed up there and found that he could see Cherry Creek where it enters the Platte—where Denver now stands. As he sat there looking he thought that he saw something moving far off, going down toward the creek. It looked like a man on foot. He sat there and looked, and pretty soon he saw a herd of horses close to where the man had disappeared in the creek bottom. He went back to the camp and said to his young men: "I have made a discovery. I have seen a man and a herd of horses on Cherry Creek, where it enters the Platte. I think we would better start to-night, and travel there. It may be a camp where we can get something to eat."

They set out, and had only gone a little way when they came to a place where there was a tree full of turkeys. It was not yet dark, and the turkeys were just flying up into the tree and lighting there. They began shooting with bows and arrows, and with guns, and killed nine turkeys. White Bull said: "We will not go further. We will go down to this little creek and cook our turkeys, and eat them to-night." They went down to the water and camped, and skinned the turkeys and roasted and ate them, and all were happy and talked and sang.

At daylight they started again to go to where they had seen the man and horses. They traveled on and got pretty close to the camp, when White Bull, who was ahead, saw a wagon. He stopped and waited, and when the others came up he said to them: "These must be white people; I see a wagon." He looked at all his people and saw that they looked like ghosts. Their eyes were sunken, and their cheeks hollow, and he thought that he would look at himself to see how he looked. He got out his mirror and looked at himself, and was almost frightened when he saw his face, for he looked like a dead man. He said to his people: "If we go into the camp looking like this we will scare the people. They will think that a lot of dead persons have come to them. You can all see each other, how you look. Let us all paint our faces, so that we will not look so queer." They did this, and went on down to the camp, and found it was the camp of a white man, a man named Poiselle, who had married an Arapahoe woman. His wife was a relative of White Bull. This man had some cattle and he gave them a beef, and told them to kill it and to eat all they wanted to. They did so. The old man gave to each one of the Indians a blanket and a shirt, and each one gave to him a horse and five robes. They stayed here with him and borrowed two horses to ride, and sent two of the party to the village to bring back horses on which they could ride home. These men were gone four days and then returned, bringing back for each man a horse to ride, and also the horses that had been given to old man Poiselle. Many of the people came back with these young men to see their relatives. This happened in 1857.

THE SPEECH OF THE WOLVES

IN the year 1858 twenty-two Arapahoes and a Mexican started to war to find the Ute camp and all were killed except the Mexican. This made the Arapahoes feel badly and they wanted vengeance; so they brought the pipe to Lean Bear, who was a leading warrior among the Cheyennes. Lean Bear accepted the pipe and smoked and asked some of his friends to join him in going with the Arapahoes to war. Still, not many Cheyennes went on this party. One of those who went was Dives Backward, a Cheyenne who could understand what the wolves said when they howled.

Two nights after they had left the village the coyotes came close to the camp of the war party and barked, and when Dives Backward heard the coyotes barking he said to them, "*Ha ho'*, thank you." Burnt All Over was in the same war lodge with Dives Backward; and when he heard him speak to the coyotes he filled a pipe and passed it to Dives Backward and said to him, "Friend, tell me what the coyotes said to you." Dives Backward took the pipe and smoked, and when he had smoked he replied to Burnt All Over and said, "This coyote says, 'The spirits have taken pity on you; they have given you seven lodges of Utes and some prisoners, and, besides that, many horses.' "

After hearing him speak, Lean Bear went outside the lodge and cried out to the other members of the party: "I have a good thing to tell you; listen to me, my friends. This coyote that you have just heard barking says that the spirits have taken pity on us and have given us seven lodges of the Utes, some horses, and some prisoners. Dives Backward has just told me this."

When the Arapaho chiefs and the Cheyennes heard this, some of them came into the war lodge to hear better what was being said, for this was good news. While they all sat there smoking, the coyotes barked again, this time closer than before. Then Dives Backward said, "This coyote tells me that we should go straight to the two mountains right beyond these mountains before us, and after we have passed them we shall find our enemies." All the Cheyennes who were with this party tell what happened in the same way. They say that it came out just as Dives Backward had told them. Before they reached the two mountains, they sent out ahead scouts to look for the camp of the enemy, and they found it close to the mountains.

The Utes were camping close under a high bluff. During the night the Arapahoes and Cheyennes drove all the Ute horses away from the camp, and long before morning they crept up near to the lodges and waited until daylight, when they charged, and took the Utes wholly by surprise. The camp was close to the thick timber with willows and logs, and the Utes all ran into this place to fight and hide. A single Ute ran for the bluff. Lean Bear counted the first coup on him, Two Lance the second, and Burnt All Over the third. Then Lean Bear and his party ran back to where the men, women, and children had run to. A great crowd of Arapahoes and Cheyennes had surrounded this place. Many of them were on foot, for the Utes had guns and were shooting at their enemies from behind logs.

Lean Bear got off his horse and walked toward a place where he heard some children crying. As he advanced, right in front of him a Ute woman with a boy on her back jumped up from behind a big log. Lean Bear motioned her to come to him and she started toward him, and just then a Ute jumped up with a gun in his hand, full cocked. The woman was walking toward Lean Bear and was between the Ute and Lean Bear, so that the Ute could not shoot at Lean Bear for fear of hitting the woman and her boy. While the Ute was trying to shoot Lean Bear, an Arapaho shot this Ute. Lean Bear took the woman by the arm and led her away from the cover, and in this way he captured both these prisoners. They were Yellow Nose and his mother. Yellow Nose was four years old at the time. The father of Yellow Nose was not killed. He had gone out from the camp very early to look for his horses and that is how he got away.

One of the Ute chiefs afterward said that he was the only man of the party who was not killed. He died some years afterward. The mother of Yellow Nose lived for many years. She ran away and went back to the Utes, leaving her son behind her. She was with the Cheyennes one year and then ran off. The first time she ran away a war party of the Arapahoes found her in the mountains with some Mexicans and recognized her, and brought her back to the Cheyennes. Lean Bear had told her that if she would let him know whenever she wanted to go home, he would send her to her people. When she ran off the second time she had gone down to the creek to scrape the hair off a deer skin; but the women of Lean Bear's lodge knew that she was going to run off. Lean Bear said, "Do not follow her; let her go." Yellow Nose was then six years old and his mother had asked Lean Bear's wife to take care of him. Lean Bear took Yellow Nose for his son, and the mother knew that he would be well taken care of. In 1863 she was at the Ute Agency, and asked a Cheyenne who was there how her boy was getting along.

Dives Backward was looked upon by the Cheyennes as a person who understood the speech of the little wolves. After Yellow Nose and his mother had been captured, another war party of Cheyennes, all on foot, again started for the Ute country. Most of them belonged to the Fox Soldiers, to which society Dives Backward also belonged. They asked him to go with them.

One night when they had come to the foot of the mountains a coyote barked near where they had camped. Dives Backward, when he heard this coyote bark, hung down his head and said nothing. Then Two Buttes filled his war pipe and handed it to Dives Backward, and said to him, "Friend, tell us what the coyote said." Dives Backward smoked and after he got through smoking with the others, he said: "I feel badly, but I must tell you what the coyote has said. He said to us, 'Look out; for someone of this party will surely be killed, if you do not change your course and go in another direction. The way in which you are going, and the place toward which you are heading, are bad.' " Two Buttes went out of the lodge and cried out what Dives Backward had said. Sun Maker, another Fox Soldier, also came out and shouted: "Why should we start out on a war party if we are going to be frightened at everything we hear or see? I believe that we should go on."

The next morning Two Buttes and forty of the party turned about to go back to their homes. Dives Backward was with this party. About twenty men, among them Sun Maker, the leader of this party, stayed where they were. They were getting ready to go on toward the enemy. During the day they also kept talking about going back. They started to go home in another direction. Before they stopped for the night, they all rested on a hill, smoking. A certain young man named Short Body, who was a good shot, was told by Sun Maker to go and kill an antelope and after he had done this he could overtake them, as they would walk slowly. He was told not to bring with him a large load of meat, but to just bring the ribs, which were light and would be a small load. Short Body said to the others, "Do not wait for me, as I shall go over and dig some yellow and white clay to take home with me." Near this hill there was a place where they used to dig this paint. Short Body said he thought he would not take the trouble to kill any antelope, so they all started for home and Short Body went his way. Sun Maker and his party walked all night to get to the camp. They said that Short Body would soon be home, but two days passed and Short Body had not come into camp. Spotted Feathers and Bull Telling Tales reached the camp the next day after Sun Maker and his party. They also had been to this place, digging for clay, but had not seen Short Body. Two Buttes and his party got in just ahead of Sun Maker and his party.

Spotted Feathers and Bull Telling Tales said that during the day while they were digging the clay they had heard something that sounded like a shot, but they could not tell the direction from which it came. On the third day a party of men went back to see what had become of Short Body. They went first to the place where he had left Sun Maker's party, and then toward the place where they dig this clay. As the party traveled on they saw in the distance wolves and coyotes that seemed to be dragging something about over the ground. The Cheyennes all started for this place on the run, and when they got there they found the bones of Short Body scattered in every direction. The tracks showed that he had walked toward a hollow in the prairie, when he was shot from there by the Utes. Several horse tracks came down this ravine, and one of the riders dismounted to do the shooting. After killing him the tracks went back to the hills. The tracks made by the moccasins were those of Utes. The Utes got down to scalp Short Body, and took everything he had, so that there was nothing left on the ground. When killed, Short Body had with him a gun and bow and arrows.

The Cheyennes declared that Dives Backward could cure anyone that might be bitten by a mad wolf or a mad coyote, if he could doctor the person immediately after he was bitten. They also said that Dives Backward, when he was severely wounded by the Pawnees, each morning would fill the pipe and light it by the sun. Several persons lately living saw him do this each morning, at the time and just after he was wounded.

A FIGHT WITH THE PAWNEES

IN 1862, when I was about seventeen years old, I went south
to war against the Pawnees. There were about seventy men
of us, Northern and Southern Cheyennes. At that time my
name was Gray Hawk, *Wōhkpi āin'o.*

After we had gone some distance from the camp an old man
harangued, calling out the names of ten men who had the fastest
horses who should go ahead during the night. I was one of those
called. The best horses were selected, so that if we found the
Pawnee camp we could charge without waiting for the others.
We were told to do this. The ten men went ahead and the others
followed and traveled all night.

The next morning after the sun was well up we came to a
place where the Pawnees had killed a buffalo, and followed the
Pawnee trail. Without knowing it we had already passed their
camp, and now we turned and followed the Pawnees north up
the creek. When we had gone some distance we came to a place
where the Pawnees had been camped but we believed that during the night they had moved camp and the trail led south. We
had followed the Pawnees up Swallow Creek and the Pawnees
who had been camped there had moved over on Turkey Creek,*
where the camp now was. It was not quite noon when we saw
some Pawnees chasing buffalo and about the same time we saw
the Pawnee camp.

When we saw this we stopped and watched for a time and
then all mounted. The oldest man of the party was called Two
Children. He told the others to fall in line with a broad front
and he would ride well in front of the line and tell them what
to do. We circled down among the hills so as to keep out of
sight, but went toward the camp. We rode at a trot, Two Chil-

* Turkey Creek, Solomon River.

74

dren well in the lead. He had said to us that he did not wish us to make a charge until he ordered it, and that he would give us the signal. Just before we reached a point near the Pawnee camp, a man near me called out: "Your saddle is slipping back and the cinch is under the horse's belly; it may turn. You will do well to get off and tighten it." I did so, and this left me far behind. I mounted and rode on, but before I had overtaken the party, the leader gave the signal to charge.

When we reached the top of the hill we saw immediately before us two Pawnees who seemed to be trying to kill a wounded buffalo cow. When they saw us the Pawnees rode away from the cow, and the Cheyennes were obliged to charge on them instead of waiting until they had come close to the camp.

I had been riding hard and had overtaken Two Children, who in turn had almost overtaken the last of the Pawnees. I passed Two Children and called out trying to encourage him not to turn from them, but Two Children seemed afraid of the Pawnees and turned away from them. When I saw this I thought that this was my chance to kill an enemy and count a coup, and I called out to Two Children, "Look out, do not go too close to him, he may kill you." When the Pawnee, turning, rushed at Two Children to fight him, his face was turned from me. I rushed in between the two and the Pawnee and I were so close together that neither could use his arms and the horses were rubbing their sides together. Now, Two Children rode up close to me on the other side from the Pawnee, who was pounding me over the head with his bow while I was trying to strike the Pawnee on the head with my lance. Then Touching Cloud rode up and called out to Two Children, saying, "Get away from there and give Gray Hawk room so that he may do something." Two Children turned his horse away and I turned my horse away from the Pawnee and as soon as there was room Touching Cloud dashed in between the Pawnee and me and shot the Pawnee with his six-shooter. After the Pawnee fell off his horse I dashed in front of Touching Cloud and caught the horse, and let it go again.

The other Pawnee was riding hard toward the Pawnee camp and I rode after him, but other Cheyennes were close behind me. As I was overtaking the Pawnee I heard Badger Bear call out, "Kill the man." He kept calling this out, but the man to whom he was speaking would not get close to the Pawnee. He made a charge and then turned off, and after he had done this more than once the Pawnee jumped off his horse and let it go. Now the man close to him made a dash toward him and struck at him with a lance, but it missed him. The next rider, Old Man, *Ma ha kĭs'*, rushed toward the Pawnee, but before he reached him, his horse turned off. Next I came. When the Pawnee had jumped off his horse he had fallen down and had turned over two or three times, but had held on to his bow. As he gained his feet he fitted an arrow to the string to shoot at me but he was a little slow. My horse struck him and rode over him, and I counted the first coup, Old Man counted the second, and Badger Bear the third. As the latter came up the Pawnee shot at him with an arrow. The arrow hit Badger Bear about the middle of the waist, struck a broad raw-hide belt and seemed to come out behind the arm. The Cheyennes thought that Badger Bear had a bad wound, but he was not scratched. This took place about twenty-five yards from the edge of the Pawnee camp.

In the camp we saw the Pawnees on their horses and charging out, so we did not stop to kill the last Pawnee. The Cheyennes wheeled and went back on the trail that they had come on. They passed the first Pawnee, who had been scalped and was now trying to raise himself on his hands, and went on up by where the buffalo was killed. There two of the Cheyenne horses gave out. Tobacco took one man on behind and at last I took the other.

When the man that I took up saw that his horse was giving

out he got frightened and began to call to the others for help. Finally he called me by name, Gray Hawk, and I returned and rode back to him. As I did so I called to him, "Jump off your horse and be ready to jump on behind me." The man did as he was told and when he struck the ground the Pawnees, who were close behind, began to yell and made the hills ring. After the man had jumped up behind me the Pawnees gained on us and were on both sides of me and behind us. The other Cheyennes had run off and left us. My horse was a good one and soon began to gain on them. We kept on, and presently the leading Cheyenne, who had matches in his pouch, began to light them and throw them on the ground, and at last he set the prairie on fire. When the Pawnees saw the fire rise they all turned their horses and went back, for they suspected that this was a signal to other Cheyennes to come up.

As the Cheyennes topped each ridge they expected as they went on to see the rest of their party whom they had left the night before. At length, after they had gone quite a long distance, they did see them. When the others saw only eight horses coming they thought that people had been killed, but they found that two were riding double.

WHITE BULL'S SCOUTS

ONE night, a long time ago, White Bull had a dream—a very strong dream. In the morning after rising he thought much about his dream, and after a time he called out, asking some of his friends and some of the principal men to come to his lodge. After they had eaten and smoked, he said to them: "My friends, I want to make up a party and go to war. I know where there are eight or ten men of some kind of people, who are coming to war this way—toward our camp. Last night I saw them as they were traveling down the Musselshell River. With them there is a chief, who wears a big silver plate tied to his scalplock."

A party of forty-one people got together for White Bull's war journey. Among them were three women.

The war party started from the village, which was on Tongue River, and traveled over to the head of the Muddy, down the Rosebud, and then over to Sheep River, and down that to the Yellowstone. There they camped for one day, and crossed, and went over to the Musselshell, and followed it up all day long. Toward night they camped and sent out a man to see what he could discover. He came back and said that he could see nothing.

Just before dark White Bull went a little way out from the camp and sat down on a hill. While he was sitting there a coyote trotted along near by and barked at him, and told him that his enemies were on the river just above him; that they had just come into camp. When White Bull heard this he went back to his camp. He filled his pipe and called some of the older men to smoke with him. They smoked, and he told them that the enemies were not far off now. After a time he said to Brave Wolf and to Prairie Bear, "Get on your horses, and go up this stream nearly to the forks, and if you get there before daylight, wait until it is day, and try to see these people, and to find out who they are."

The men went as he had directed and hid themselves and their horses near the forks, and lay down and went to sleep. They slept too long, however, and did not awake until the sun was up. Then they jumped up, and mounted their horses and rode up on a hill, and looking over discovered a little smoke, where there had been a fire. They rode around behind a hill close to the smoke, and when they looked over, they saw what had been the camp, but the people were not there. They had gone. The two men rode down to the camp and found a war lodge, and where people had cooked and eaten, and their tracks.

Early that morning White Bull with the party started up the creek, and it was nearly noon when he met Brave Wolf and Prairie Bear coming down. They told him what they had seen, that the people had left their camp and were coming downstream toward him, but that they were not following the river, but had gone out on the prairie as if intending to cross toward the Yellowstone. Then the Cheyennes started across to look for the trail, and soon found it. The enemy were on foot, but the Cheyennes on horseback. The Cheyennes followed them all day, and camped on the trail. The next morning they continued to follow the trail, which kept on toward the Yellowstone, and when they reached the river they found that the enemy had crossed. The Cheyennes crossed, and kept on to a small stream which had timber growing on it, and followed it up. It was now nearly dark, and had begun to rain, and they could see by the tracks that they were close to the enemy. White Bull said to his people, "Now it is getting dark, and is going to rain; let us camp here, and look for these people in the morning."

In the morning, just as it began to get gray, White Bull called to his people to get up, and said, "Come on! We will start again on the trail." They had gone only about a hundred yards, when they met a coyote trotting along. He barked at them, saying to White Bull, "Your enemy is right close here, now." White Bull turned to his people and said, "Get ready: get out your shields, and your arms, and make ready, they are close by here; right close." All stopped there and painted themselves for war, and tied up their horses' tails. He had put down his pipe on the ground, and just as they were getting ready to start, a magpie flew up and alighted on the ground just beyond his pipe, and called to him loudly, saying: "White Bull, hurry! hurry! your enemy will see you. They are close by. Just under those pines," nodding his head toward

some pine trees a quarter of a mile away, "is your enemy."
Then the bird flew away.

The enemy had discovered them. They had seen the Cheyennes, and then had crossed the creek and gone down on the
other side toward the Yellowstone. The Cheyennes made a
charge toward the camp, looking everywhere for the enemy,
and finally White Bull rode right into the camp, but no one was
there. Meat was roasting over the fire, and some of the Cheyennes took it and rode on, eating as they rode. They hunted
about, looking everywhere for the people, and at last found
their tracks going down the stream. They followed the trail to
the banks of the Yellowstone, White Bull and old Two Moons
being ahead of the others. At the bank, Two Moons ran into
some brush, and there, face to face, met the chief of the enemy,
who wore a silver plate on his head. Two Moons was a chief,
and over his forehead tied to his hair he wore a large feather
with a piece of buffalo horn on it. When the two met the enemy
shot and hit this feather, but Two Moons shot the enemy through
the head and killed him dead. He counted coup on him and so
did White Bull.

In the Yellowstone at this place is a little island covered with
bushes, and most of the Cheyennes crossed over to this and were
searching in the brush, when, from the shore they had left, a
young man on a hill called out and said, "They have all crossed
the river!" They looked over to where he pointed, and saw the
enemy standing naked on the bank. They followed them no
farther.

The chief killed was dressed just like the man White Bull
had seen in his dream. He was a Blackfoot chief named Red
Eagle, a great warrior.

STORIES OF MYSTERY

SEES IN THE NIGHT

THE camp was moving, but every stream they came to was dry. They could find no water. They kept on until they reached a creek, where they found water by digging holes, and here they camped. The next day they moved on and set out for the big river. At the camp they left behind an old dog with a litter of puppies. The people came to the river and crossed it and went up on the other side.

A poor boy who had no home crossed with the rest, and when they had come out of the river he lay down under a tree and went to sleep. The dog with her puppies was following up the trail of the camp. The boy who was asleep heard the dog coming, singing; it sounded like a young woman singing. She sang a song over twice, and after each song she stopped and howled four times like a wolf. When he first heard her the boy thought it was a wolf.

The dog kept coming closer and closer all the time, singing the same song. As she came on she began to sing another song different from the first one and again howled four times like a wolf.

Then she spoke and said: "Do not harm my children. Take pity on my children; carry them across the river." Then she sang another song, the same as before, and howled four times like a wolf and spoke again saying, *"Wŭ hŭ ĭs tăt' tăn,** do not harm my children. Take pity on my children; carry them across the river safely. I know that you are a poor boy and have no father. You have no home; you are on the prairie. I know the man road and the war trail. I am a woman. I know the woman trail. If you take my children across safely, I will take pity on and help you."

* *Wŭ hŭ ĭs tăt' tăn,* human being.

83

The young boy was very poor. He had only an old wornout robe and every part of his clothing was bad. When he heard the dog coming he got up and looked across the river, and when he saw her he held up both hands. He wanted the dog to take pity on him.

When the dog reached the river bank, the boy waded over to meet her and took two of the puppies and carried them over, and then went back again and took over two more, and then again, and took the last two across. When he carried over the last two, the mother jumped in and swam across. When she had reached the other side of the river she said to the young boy, "Where is the camp?" He replied: "It is right below here; right around that bend. There are some of the people coming out in little parties. Perhaps they are going out to chase buffalo."

The dog spoke again to the boy, and said: "I know that you have no home, and therefore I am going to take pity on you. Look at your moccasins and look at your robe; both are full of holes. You shall have a name, and your name shall be known everywhere. You shall have friends, and you shall have relations. Two or three or four days after a war party starts, you must follow after it, and must sing these songs that you heard me sing."

The dog said to him: "You must do just as I tell you. You must start out two or three or four days after a war party starts. You must go then, even if you have to start at night. If you go at night it will be to you just the same as day. You can follow the trail. I am a woman, and I know that you will have relations."

The dog went on to the camp. After she had gone a little way the boy saw an old woman coming. She took up the puppies and carried them on. The people were about to go out on a buffalo chase.

The young lad had never been to war. He told no one what the dog had said to him; he kept it secret to himself. He used to go out among the hills at night and cry and pray for help and good luck. After a while he grew up to be a young man. A war party was about to start, and he thought to himself, "I wonder if that dog told me the truth." He determined to wait three days before he followed up the trail of the war party. He said he would go with the war party, and after it had started people began to ask him when he was going to start. He replied to those who questioned him, "I shall follow the war party after a little while."

Three days after the war party had started, he followed it. That night he camped. Next day he went on, following the trail. Night came on, but he traveled during the night, singing the songs which the dog had sung, and to him the darkness was like daylight. He could see the buffalo on each side of the trail. He did not travel all night. The third night he traveled, singing these songs, first the first song the dog had sung and then the second song, and after each song he howled like a wolf, four times. The following night, about the middle of the night, he came to the camp of the war party. Some of the people were still awake and when he reached the camp they called him to the war lodge to which he belonged. A man said to him, "We have been expecting you, but at the last we thought you were not coming." "Oh," he said, "I thought I would wait about three days before starting."

The next morning they went on. They camped three or four times before they found the Crow camp. When they reached it, they waited until night so as to try to take horses. Then they separated to look for the horses. He and a young man whom he knew well went together. He said to his companion, "Let us go this way." No one knew that he could see as well by night as by day. They came to a bunch of horses and he said to his friend, "You take these, and I will go across and see if I can find others." Across the stream he could see another bunch of horses. He was selecting those that he wished. He brought back all these horses to the Cheyenne camp. He helped the people who had taken care of him when he was little, for he gave them some of the horses he had brought.

Some time after this another big war party was about to start out, and he was going with it. His moccasins were made and he was ready to go. He told his people at home that he would wait four days before he followed up the trail. After four nights he followed the party, singing his songs as before, and each time after he had sung he howled like a wolf. He overtook the war party after it had been out six nights. They went on and came to a camp where they could take some horses. They separated as usual, two or three going together. The people did not yet know that he could see at night as well as in the daytime. He took with him the same young man that he had been with before, and said to him, "Let us go down this way." They came to a great big herd of horses, and he told his friend to drive them in. Each caught a horse, and they ran them off.

When he got back with these horses to the camp the young man was made a soldier chief. After that whenever a war party was starting out, there were always two or three young men who wanted to remain behind and go with him. They wanted to see what he did on his journey; they were trying to find out about him.

They started on another war party, and two or three stayed behind to go with him. After the party had started, these young men kept persuading him to start, saying, "We do not believe that you are going." But he said, "Wait; we will overtake them." When they started, he taught these young men his songs and they did just as he did. They took some more horses. When they came home, the chief of the camp said, "I would like to have that young man for my son-in-law." When the people he lived with heard of this, they sent horses for the girl, and he married her. Now he was rich, and had a big skin lodge and had plenty of friends and plenty of relations. He was made a big chief. He never had any bad luck. He always had good luck on his warpaths. Everything the dog had told him came true.

THE BUFFALO WIFE

I

ONCE the tribe was scattered out, camping in small parties in different places. In one of the camps there was a very handsome young man. His father loved him dearly, and used to put up for him a lodge in which he lived by himself. Several girls had wanted to marry him, but he refused them.

One day a girl came to his village—a very beautiful girl—; she had yellow hair. He liked her and took her to his lodge and married her. Afterward another girl came in. She too was very handsome. Her hair was dark. He married her too. The first girl was an elk, and the second a young buffalo cow; but the young man did not know this, for they were human in shape. The young man lived with these two wives. After a time each had a child, and these boys grew up until they were big enough to run about and play together. One day they began to dispute about something, and soon they were fighting. From this time on the two women began to dispute, each one taking the part of her child. One day they quarreled and the elk girl became angry, and went away from the camp, taking her boy with her. The buffalo girl declared that she would not stay there, and she too went away. This happened while the young man was out in the hills looking for his dogs.

When the young man returned to the camp and found both his wives gone, he felt angry and said to his father: "Why did you let those women go away? Why did you not stop them? I saw them going over the hill as I came into the camp."

The young man got together some moccasins, and said to his father, "I am going after one of them, to see if I can get her

to come back." He left the camp and climbed the hill, and
when he had reached the top he stood there for a time considering, trying to decide which one of his wives he should
follow. He determined to follow the buffalo woman, and set
out after her. He followed the trail a long way, and at length
the tracks of the woman and the child disappeared and he saw
only the tracks of a buffalo cow and calf. He followed these
until late in the evening, and at length saw before him, far off,
a lonely lodge, and went down toward it. It was his wife's.

The little boy was playing about outside, and saw his father
coming, and went in and told his mother, saying, "Mother,
my father is coming." His mother said to the child: "Go and
meet your father, and tell him to turn back and go home. Let
him come no further than where he is when you meet him.
Tell him that I am going to my home, far away." The boy went
as he was bade, and when he met his father he told him that his
mother wished him to turn about and go home, that his mother
was going to some great place far off. The young man refused
to go back. He said, "No, I love you, son; I am following
you." He went into the lodge. Everything was nicely arranged.
At night when he went to bed he lay down to the left of the
door, by his little boy. His wife lay to the right of the door.
When he awoke in the morning there was no one there. There
was no lodge; he was lying on the open prairie.

He arose and looked about for the trail. He could see the
trail where the lodge poles had dragged along, and he followed
it, crying. For a little distance he followed the lodge pole trail,
and then it disappeared, and there were only the tracks of a
cow and her calf. All day he followed these tracks and at night
he saw before him a stream, and by it stood a single lodge—
his wife's. His boy saw him coming and told his mother, who
sent him to meet his father with the same message as before.
Again the father refused to turn back, saying: "No, son, I am
following her for your sake. I love you." That night he again

lay down by his son, and put his arms around him and held him close, so that if they moved during the night he would know it. But in the morning, when he awoke, he was lying on the bare prairie. There was no lodge there.

That day he followed the trail, mourning and crying. At night he saw a lodge. The boy saw him, and again came out with the same message from his mother. He added: "We are going to have a hard time to make a living. It is pretty bad there. You ought to go back." His father said, "No, my son, I am going to follow you and your mother." That night when he lay down to sleep, he tied his little boy to his belt, thinking that thus he would know if they moved, but the next morning they were gone as before.

Again he followed and overtook them at night. Before he reached the lodge, the woman sent him word to turn back. "She says," said the little boy, "that we are getting close now; that my grandfather and grandmother are powerful people. They may kill you." The man would not go back, but spent that night in the lodge. His wife lay down beside him. He tried to stay awake all night, but the next morning they were gone.

Again he followed the trail, and again the boy came back to him, and told him that he must turn back. He said, "Where my mother is going is a bad place; it will be dangerous for you; you ought to turn back." The man said: "No, my son, I will not turn back; I am going to follow you and your mother. I love you, and I will not leave you." "Well," said the son, "it will be better if you go back; this is a long journey that we are going on, and you will very likely suffer for water, for the country is dry." "No, my son," said his father, "I am going to follow you."

"If you are determined to come," said the boy, "watch our tracks, and wherever I step to one side, follow the track, and where I have stepped there will be water in my track. Beside this I will leave a bowl of meat for you. After a while you will reach that place where we are going, and when you get there sit down on this side of the place. My relations will come back toward you, and will charge on you, but you must not run from them; you must not move."

The man remembered what his son had said to him, and as his son had said, so it was. The cow and her calf ran far, and the man followed fast, and grew very tired and very thirsty, but several times in the calf's tracks he found water, and he found also food that his son had left.

That day the woman and the little boy reached their home—the buffalo home. When the buffalo saw her coming, they said to each other: "The buffalo woman is coming, and she is bringing a person with her. What shall we do?" They talked among themselves, trying to make up their minds what they should do with this man, and they determined that, unless he went away, they would kill him. They sent his son to tell him this.

When the woman reached the place where the buffalo were, the man was a long way behind; and when he came in sight of them he stopped on a hill and sat down, and stayed there mourning and crying for help. After a time the little boy came to him on the hill, and spoke to his father and said to him: "You had better go; my grandfather and uncles are very bad. They will kill you." His father said: "No, my son, I am following you. I love you, and I am willing to die for your sake." The boy returned to the buffalo and told them what his father had said.

The chief of the buffalo sent up his son to kill the man. The young bull went up the hill slowly, often stopping and pawing the earth, and making a great dust. When he had come near the man, he put down his head and made a rush at him, but the man did not move; he sat there motionless. Before his brother-in-law reached the man, he stopped and looked at him and said, "*I yo hoh'*; my brother-in-law has a strong heart." Then he turned about and went down the hill. Next the man's father-in-law went up to kill him. He did just what his son had done, pawing at the dirt, and tearing up the ground with his horns; and when he got near the man he made a rush at him. The young man did not move, and before the old bull reached him he stopped and said, "*I yo hoh'*; my son-in-law has a strong heart." Then he went back down the hill.

Now the buffalo counseled together again, and after they had come to a decision, they sent the man's son to tell him what they were going to do. His son came to the man and said to him: "Father, they are going to call you down to the herd, and if you cannot pick out my mother and me and your other relations from among the buffalo, they will kill you. Now I intend to try to save your life. When you are looking through the buffalo to find me, I shall be on the left of the other calves, and will keep moving my ears. I will put a big cockle burr on my mother's hump, a burr on the middle of my grandmother's back, one on my grandfather's head, and one on my uncle's rump, close to the root of his tail. Look closely for these."

The chief of the buffalo told all his people to stand in rows; the young calves in one row, the young cows in another, the young bulls in another, the old cows in another, and the old bulls in another; and sent word to his son-in-law to come down and pick out his son, wife, brother-in-law, mother-in-law, and father-in-law. The man went down and picked them all out. After he had done this the buffalo were astonished, and said to each other, "*I yo hoh'*; this man is great."

On the prairie where the buffalo were camped were many possible sacks, containing their possessions, and these possible sacks were all ornamented with quills. The boy said to his father: "They will ask you to look among these for my mother's possible sack. I will put a little bit of a stick on that sack, where the strings are tied, so that you may find it." When the buffalo told the man that he must find his wife's possible sack, he looked among them, and by the little bit of stick he found it. The buffalo had many quilled cushions and pillows. The calf told his father that they would ask him to look for his wife's cushion, and that he would put a little stick on the end of the cushion, so that his father might know it. The man found it at once. The buffalo were still more astonished, and now they let him stay with them.

This man's father-in-law told the people to put up a lodge for his son-in-law. He said: "How shall we support this man? What can we give him to eat? We have none of his food, and he cannot eat the grass, like buffalo. Let a buffalo be killed, and let him taste it and see if he likes it." They killed a buffalo, and the man ate of it. The old bull asked his daughter if her husband liked the meat. She said: "He likes it. It is good."

While all this was going on, war parties of buffalo were continually starting off from the herd, looking for the camps of the people, and fighting them. Often when the man walked out in the hills, he would see far off great dusts rising where the war parties of young bulls were going off to look for people. In those days the people had no bows nor arrows; all they had to live on were roots, mushrooms, the fungus that grows on the trunks of trees, and the soft inner bark of the trees. In those days, too, the buffalo used to eat the people. One day the man went to where the buffalo had been fighting, to see what they were doing. The buffalo had killed a number of people, and were hanging up the hind quarters. It made the man feel badly to see so many of his people dead.

One night the man dreamed of something—a tool that could be used to pierce things a long way off. He went out in the hills and thought about this for a long time, and at last he devised it. He took sinews from the buffalo that had been killed, and a stick, and made a bow—the first that had been made. After he had made it, he did not take it into the camp, but left it out in the hills. As yet he had no arrow; but he got small sticks, and took more sinews, and found some feathers, and looked through the hills for sharp stones, and bound them on his arrows. When his arrows were finished, he left them hidden out in the hills, and went home. Every day he used to go out and shoot with them, learning how to use his new weapons.

One day when the man was out far from the camp he saw a herd of buffalo charging over a hill. He went far around and crept up carefully to see what they were doing. When he had come close to them he saw a group of people fighting behind breastworks, and the buffalo fighting them. The buffalo charged, and the people fought them off with clubs; and because of the breastworks, the buffalo could not get at the people. When he got near to the buffalo, the man rushed toward them, and began to shoot them with his arrows, and some fell down and died. The others called out, "Run, run! Here is some great person who is armed." The buffalo had already killed some people, and had some meat and fat. They called out to each other, "Hide what you have, and run." They hid it about their necks and ran. That is why we call this (the sweetbreads) "human fat," and do not eat it now.

The man said to the people that he had helped: "Cut up these dead buffalo, and eat their flesh. I have already eaten of this food, and it is good."

He made many bows and arrows for the people, and from this time forth they began to scatter out and roam the prairie —to live like people. The buffalo ran away, and after that never attacked people. The man told them to eat of all fruits that grew—all cherries, plums, and berries. He was a man of great power, and saved the tribe. That was when we first began to live.

II

THE whole camp was moving. They came to a big river and intended to cross over to the other side. The people began to cross and soon nearly all of them were on the other bank. The last family about to cross saw an old woman sitting by the water, and the woman of the family said: "My, my, here is an old woman who has been left on this side of the river. Get on the travois," she said to the old woman, "and I will take you across."

"No," said the old woman, "I will wait here for a little while." She remained sitting there and would not cross. The woman went on, leaving her. When the woman reached the camp, most of the lodges were already set up in the circle.

As usual there were stragglers following behind the camp—young men and boys on foot. At last these reached the river and some of them, seeing the old woman, said, "Well, well, they have moved off and left the old woman on this side of the river." They sat down and began to take off their moccasins and leggings before wading the stream. One of them said to the others, "Let us carry the old woman across the river." They talked and joked about it for a little and finally one said, "I will carry her over." He spoke to the old woman as she sat there with her staff lying on the ground before her, and said, "Old woman, I will carry you over." She said, "No."

While these young men sat there talking, another crowd of young men and boys came up and began to get ready to wade across. The first lot, as they walked into the river, called back to the others, "Bring your grandmother over the river." The second lot began to say to one another, "Go to the old woman and carry her across." One by one they went to her and offered to carry her across to where the camp was, but she refused them all. Among them was a handsome young man, very quiet, who carried a contrary bow. The young men spoke to him and said, "You go and ask her to let you carry her over." The young man walked up to her and said, "Grandmother, let me carry you over." She said to him, "Yes, yes, grandchild, carry me over." He was the one she wanted to have carry her over.

The young man turned round and gave his moccasins and robe to another man to carry for him, sat down on the ground, and said to the old woman, "Put your arms around my neck." When she had done so, he rose to his feet, went into the river, and carried her across.

When they had reached the other bank he said, "Now, get off here." The old woman did not answer, but she did not get off and he could not get her off. She would not speak a word. The young man went to his close friend and said to him, "Friend, try to get this old woman off my back." His friend tried but he could do nothing; he could not even get her arms loose. Then the young man said, "Put on my moccasins for me," and they did so. They all started toward the camp and as they went on the young man who was carrying her felt ashamed, and said to himself, "The people will all look at me when I come to the camp carrying this old woman." When they reached the camp the young men told him to go to the center of the camp, that they would find some way to get her off his back there; but all the other young men turned off and went to the places where they belonged. The young man who was carrying the woman went to the center of the circle and sat down there.

The young men went about the camp telling the people that Contrary had an old woman stuck fast to his back, and that something ought to be done to get her off. An old man went about the camp crying out that in some way this old woman should be got off Contrary's back. Then the people all came to the center of the camp and tried to pull her off, but they could not do it.

At last they gave up the attempt; but one man spoke up and said: "Wihio is in camp. He may have some plan for getting her off this person's back. Send for him." They found Wihio and brought him up there.

When he heard what the matter was, Wihio said, "All you young men carry up wood here and build a big fire, and place this young man with his back toward the fire, and when the old woman gets real hot she will fall off."

All the young men ran to bring up wood. They were all glad to do it, because everyone liked Contrary and wanted to help him. They built the fire, and put the young man close to it with his back toward it, and at last the fire burned up and grew hotter and hotter. When the old woman got really hot she began to move this way and that, and finally she fell off the young man's back and coiled herself up as women do and sat there with her staff in front of her and her head hanging down.

The people said, "Come away and leave her; give her nothing to eat; let her starve." They all moved away and left her sitting there by herself. Contrary went home to his lodge.

Night came on. After it was dark the young men went about through the camp playing and singing and yelping and calling out, as young men do, but toward midnight these sounds grew quiet and there was no noise in the camp. The young man who had had this burden on his back was in bed and asleep. About the middle of the night he awoke and felt that he must go out. He was tired and wanted to rest and sleep, but yet he felt obliged to go out. He could not resist the feeling and he got up and stepped out of the lodge. When he looked toward the center of the camp he saw standing there a great big skin lodge with a light in it. He looked at it astonished, and as he looked at it he heard a baby crying, and a woman singing to the baby. He wondered who could be camped there, and said to himself, "I believe I will go over and look into that lodge." But he did not go. He went back into his own lodge and lay down. As he went in he said aloud, "Someone is camped in the center of the circle; there is a big lodge there with a light in it." The next morning when he looked out of the door, there was no lodge in the middle of the circle, but the old woman was sitting in the same place where she had been left.

That day the people kept talking about what they should do with this old woman. They were wondering about it, and toward evening they held a council over it and finally decided that they would move off and leave her there and let her starve to death.

That night late—some people had gone to bed and some were still up and about—an old man stepped out of his lodge and saw a lodge standing in the center of the camp. He called out, "Look at this lodge in the center of the camp, with a light in it."¹

After all the people had gone to bed, Contrary said in his mind: "I think I will go and look into that lodge." He arose from his bed and went out, and again he could hear the baby crying and someone singing to it. The voice said: "Hush, hush, baby, your father is coming; he will be here soon. You must not cry."

The young man went over to the lodge and looked in at the door, and saw, sitting on the left side of the lodge, a handsome girl with long black hair, holding a little baby in her arms. The lodge was finely furnished, with back rests, and buffalo robes hanging on the back rests.

The young man entered the lodge. The girl looked at him as he went through the doorway, and followed him with her eyes until he said to her, "Hand me my son." Then she put the baby in his arms. He felt happy to see the child. She felt with her hands behind the bed and brought out some nice pemmican and gave it to her husband. Then they got ready to go to bed. On the beds were fine robes garnished with porcupine quills. They went to bed. He slept with the child.

The next morning when Contrary awoke he found himself alone lying on the grass in the center of the camp circle. There was no lodge, and no furnishings, and no people. This was the time the camp had intended to move, but when the people awoke that morning the old woman was gone. Contrary went home to his lodge. He wondered which way his wife had moved and before anybody had started out from the camp he went out to look for signs, any tracks which his wife might have made. In the camp there were no tracks, but at the opening of the circle he saw the tracks of lodge poles dragging and followed them. He did not turn back.

He followed the tracks the whole day long. Toward evening he began to get tired, and from time to time he stopped to rest. He passed over a hill and saw beyond a little creek, on which grew some timber, and standing all alone by the stream bank, a lodge. When he came in sight of the lodge he stopped and sat down, for he thought that he would not go in at once, but would wait a little while. At length he went down to the lodge and when he had come pretty near to it, the woman came out of the lodge and began to move the poles that held the wings. She spoke to the child, which was now large enough to sit up, and said, "Your father is coming."

Contrary went in and sat down on the bed at the left of the lodge—on the south side—and took the child in his arms. His wife gave him something to eat, back-fat and buffalo meat. At night they sat up for a time and talked to each other.

Next morning when Contrary awoke he was lying on the prairie. The lodge had gone; he did not know which way it had gone; all that he could see leaving the place were the tracks of a buffalo cow and calf. He followed these and after they had gone a certain distance they turned into a travois trail and he followed that. That day he rested quite often on the trail.

In the evening he saw a lodge a long way off. As he drew near it the woman came out as before and fixed the wings. When he had got close to the lodge he saw the boy toddling around, walking. The mother spoke to the child, saying, "Your father is coming." The child laughed and ran to his father, holding out his hands. He took him up in his arms and carried him into the lodge. His wife gave her husband something to eat.

The man said, "I am tired." They talked for a little while and then went to bed.

The next morning when Contrary awoke the lodge was gone. He did not know where they had gone, but by this time he had learned that they were going in one direction—toward the sunrise. He found the trail and followed it. Before him he could see far off some blue ridges and when he reached them he stopped and sat down. Then he went on again and ahead of him he saw another distant ridge, and he went toward this ridge. It was getting toward evening when he reached the second ridge. When he had climbed to the top he saw on the creek down below the camp. It was now very late in the evening and he went down to the camp. The little boy saw him coming and called out to his mother, "My father is coming." When Contrary had come near the lodge the boy ran out and met him. His wife was just bringing in some wood for the fire. He went in. His wife cooked him something and gave him to eat. After he had finished eating he said, "I am very tired."

The woman said to him: "I came for you. You are the one I came for." They went to bed. He was very tired and slept sound and long, and the next morning he was so tired that he did not wake up in time and again the woman and the camp were gone.

He followed up the trail all day long, but rested four times during the day. That evening after the fourth rest he again saw a lodge, his wife's camp. The little boy was now quite large. He was playing around the lodge. When he saw his father coming the boy called out, "Mother, father is coming," and then ran out and met him. He took the boy by the hand and led him back and went into the lodge and sat down on the bed. His wife cooked something for him to eat.

After he had finished eating the woman explained to him how it was that she had come for him. "My father gave me to you," she said, "and sent me for you. Before this I have been sent in the same way. Whatever may happen do not get frightened; do not give up; be strong."

"In the morning if you look off in that direction"—pointing—"you will see a blue ridge a long way off. It is from there that I was sent for you."

The little boy felt glad to have his father again. He played and ran all around the lodge, he was so glad. Then he ran to his father and threw his arms around his neck.

The woman continued speaking and said: "Over there are many of my people and we all look alike. All the little ones look alike—the little calves that are still yellow. You will be told to look for your wife. My father will be the one who will tell you. My father will tell you to look for your son, too."

The little boy spoke to his father. He said: "Father, when you come to look for me I will shake my tail and start toward my mother to nurse. Then you can say, 'This is my son.'"

The woman said: "When you are told to look for me I will move my right forefoot just a little and will move my right ear." She added: "It is a long way to where we must go to-morrow. There is no water between here and there."

His boy said: "As you follow my trail to-morrow, father, watch it closely and after we have gone a long distance you will see when we are crossing a dry creek where I will turn off. Follow my tracks and I will stamp on the ground and put a stone over the track. Lift up that stone and under it you will find water to drink."

The woman said: "I have been sent off in this way several times and have brought back husbands, but always they got frightened and were killed. If they get frightened my people just stamp them to death. When you have come on top of that ridge you will see the buffalo scattered all over the flat beyond. When you get to that place wear your robe hair side out. Do not get frightened and do not dodge. When you have come to this ridge and are in sight of my people, my father will charge on you four times. If you do not get frightened or move when the four charges are made, you will save yourself." After they had finished talking they lay down to sleep.

The next morning the man awoke and found himself lying alone on the prairie; he started to follow on and after a time he found the lodge pole trail and followed it, but at length the lodge pole trail disappeared. When the trail disappeared, there were the tracks of two buffalo—a cow and a calf. He followed these until he came to the dry creek. By this time he was growing thirsty, but he had not forgotten what his son had told him. When he came to this place he began to watch the tracks closely and soon he saw where the calf had turned off and gone up the creek a little way. He followed the tracks and soon came to a stone and said to himself, "This must be the place," and lifting up the stone he saw a nice pool of water.

He drank and sat there until he was rested. After he had drunk and rested, he took the trail again and followed it. He kept on until he had come to the hill about which his wife had told him. He looked over, and saw all the land covered with buffalo. He sat down there wearing his robe with the hair side out. When he came in sight and sat down, the buffalo began to move about, to go around in a circle. They made much noise. When they made this noise, more buffalo seemed to come from all directions toward this big flat.

After a time a bull came out of the herd and came slowly up toward him. The young man made up his mind that this must be the one of which his wife had spoken, and he began to get ready and to try to have a strong heart. He sat there with his robe around his knees, and one elbow resting on his knee and his hand over his eyes. The buffalo was now coming closer. When the buffalo had come near, he stuck his tail out stiff and began to paw the earth and to put his head down and blow. The young man did not move, but sat there. The buffalo came toward him, pawing the earth, sometimes advancing with one side toward him and sometimes with the other; pawing the earth and grunting. Then he made a fierce rush toward the young man and almost touched him and then turned off. The young man did not move. Then the bull said, "*Ē hē hēh'*, my son-in-law has a strong heart."

Four times this was repeated, and the young man did not move. The fourth time the bull said, "*Ē hē hēh'*, my son-in-law has a strong heart. He possesses spiritual power (*Mā ĭ yŭn ĭv'*). He has saved his life." Then he spoke to the young man and said to him, "You can get up now and go to your wife."

The bull went off and threw himself down on the ground and rolled, and then rose and shook himself.

Then the young man stood up and started down toward the buffalo. After he had gone a short distance, he saw a big lodge and went into it and sat down. His mother-in-law gave him something to eat. His wife was not there. His mother-in-law said to him, "In four days from now you will search for your wife."

Contrary remained four days at the lodge. During all this time the buffalo stayed close about the lodge and made noises, grunting constantly. Contrary sat there and was not frightened. He could look out of the lodge and see close about it the great crowds of buffalo. He wore his buffalo robe and was painted red over the whole body. For three nights the buffalo made their noises, as if they were trying to frighten him and to get him to run away. The morning after the fourth night, he was told that now he must find his wife and child among all the buffalo.

A buffalo set out and made a circle among all the great herd and after he had done this all the buffalo began to crowd toward this lodge. Then they separated by ages—the sucking calves all together, the yearlings, the two-year-olds, the cows, and the bulls, all came together by ages. The young cows were all put in a line; the yellow calves were all put in line. The rest of the buffalo were not put in line but stood apart, crowded together by ages. Contrary was still in the lodge; he had not come out. His father-in-law now sent for him. He said: "Come out now, son-in-law, and look for your child. You must do this, and if you cannot recognize your wife and your child you will be killed."

The young man went out and first passed down in front of the line of little calves. When he was passing in front of them he went down the line slowly, and looked at each one of them; and in the same way when he passed behind them, he went slowly. The calves all looked just alike. As he passed he looked carefully as his son had told him, and at length one of the calves shook its tail and moved its head as if it wanted to nurse. The man put out his hand and touched the calf and said, "This is my child."

When he put his hand on it his father-in-law said, "*Ē hē hēh'*, my son-in-law is *Mā ĭ yūn ĭv'* (has spiritual power), he has recognized his son."

When he had picked out his son the calves left the line and all scattered out, following along toward the cows as if to go to their mothers. But the man's son was slow in going, he seemed to feel uneasy, hesitating whether to go on to his mother or not.

His father-in-law now told Contrary that he must look for his wife. The young man first passed down in front of the line of cows. By this time some of the calves had reached their mothers and were nursing. When Contrary got around behind the line of cows he walked slowly, and pretty soon a calf dodged in front of him and made the motions of which his son had told him some days before; it shook its tail as his son had done and started to try to nurse. When the calf went in to nurse, the young man went very slowly and watched the cows' ears and their feet. He came to a cow that this calf was sucking and that moved her ear and her foot as his wife had told him she would do, and he touched her with his hand and said, "Here is my wife." Again his father-in-law said, "*Ē hē hēh'*, my son-in-law is *Mā ĭ yūn ĭv'*; he has recognized his wife." Then the buffalo scattered out and the young man and his wife and child were left alone.

(The end of this story appears to have been forgotten.)

BLACK WOLF AND HIS FATHERS

BLACK WOLF was a fine-looking young man and many girls liked him, but his father did not wish any of them as daughter-in-law. He used to say, "I do not want my son to get married."

Every day Black Wolf used to go up on the hill and sit there on a white buffalo robe, looking over the valley.

There was talk in the camp that they were going to move. Black Wolf's father said: "If the camp moves, I shall stay here. The people give me too much trouble."

He did not like it because so many young girls wanted to marry his son.

Two girls, who thought they would be smart, determined to play a trick on Black Wolf, and agreed that when the camp moved they would stay behind. They said, "We will see what we can do to this young man who thinks he is too nice for any girl."

The robe on which Black Wolf used to sit was never moved. It lay always in the same place on the hill. One night after the camp had gone the girls, who had remained hidden during the day, went up on the hill and took the robe from its place, and where it had lain they dug a deep hole. They worked all night, digging the hole and carrying the dirt far away, so that it could not be seen. When they had finished they spread the buffalo robe smoothly over the hole, just as it had been before.

Next morning Black Wolf went up to sit on the hill and when

he sat down on the robe he fell into this deep hole. He could not get out.

When night came and he did not return to the lodge, his mother said to her husband: "Where is my son, that he has not yet come in? He must feel lonely since the camp has left. My son wanted to follow the camp, and if you had had good sense you would have done as he wished. Let us pack up now and follow the camp."

They packed up and started, and when they reached the main camp the mother said, "Is my son in camp?"

The father said to his friends, "My son got lonely and followed up the camp." Both supposed he was there.

The two girls were watching the lodge, and after the father had moved his camp, the girls came to the hole on the hill and looked down into it and saw the young man sitting there. He could not get out. The girls spoke to him and said, "You were very hard to get, but we have got you now."

Black Wolf answered them, saying, "If you will take me out of this hole I will marry you both."

"Very well," said the girls; "but first hand us up the white buffalo robe. If we should take you out first, there would be no way of getting the robe."

After he had handed the robe up to them they said, "Now we have you where we want you." Close by were many buffalo bones, and they gathered these and threw them down at Black Wolf and hit him on the head and shoulders so that he was bleeding from many places. They did not take him out of the hole. They went away and left him there suffering. His parents in the camp kept asking people if anyone had seen their son, but no one could tell them about him, and at last they concluded that he was lost and began to mourn for him.

One night a big white wolf that was trotting along the hill-side smelled the man and following up the scent found the hole. When he had looked into the hole the wolf said, "I have found a human being.* I will take him for my son."

Another wolf, a mad one,† came up, looked into the hole, and said: "I have found a human being. Now I shall have something to eat."

The white wolf wanted the young man for his son, and the rabid wolf wanted to eat him. They disputed for a long time as to what should be done with him, and finally they agreed that each one should dig down to the man, and that the one that first got to him should have him.

They began to dig, and the man, who had overheard the dispute, took one of the buffalo bones that had been thrown into the hole and began to dig on the side where the white wolf was digging and so helped him, and the white wolf got first into the hole.

When both wolves had dug into the hole they again began to dispute, for the rabid wolf still wanted to eat Black Wolf. Then they began to discuss how they should get out of the hole and up on to the ground again. The rabid wolf said to the white wolf, "I will first creep out of the hole and then the man may follow, and you can come last."

"No," said the white wolf, "that will not do." He turned to the young man and said, "If you come following him out of the hole he will turn around and bite you and begin to eat you." At last the rabid wolf gave up to the white wolf and let him have the man. The rabid wolf said, "You go ahead and our son can follow you and I will follow him."

"No," said the white wolf, "this human being may be a great help to us. We must protect him so that he can help us. You go out first, I will follow, and our son can follow me."

The mad wolf went first and the white wolf followed. When

* *Wŭ hŭ is tăt′ tăn.*

† *Wŭn stāh′ wŭn nē* = "loses his heart, sense, mind, or intelligence wolf"— the name given to a rabid wolf.

he got to the entrance the white wolf just put his head out of the hole and the rabid wolf, who had already turned around, started forward to bite him and then when he saw who it was stopped and said, "I have made a mistake." The man came out last and all three stood there together.

The white wolf said to him, "Now, we will take you to our home."

"Yes," said the mad wolf, "you will go to our home. There you will see many fathers."

They started and pretty soon the mad wolf began to edge closer and closer to the man and to act as if he wanted to eat him. As they went the white wolf said to his son, "We live inside a big round hill."

The mad wolf said: "Our son has traveled a long way. He must be getting hungry. Why do you not go off and see if you can find something for him to eat."

The white wolf would not go away from the man. He said to the mad wolf: "No, you are a better hunter than I, and always have better luck than I. You go and get something for our son. He is getting very hungry."

"Yes," said the mad wolf, "I will go. You see that hill ahead of us,"—pointing—"you try to meet me there."

The mad wolf went off and as he went over the hill the white wolf said to the man: "There are four of us just like him, and they are very cross and ugly, and there are four of us just like me who have taken you for my son."

Just then the mad wolf came back, and said to the white wolf, "Have you been telling our son bad things about me—abusing me?"

"No," said the white wolf, "I have just been telling him what a good hunter you are, and how you never get tired."

The mad wolf went off again, and as they were going along the white wolf said to the man, "He will carry the news to where we are going and there you will see many wolves and they will all be your fathers."

When the mad wolf came back to them, appearing over the point where he had said he would meet them, he carried in his mouth a buffalo kidney for the man to eat. Black Wolf took the kidney and the white wolf said, "I told you that your father was a great hunter and that he would bring you something to eat."

The mad wolf said, "I think you have been telling this man all about me."

Where they met they slept that night. The mad wolf said, "I will sleep next to our son."

"No," said the white wolf, "I will sleep next to my own son." The mad wolf always seemed to be wanting to get near the young man to harm him.

Next morning they started again, and the mad wolf said to the white wolf, "Now, do you go off and get something to eat for our son."

"No," said the white wolf, "you go. I have told you once that I have taken this person for my son, and I shall not leave him."

The mad wolf started, and before he left the white wolf told him the direction they were going and where they should meet. When they met the mad wolf had in his mouth a piece of liver for the man. That night they stayed at the place of their meeting.

Next morning they started, and the white wolf said to the young man, "To-night, at the next camp we make, before we get home, you shall have a robe."

As they traveled that day the white wolf said to the mad wolf, "Now, try again and make another hunt, and get something to eat."

The mad wolf started off and then turned back and said, "No, I have gone twice; you go now."

"No," said the white wolf, "I have told you that this is my son and I will not leave him. Besides he is going to have a robe at our next camp." So the mad wolf went off to look for food. When he met them he had in his mouth a tongue, cooked, and the young man ate it. After the young man had eaten the tongue, the white wolf said to the mad wolf, "Our son now must have a robe so that he can sleep warmer."

The white wolf lay down and rolled on the ground and when he rose to his feet, he left a wolf hide lying on the ground. He said to the young man, "Now, take the front and the hind feet in your hands, just as you would pick up a robe to place on your shoulders, lift the hide straight up, and give it one shake."

The young man did as he had been told and when he had given the hide this one shake, he was holding in his hands a nice big robe, made of four large wolf hides sewed together.

The white wolf told him to put the robe on. They stopped here all night.

Next morning as they started, the white wolf showed the young man a great butte, away far off. "There is where we are going," he said, "but we shall not reach it to-day."

The mad wolf said, "Now, do you go out and hunt, and we will meet halfway to the butte."

The white wolf answered him as before, and then the mad wolf went off to hunt. After he had gone the white wolf said: "When we get to that place where we are going, the mad wolf will ask you to pick out your father from among the other wolves. You cannot do this, for there are four of us just alike, and if you do not do it they kill you and eat you. I will refuse to let you do it. When I refuse, perhaps they will say that you must do it. If they do so, when you look at me as we stand in the line I will try to wink my right eye and you must take hold of me and pull me out of the line and say, 'This is my father.' The first time you try to pick me out I will wink my right eye, but then we will all mingle and walk about and howl. Then

we will form in line again. The second time you have to choose
me I will move my right ear and you must say, 'This is my
father.' The third time we will again mix up and howl and when
they fall in line that time I will move the third toe of my right
foot. The fourth time after we mix up and howl, we will all sit
down on our tails with the tails sticking out between our fore-
feet and as we sit there I will move the tip of my tail. Then
choose me."

That night the mad wolf met them with a piece of roasted
meat. They were then very near to the butte. The white wolf
again pointed to it and said, "There is where I am taking
you."

When they started next morning, the mad wolf left them
and went on fast to the butte to carry the news. When he got
there he said, "We are bringing with us a human being who
will be a help to us wolves."

As the white wolf and the young man approached the butte,
there seemed to be a wave of wolves and coyotes rushing toward them over the prairie. When they reached the butte they
found there four mad wolves just alike and four white wolves
just alike. The ground inside the butte was beaten down hard.

The man-eating wolf said to the white wolf, "If this son of
yours can pick you out every time for four times, then we will
all take him for our son."

The white wolf said, "Yes, we will have our son look for
his father."

They told the young man to cover up his head and all the
wolves moved about among themselves and howled. Then they
walked in a circle and the four white wolves fell into the center of the circle and stood in a row. Now the son was told to
uncover his head and to look for his father. The four white
wolves stood there in a row in the center of the circle. The
young man looked at the four and watched their heads and
presently he saw one of the wolves wink his right eye. The

young man said, "This is my father," and the man-eating wolf gave a grunt. He did not like it.

Again they told the young man to cover his head, and the wolves all walked around and howled as before and when the young man uncovered his head and they said, "Now look for your father." He looked again and one of the white wolves moved his right ear. The young man said, "This is my father," and again the man-eating wolf gave a grunt. He did not like it.

The same thing happened again, and when the young man looked for his father he chose the white wolf that moved the third toe on his right foot. Again the man-eating wolf gave a grunt of anger.

The same thing happened again, but before the young man chose, the man-eating wolf said, "This is your last choice." The young man chose the white wolf that moved the tip of his tail that was under him. After he got through, the man-eating wolf thought more of the son than the white wolf did.

The white wolf said: "Now, our son has been here a long time and so have we, and we are all hungry. We must send off for a bow and arrows. We will send Walking Rabbit (a jack rabbit)."

"No," said Walking Rabbit, "do not send me, they might hurt me; send Standing Rabbit."

Standing Rabbit went and found a camp of people and went close to it and presently people began to shoot arrows at him and he went so close to some people that they even threw their bows at him. He dodged the arrows and the bows, and managed to pick up all these things, and to carry back with him to the butte the arrows shot at him and bows thrown at him. When he returned he had a lot of arrows.

The young man was glad to get these things. He began to try his bow to see how strong it was, and when he snapped it he frightened the wolves and they began to run away.

"Look out," said the white wolf, "do not frighten your fathers; they are easily scared."

"Very well," said the young man, "but let them get some buffalo here so that I can try my bow on them."

The wolves went to drive the buffalo up and soon did so.

The young man had twenty arrows, and he killed twenty buffalo. Then they needed a knife to cut up the meat and decided to send the Swift Fox for it, for he could go fast and would make a quick trip.

Before long the Swift Fox got back, bringing a knife with him. They did not know how he got it but supposed that it was thrown at him.

The young man was glad to get the knife and went out and cut places in the buffalo, so that the wolves could eat. He took the tongues for himself.

Now the wolves said: "Our son needs something to cook with. He must have fire."

To the Coyote they said, "Now, you are sly; you go and get fire."

Presently the Coyote got back with a whole sack of punk and some flint stones and he went to the young man and gave these things to him saying, "Now, here is something to make fire with, if you know how to use it."

The young man made the fire in the lodge where he was, and the smell of the fire frightened the wolves almost to death. The white wolf said to him: "My son, you are frightening all your fathers. After this you must build your fire outside."

So Black Wolf built his fire outside that night and was sitting by it roasting his meat when a wolf came up that had been into a buffalo pound where people were, and had been shot. The arrow was still sticking in him. The white wolf told his son to pull the arrow out. Another wolf came with an arrow sticking in him and again the white wolf said, "Go and pull the arrow out of your father, for you understand how to do this."

One day the young man said to his father, "I will go to that place where my fathers got wounded." He did so. After the buffalo had been surrounded and killed, the wolves went down to the buffalo and began to eat, and the young man went with them. He acted wild and seemed to be afraid of the smell of people. Some of the people saw him and said, "That looks like the young man who was lost." These people took the news back to camp saying that among the wolves that came to eat was one who walked upright and acted like a human being. Black Wolf's father said: "That must be my son. I want you to try hard to catch him so that I can have him back."

The next night the wolves decided to go back to feed on the buffalo and the man went with them. The news had gone through the camp that the lost young man had been seen with the wolves, and all the people went out and got around the pound and when the man tried to run away he found that they had surrounded him, and they caught him. He acted very wild and tried to bite them. He had big tusks like a wolf. For a long time he struggled, but the people talked to him and told him that his father wanted to see him, and at last he became quiet. After they had taken him to camp, he still tried to get away and his father talked to him and asked him where he had been and why he was living with the wolves, and at last he became quiet, but the people still held him.

All the wolves went home crying and said that they had lost their son; that the people had got him. When they told this at the butte, the wolves all said that they would go to war for him to-morrow.

A wolf came near to the camp and howled, telling the young man that the wolves had gone back to notify the others, and that they would come for him next day and would surround the camp and make a charge on it.

The young man said to the people: "That one that howled has said something very bad. There are a great many of those people that took me for their son. None of you should wander out from camp in the morning. There are many of those people, and they will eat you up. On the place where I used to sit on the hill on my white buffalo robe I was treated very badly and I felt angry about it. No one ever came to look for me."

The next morning the wolves were thick about the camp. The young man said: "Father, I was treated very badly by two girls. I have promised them to the wolves to eat and when I have given them to the wolves, I will tell the wolves to go away."

He asked if he might go out to speak with the wolves but his father said, "No, speak from where you are." Then the young man howled like a wolf and the wolves all began to go away.

Black Wolf went out of the lodge with his father to walk about and as he was walking he saw the two girls who had thrown him into the hole, at work scraping on a buffalo hide. They saw him and, as he passed, nudged each other.

"Father," he said, "if you will give me those two girls for my fathers to eat, I may remain with you all the time."

He said, "Father, let us go back to the lodge."

When they had entered he said, "Father, give me two arrows." When they had been given to him he went out and killed the two girls. He asked his father to have dried meat piled up in the center of the camp, and the father had an old man cry it through the village to have dried meat so piled up. After it had been piled up, he told the people to carry it outside the circle and to make four piles of it to the four directions. After that, he cut up each of the girls in two pieces and put one piece on each pile. After that was done he told his father that he was going to call the wolves and that none of the people should go out of the lodges, but they might look out of the holes. Then he went to the center of the camp and howled four times, and wolves appeared all about the camp. In his howlings he said, "My fathers, I give you human beings to eat."

When the wolves began to eat he went among them. He called out to the people, "Now, you will see me with my four fathers," meaning the four white wolves.

His four fathers stood close to him all the time. After he came back to the camp from the wolves he said to his father: "Father, I will now stay with you, but not all the time. Whenever my other fathers call me I will go back to them and kill them something to eat. After I have killed some buffalo for them, I will come home. I will live part of the time with each of you."

THE BEAR HELPER

ONE autumn, about the year 1835, when the leaves were just beginning to turn yellow, a large village of Cheyennes and Arapahoes was camped on Crow Creek, near the South Platte River. Game was scarce and there was not much to eat, so that the people began to get hungry.

One day a man named Plenty Crows said to his wife, "I will take my gun and go up into the hills, where perhaps I may find a deer, or a bull, or an antelope, or something else to kill." He started out on foot and went up into the hills where a few pines grew, and after a time, as he was going along, he saw two bulls lying down. He crept up close to them and killed both where they lay, and then skinned and cut them up. He took a piece of meat to carry with him to the camp, put the rest in a pile and threw the hides over it, and putting his meat on his back went to the camp. When he reached his lodge, he told his wife that he had killed two bulls and butchered them, and that the next morning they would go after the meat. That night they tied their horses close by the lodge, and the next morning saddled a horse each, and took a pack horse, and went up to get the meat.

BY CHEYENNE CAMPFIRES

After Plenty Crows had butchered his meat, and gone to the camp, a war party of Crows had passed that way, and found the pile of meat. When they saw it, the Crows said to each other, "These persons will come back for this meat in the morning, and we will wait here for them, and kill them when they return." So they went over a little hill and stayed there all night.

Plenty Crows and his wife rode up to the meat, and got down from their horses, and packed all three of them with the meat, those that they were riding as well as the pack horse. The Crows were watching, and as soon as the horses were packed, they charged down on the man and his wife and began shooting. For some time Plenty Crows fought them off, but at last they killed him and took the woman prisoner, and went away with her and the horses.

They traveled north, and at last came to the Crow village on Sheep* River. The Crow man who carried the pipe of this war party took the woman as his wife. He already had two Crow women, so she was his third wife. These two Crow wives did not like the Cheyenne woman, and whenever the man was not near they abused her, whipping her with quirts, and hitting her with sticks and stones. They made her work hard, packing wood, dressing hides, and making moccasins all the time.

In this lodge there lived a young man sixteen or seventeen years old, who was a servant, and herded the lodge man's horses. This young man took a liking to the Cheyenne woman, for he felt sorry for her. One day when no one was in the lodge except these two, he said to her: "These women abuse you, and it makes me angry. Go to work now and make moccasins for yourself, and hide them away. When you have made enough, you must run away and try to get back to your people. I will help you. If you get a chance to do it, wrap up some dried meat, and hide it away, so that you may have something to eat. Some time when they go out after buffalo, this man will take his

* Big Horn River.

women with him, and you can get away." The woman remained with the Crows all through the winter, and until the snow began to go off in the spring.

One day all the Crows went out for buffalo. The woman's husband went, and took with him his two Crow wives, and the young man also started with them. After the young man had gone a little way out from the camp he stopped, turned, and went back. He rode around the Crow camp until he was on the other side of it, hid his riding horse in the timber, and tied him there. Then he caught another horse and rode into camp. Some of the people who saw him coming in on this horse said to him: "Why, what is the matter? We thought you went to kill buffalo."

He answered: "My horse threw me off and ran away, and I could not catch him. He has my blankets on the saddle."

He got off his horse and went into the lodge, and found the Cheyenne woman there. He said to her: "Hurry now, and get your things. I have hidden my horse in the timber down the creek, and you can get on him and go home. I will go with you and show you where the horse is. I have told these people a lie. I said my horse had thrown me off. I have a horse here, and I will get on him and ride down the creek a little way. Do you come on as soon as you can. I will wait for you."

He rode away out of sight of the camp, and stopped there and waited. Pretty soon he saw the woman coming, and at last she reached him. He said to her, "Jump up behind me quickly, before anyone sees you"; and they went on down the creek to where the horse was tied. Then he said to her: "Now tie your things on that saddle. There is my blanket. Take it. Get on now, and take this horse also, and lead him, so that you will have two. You must go fast. I will go back to the camp, and will say that my horse has run off and I cannot find him; and when I look for the horses in the morning, I will tell them that there is another one lost."

The woman started and traveled and traveled. When she got

too tired, she got off and unsaddled, and let her horses feed. She went on and on, until she had passed the Pumpkin Buttes; then she made a camp and lay down and slept. That night her horses got frightened, and broke their ropes, and both of them ran off. She made up a bundle of her things, and started on afoot. All that day she walked on, frightened, and crying all the time. That night she lay down and went to sleep, and at daylight she started on again.

She had gone only a little way when she happened to look back, and there following close behind her was a great big bear. That frightened her still more, and she began to run, crying as she ran. She ran until she was exhausted and could go no further, and still the bear kept just about the same distance from her. At last she turned about and talked to the bear. She called him by name, saying: "O Bear, take pity on me. I am a poor woman, and am trying to get back to my own people." Then she would hurry on a little further, and turn around and talk to him again in the same way. At last she was so tired that she determined that she must sit down and rest, even if the bear should kill her. She did so, and she was so tired that notwithstanding her fear of the bear she fell asleep at once.

While she was lying there asleep, the bear spoke to her. She could hear his voice when he said: "Get up and go on to your people. I am following you only to watch and protect you. I am following you, stepping in your tracks, so that the enemy cannot trail you."

After a time the woman got up and started on. The bear was sitting close to her looking at her; and even though he had spoken to her in this way she was still afraid of him. She walked on until it was a long time after dark, and then she lay down and went to sleep.

In the morning, when it was light enough to see, she got up and looked about her, and there, a little way off on top of a small butte, she saw the bear sitting. She started on her way, and as soon as she moved off, the bear came down from the place she had left, and followed in her tracks. That night she ate her last piece of meat, a very small one. Early the next day she reached the Platte River. The stream was full from bank to bank. She sat down on a hill a little way from the river, and looked and thought and thought, to see if there might be any way by which she could cross. She said, "If I were only on the other side now; but how can I ever get there?"

While she was sitting there, the bear came up and walked in front of her. Then he turned about and backed toward her. She could not think what he wanted. She turned aside to get away from him, but he walked around in front of her, and backed up to her as before. He did not speak. Suddenly she thought to herself: "I wonder if he does not want me to get on him and ride him. Now I will get up and go down to the river bank, and sit down close by the edge of the water, and see what he does." She walked down, and sat down close to the bank, and the bear came after her and got in front of her, and backed up toward her. He kept looking back at her over his shoulder, as if to see what she was doing. The woman said to herself: "I think he wants to carry me across the river. I believe I will get on him and try what he will do." Then she said aloud, "Bear, I am going to get on your back, if you will take me across the river." She prepared herself, and tied up her blanket. Then she crawled on his back, and put her arms around his neck, just in front of his shoulders. He looked back as if to see if she were ready, and then he gave a snort and jumped into the water. She held firmly to him, and he swam strongly, and took her safe across to the other side.

When she got off his back, the bear shook the water from himself and rolled on the ground, and the woman started on, and the bear followed her just as before. She walked on and walked on, and at last got tired and sat down to rest. She looked around and saw that the bear had stopped close to her and then he sat down. She was feeling very tired and hungry, and she said, "Oh, I am hungry, and I am tired, and I think I shall starve to death before ever I get to my people." Then the bear spoke and said: "You will get there. Go on." She got up and started on, the bear following behind her. The woman walked and walked until she was very tired, and again she stopped to rest, sitting down on a little hill. Just beyond the hill was a creek, and along the creek were many buffalo. The woman said, "There are buffalo, but I cannot get any to eat."

The bear said to her: "Sister, you shall eat. Stay where you are until I go and kill a buffalo." The bear went down into the timber in the creek, where the buffalo were. He crept about for some little time, and at length he got close to a yearling and jumped on it, caught it, bit it, and killed it. The buffalo then all ran away, and the woman arose and went down to see what had happened.

When she got there, she found what the bear had killed, and saw him sitting on the ground a little way from it. She skinned and cut up the buffalo, and took her flint and steel and made a fire, and cooked and ate. While she was doing this, the bear went up to the top of a high hill and sat there watching.

When the woman had finished eating, she took what meat she could carry, and made a pack of it and put it on her back. "Now," she said, "I will leave the rest of this meat for the bear. Let him come down and eat it." She started on, and when she started, the bear came down and ate of what she had left. After he had eaten he followed on, and soon overtook her. They traveled on all that day, and at night she camped, cooked, and ate. She took a piece of meat out a little way from the camp and put it down on the ground, and the bear came and got it. He would not come up close to her and eat.

The next morning they set out again, and traveled all day, and then camped. The bear followed her all the time. The fourth morning she started on again. About noon that day they

A PAUSE IN THE MARCH.

came to a hill, and from it she could see the Laramie River. There she saw a big village—many lodges. She said, "There are many people, but I do not know whether they are my people or not." The bear went up close to her and said: "Those are your people. Go now into the camp, and I will go down into the thick timber below the camp. Go to your people and tell them that I brought you home safe. I want you to get a fat buffalo hump and have it cut into four pieces, and send it to me to eat. I will wait for it in the timber below the camp."

The woman went on into the camp, and when they saw her, all her relations were glad. She told the people that the bear had brought her home in safety, and that he was in the timber and wanted a fat buffalo hump. They got the hump, cut it into four pieces, and her relations and many other people in the camp went down to the timber. They took with them a fine robe, great strings of beads, and nice feathers. They found the bear there and gave him the meat, put the robe over him, and hung the strings of beads about his neck. Then they went away and left him.

SAND CRANE

IT was in the fall of the year, when they moved the village to a warm place, and built about it a fence of brush to keep the cold wind from the camp.

Sand Crane was a young boy. His older brother had two wives, one of them a very beautiful girl. One day Sand Crane killed a prairie chicken not far from the camp, and the youngest wife was out near him, and she got the arrow from the chicken and gave it back to Sand Crane, and said to him, "You ought to give me a present for getting your arrow for you." Sand Crane did not answer, and went away. This made the girl angry, and she thought about it a good deal. On her way back to the camp she scratched her face and tore her dress all to pieces, and when she reached the lodge she cried and told her husband that his brother had treated her badly. After a time Sand Crane came back to the lodge, and his brother told him to go out now, that he was going to call some men to a feast. So Sand Crane went out and sat on a hill near the camp.

When the invited men had come to the lodge, the brother told them that he intended to go to war, and to take his brother Sand Crane with him; that Sand Crane had treated his wife badly, and he was going to cross the Big Water, and throw him away on the other side. Wihio was present, and the brother told him privately that if he would make him a boat and carry him across the Big Water he might marry his sister. The chiefs knew about this, and the brother's wives, and, in fact, the whole village knew what was going to be done to Sand Crane.

The brother and Sand Crane started to war, and Wihio went too and carried the moccasins. When they came to the edge of the Big Water they made a boat and got in it, and Wihio paddled it toward an island. When they reached the island, the brother told Sand Crane to take his bow and arrows and go to the end of the island, and they would go through it and frighten the deer and the antelope toward him, and he could kill one as they came by. Sand Crane took his bow and arrows in his hand and started, leaving his clothing and even his moccasins in the boat. As soon as he was in the bushes they pushed off from the shore.

Sand Crane went on, but as he heard no sound of anything coming, he went back to the shore, and saw the boat going off. It was far from the shore, but near enough so that they could hear one another call. He cried out: "Brother, where are you going? You are throwing me away. Why are you doing this? Only we two are left." His brother did not answer, but Wihio called back a bad name. The boat went on, and the young man walked up and down the beach, mourning and crying.

When the brother and Wihio landed, they left on the shore Sand Crane's bow case, quiver, moccasins, and other things.

"Now," they said, "what story shall we make up to tell about Sand Crane when we get back to camp? Let us tell them that he went out to look for buffalo and did not return. We suppose he was lost." They did this. After they reached the camp, Wihio married Sand Crane's sister, and they lived together. After they were married a big snow came. Much snow fell, and the wind blew hard.

As winter came on, Sand Crane had nothing to eat, and began to starve, and all birds that eat flesh began to gather about him, and to alight near him. One would say to another, "I hear that Sand Crane has been thrown away; I shall get the thick part of the neck to eat, or the head." Sand Crane grew weaker and weaker, and at length he lay there and could hardly move.

After all this had happened, five large birds took pity on Sand Crane. The first to tell him that his grandfather had taken pity on him was the buzzard. The second was the speckled-tailed eagle, who said, "Your grandfather says that you shall live to see the man that threw you away." The gray eagle, the bald eagle, and the magpie—who was a messenger—each told him the same. After all had told him this, the four big birds said to the magpie: "Our grandfather told us to do this; now you can go and bring him. Tell our grandfather that Sand Crane still has plenty of life in him. He still can move pretty well." The magpie went to the grandfather and told him the news, and he told the magpie to go back to Sand Crane, and to say to him: "Your grandfather is coming. You must try to move; you must try to sit up." After the magpie had returned to Sand Crane and had told him this, they could hear the grandfather coming; his wings made a big rustling noise. He was a big raven. He was as big as a man, and was the grandfather of all the ravens.

When he got to the place, he told the other birds to try Sand Crane to see whether he was living or not. The birds hopped up to Sand Crane and pecked him on the feet, but his feet seemed numb, and he did not move. Then one of the birds stepped around beside him and pecked him on the breast, and he flinched. The big raven said: "Why, he has plenty of life in him. Let him get up." When Sand Crane heard the raven say this, he moved a little, and turned over on his side, and got up on his knees. "Now," said the raven, "do you four big birds try to see whether you can carry him."

The buzzard tried first. Sand Crane put his arms about the buzzard's neck, and clenched his feet around its tail, and the buzzard rose in the air and flew around once in a circle, and then came down to the ground. He could not carry him. Then the speckled-tailed eagle tried. He made two circles in the air, and then he came down. Next the gray eagle tried; he made three circles above their heads, and then came to the ground. The bald eagle tried, and made four circles and then came down. None of the big birds could carry Sand Crane.

The big raven said to all the birds that eat flesh: "I am the only one left. If I cannot carry him, you will all have something to eat."

"Now," said the raven to Sand Crane, "stand up on your feet, and put your arms about my neck, and clasp your legs over my tail. You must hold on tight, and when I start to fly, you must keep your eyes shut until I tell you to open them. Now, I am going to start. If I can sail eight times about the island, carrying you, you are saved." The raven flew high up in the air with Sand Crane, so far that the other birds could hardly see him, but at last he came down, and as he reached the ground he said to Sand Crane, "You are saved."

"Now," said the raven, "I will take you across this water. While I am going over I will rest four times, and when I lower myself toward the water, you must hold on tight with your legs, and when I rise higher, you must hold on tight with your arms. When I reach the other shore I will tell you to open your eyes."

They started, and at length after a long time the raven told Sand Crane to open his eyes, and when he did so he found that they were on the other side of the water, just where the boat had started from.

Sand Crane looked about a little on the shore, and soon found, lying at the foot of a tree, his bow case, leggings, and moccasins. When he took up his moccasins to put them on, he found in them some dried meat, for in the olden time they used to carry meat in their moccasins when going to war. Then he ate, and this was the first food he had had since his brother threw him away.

After he had dressed himself, the raven said to Sand Crane, "Now, I will teach you what to do as you are traveling back to your camp, and how you shall act when you reach it." He talked with Sand Crane for a long time, telling him what he must do, and then he left him, and Sand Crane started on his way.

As he was traveling along on his way back, he saw some trees before him, and as soon as he saw them he began to hurry, trying to get to them as quickly as he could, for so the raven had told him. When he had come near to the trees he heard a low rumbling noise, like thunder far off, and looking behind him he saw a mist coming, like a storm, and he hurried still more, for this mist was the wings of a great mosquito that was coming to kill him. He saw a big tree lying on the ground, and, just before the mosquito overtook him, Sand Crane dodged under the trunk of this tree, and the mosquito struck at him, but instead of hitting Sand Crane, the mosquito's bill pierced the tree, and the mosquito was held there. Then Sand Crane got up and killed the mosquito, and cut off his bill, and carried it with him to use as a club, as the raven had told him.

He started on again, traveling against the wind, and listening, as he had been told to do, and pretty soon he heard, far ahead of him, someone crying out, saying, "Come on and eat." Sand Crane kept right on, and before long he saw an old woman standing, calling. He went around and slipped up behind her, and placed the bow case on her back, saying, "Grandmother, carry this for me." When he did this, many bears started up all about him, and rushed at him, as if to tear him to pieces. The old woman cried to the bears: "Hold on, stop; this is my grandson. Grandson, where are you going?"

"I am going home to my camp," said Sand Crane.

"Well," said she, "I am going in another direction; so you had better take your bow case with you, you may need it." He took it, and the old woman made motions to the bears to move out of his way; and he went on.

After he had passed the old woman a great snowstorm came up and it was very cold. The wind struck him on the side. While the storm was blowing, he came close to where the people were wintering. He knew the stream, and walked down it on the ice. After he had gone some distance, he saw something black on the ice, and walked up to it, and saw that it was a woman. He said to her, "Who are you?" It was his sister; and when he spoke she knew him, and said, "Why, is that you, Sand Crane?" He said, "Yes, it is I."

His sister said to him: "I heard they took you to throw you away, and they promised that I should marry Wihio. Now, he has sent me down here to stir the water in this hole in the ice all night, to keep it from freezing."

"Tell me how your husband treats you," said Sand Crane. "Tell me all about it."

"He does not treat me very well," his sister answered. "Every morning I have to carry water to him, and he makes me carry it very slowly. If I do not carry it slowly, he calls out to me that I am bringing his water too fast. When I light his pipe, I have to take the coal from the fire with my bare hand; that is why my hands are all burned and sore."

"Well," said Sand Crane, "wait here with me during the night, and in the morning when you take your water to Wihio, I will go with you. When you carry the water, do not go slowly, hurry with it, and let it spill out as it may. When you go into the lodge with the water, your husband may say to you, 'Sand Crane has come back.' Do you say to him, 'He has come back' and throw the water over him, and the water skin on him; I will walk in afterward. Do not be afraid; he will not say or do anything."

The next morning she went into the lodge with the water, shivering with cold and nearly frozen. The water was slopping out of the water skin, and Wihio said: "Here, you are spilling my drinking water. Sand Crane must have come back."

"He has come back," she said, and threw the water over him, and the skin on him, as he lay there in bed. After this, Sand Crane walked in close behind her, and Wihio jumped up out of bed, all wet, his buffalo robe wet, but laughing, and said: "Brother-in-law, this is the way your sister has been treating me ever since we were married. Brother-in-law, come around here and sit in the back of the lodge and smoke with me."

"It is good," said Sand Crane. "I will. Since you threw me away, I smoke only in a medicine way."

Wihio filled a pipe and passed it to his brother-in-law; and Sand Crane said to him: "This is my medicine way of smoking. You must rake a coal out of the fire with your bare hand, and hold it while I light my pipe." Wihio had to do so.

While he was sitting here smoking, the news that Sand Crane had returned got out in the camp, and his brother came to the door of the lodge and said to Sand Crane, "Come out, and come over to the lodge and have something to eat." "Yes," said Sand Crane, "I will come out. I will go over to your lodge." He went to his brother's lodge, and went in; and the brother said, "Ah, friend, come over here and sit down by me and eat." "No," said Sand Crane, "I do not wish to eat now; I wish to go into a sweat house. Go out and get me four bowstrings." His brother hurried out, and soon came back with the four bowstrings. "Now," said Sand Crane, "I want you and Wihio to go out and gather willows for the sweat house, and to carry them across your shoulders with these bowstrings. I will go with you and show you where to get them."

They went out, and he with them, and the brother and brother-in-law each cut fifty willows. He fixed the packs on their backs with the bowstrings, and had the strings pass about their shoulders and over their naked breasts. They carried them home thus, and when they got there their breasts were all gashed where the bowstrings had cut them. When they got back to the camp, and had dug the holes and built the sweat house, he took out his two sisters-in-law, to bring in the rocks, and took with him the same bowstrings. He tied the stones up in a robe, and made the women carry them in. The loads were so heavy that the women were staggering from the weight, and their chests also were cut. They left the stones at the sweat house. After they had come in with the stones, he sent the same women after bark, but this time he did not punish them. They brought in the bark with hide ropes, as was the custom. Next, they brought out robes and covered the sweat house; and now he destroyed all the people in the camp who had been cruel to his sister or to him. Sand Crane and his sister alone remained alive.

After this he told his sister to unbraid her hair. While she had been married to Wihio he used to pull hair out of her head, to use for his moccasin strings, and her hair was now very short and ragged. Sand Crane gave his sister a long forked stick, and told her to bring some of the hot stones into the sweat house. She brought them and brought some water, and they crept in under the coverings and took a sweat. Then Sand Crane told his sister to take sage and fan herself all over with it, and to rub herself all over wherever she was sore, and when she came out of the sweat house her sores were all healed and her hair was long, just as it had been before she was married.

Then Sand Crane and his sister started off to look for the other part of the village.

THE STOLEN GIRL

THERE was once a young girl who had many men coming to court her. She was the daughter of a chief, and his lodge was pitched in the center of the circle. Many young men came to see her, but she refused them all. She did not care for any of them. She wanted a young man that she could love.

One evening as she sat in the lodge, she perceived a very pleasant smell in the air, and wondered what it came from. She wanted to look out and see, but did not wish to go to the door and herself be seen; so she took her mother's awl and pierced a hole in the lodge skins and, peeping through the hole, she saw a young man standing not far off.

When she had looked at him for a little while, she liked him, and determined that she would go out to see who it was. She did so, and as she walked past him he spoke to her, and she stopped. Then they talked to each other, and the girl asked him who he was, and why he had come; for she saw that he was a stranger. The young man said: "The home of my people is far from here, and I have come to get you. Come with me, and we will go to my father's lodge."

The young man spoke pleasantly, and the girl, after she had thought a little while, said to him: "Very good, I will go with you. Other young men want me, but I do not want them. I will go only with you. First, however, you must let me go back and get my awl and sinew and my quills." The girl went into the lodge and made up a bundle of her things, and then came out again and said to the young man: "Now, I am ready. Which way do you live from here? In which direction must we go?"

"I live toward the rising sun," said the young man. "There are many camps of my people there." They set out toward the east.

As they were going along, she said to him: "What is your name? What do they call out when you ask your friends to come to a feast with you?"

"My name," he said, "is Red Eye."

They traveled along for some time, and it was almost night when they came near to the camp. There were many trees where the camp was pitched, and all among the trees you could see the light shining through the lodge skins. They passed into the circle of the camp, and went up to a big lodge standing in the center, and when they got to the door, the young man and the girl stopped. Through the lodge skins they could see the shadows of many men sitting about the fire, and could hear them talking and laughing. The young man's father was speaking. He said to the others: "My son has gone far away. He has gone to get a chief's daughter to marry. He has seen her and liked her, and now he has gone to get her. After a time, if he has good luck, he will return with her." So the old man talked about his son.

At last Red Eye said to the girl, "Come, let us go in." He first went into the lodge. When his father saw him he was surprised. He said to him: "Why, my son, I did not think to see you again so soon. I hope you have had good luck."

The girl followed the young man into the lodge, and went over and sat on the women's side. She saw her father-in-law speaking to her husband, and she noticed that he had a very sharp nose; and after a time, as she looked about, she saw that all the men sitting around the lodge had sharp noses. The lodge was nicely fixed up, and the linings handsomely painted. On the beds were many nice warm buffalo robes.

At the girl's home there was great trouble. The chief's daughter had disappeared, and no one knew what had become of her. Her father and mother were crying because their daughter was lost. All the young men were out searching for her. They could not find her, nor any trace of her. When they could not find her,

her father felt still worse, and said to the young men who were searching for her, "The young man who finds my daughter shall marry her."

When the girl awoke in the morning, she found that she was in a big hollow tree, and all about the tree were sitting mountain rats. The buffalo robes on which they had been lying were grass nests.

A young Cheyenne man was out looking for this girl, and as he passed a great hollow tree the girl came crawling out from it.

"Girl," he said, "where have you been? Everyone in camp is in great sorrow because you are lost. We have been searching for you everywhere."

"Friend," said the girl, "the rats stole me away, and brought me here to this tree." Then the young man took her back to her father's lodge, and afterward he married her.

That was the beginning of rats stealing things from people.

AN EAGLE'S TEACHING

IT was a long time ago. I was a young man and the people were camped on the south side of the Platte River. My brother went out hunting and killed a buffalo and an elk, and broke the leg of another elk. He took all the meat of the elk, but only part of that of the bull.

That night my brother said to me, "Come out with me to-morrow; you can trail up the elk that I wounded and can take part of the bull and make an eagle trap with it."

We started at daylight, and at last came to a hill, and down below we could see ravens flying, and my brother said to me, "I killed the bull down there where you see those ravens." When we had almost reached the place, my brother said: "Go over and see what is there, but go carefully for there may be a bear feeding there, or perhaps an eagle. If an eagle is there, wait, and perhaps it will eat so much that it will not be able to fly." When my brother had said this to me, he went on further.

I rode carefully up to where the buffalo was lying, and peeped over the hill, and there, perched on the carcass, was an eagle feeding on the meat. I drew back and waited a long time, peeping over the hill now and then to see the eagle still there, feeding. Presently I looked over the hill and saw the eagle sitting with its head up, and I thought that perhaps it had eaten all it wished to, so I crept about a ridge and came quite close to it. At first I was going to shoot it with my arrow, but just then it flew a little way very heavily, and I saw that it could not go far. Therefore, I dropped on the prairie everything that I carried, except my bow and arrows, and ran after it. Again it flew a little way and then dropped down on the ground and flapped its wings. It had eaten so much that it could go no further. It lay there on its breast with its wings outstretched, and I was just about to send an arrow through its body, when the eagle spoke to me, saying, "Hold on, friend, wait; do not shoot." When the eagle spoke, I was astonished, and stopped and unstrung my bow. Then the eagle spoke again and said, "Look at this," and I saw in the eagle's back a hole with blood oozing out of it.

The eagle said to me, "If you do not hurt me, you shall be able to cure all wounds like this one that you see." Then I said to myself, "I will keep this bird and will ask him some more questions"; so I tied my bowstring about his wing, and led him over to where my blanket was. This was a young speckled-tailed eagle.

After we had come to where the blanket was, we talked for a time. The eagle said to me: "You see my wings and tail are speckled, your horse shall be so too. You shall be named from the animal that has been killed here; you shall be called White Bull and everybody will know you by that name. Now I should like to have you let me go, and before I go, I will give you some of my power. You shall be great in fights. The bullets shall not hit you."

"No," said I, "I do not wish that."

"Well," said the eagle, "when you are on the warpath, you shall always know where your enemies are."

"No," said I, "I do not wish that."

I did not intend to let the eagle go easily.

The eagle said to me, "There are a great people who are making many guns; perhaps, if you fight with them, you may pull through without being hurt." Some years afterward I did have a long hard fight with the white people, but they did not kill me.

At last the eagle said to me: "Friend, you will live to be quite an old man, and you shall never be poor or in want. Now, if you are ever wounded in the head or in the body, you must sing a certain song, one song for the head and a different one for the body." He taught me to sing those songs and how to cure myself and other people.

I stayed there all that day and all that night, talking with the eagle, and during all this time I had no water.

Meantime, the camp had seen a war party of enemies, and the people thought that I must have been killed. Men sent out to look for me went back to the bull, and reached the place before day, but did not find me. When day came, they saw me far off in a flat, and rushed toward me. When I saw them coming, I said to the eagle, "Friend, enemies are rushing on us."

"No," said the eagle, "those are your own people." Before the people reached me, I set the eagle free. It rose to go away, but before doing so, it flew about my head and said: "That is the way people will charge upon you, and you will charge upon people. But when you are in fights, you must always imitate my cry. Also, when you go into battle, you shall tie one of the middle tail feathers of an eagle in the tail of your horse, and tie a horn of an antelope about his neck, for an antelope is a fast-running animal and long-winded, and your horse shall be long-winded too." Then he said to me, "Friend, now I am going, but remember that you shall have a long life."

Since that time, when in fights, I have always imitated the eagle.

A WAR PARTY OF SEVEN

THE Turtle planned a war party, and sent word to some of his friends asking them to go with him. Those who went were the Grasshopper, the Water Snake, the Mouse, the Frog, the Skunk, the Diver, and the Rabbit—eight in all.

They came to a big stream, and in crossing it the Grasshopper's leg stuck fast in the mud, and, in trying to get it free, he pulled off his leg and had to turn back, leaving seven in the party.

The Turtle was the leader. The Mouse acted as the scout. The enemy were the people.

After the party had crossed this stream the Mouse was sent ahead to find the enemy's camp. The Mouse scouted at night, for mice do not sleep in the night-time. At length he came back and reported that not far ahead there was a camp in which a man was sleeping alone, in an earth house. The Mouse said that this man was sound asleep—they could easily kill him. The Turtle, being the leader, was told to go on and kill him. He rubbed his shell against the ground until its side was very sharp, and started. The Mouse kept running ahead and led them to the earth lodge, which they entered, and there saw the man asleep on his back. The Turtle crawled up on the man's breast and with the sharpened edge of his shell cut off his head. Then they said to the Mouse, "Go and scalp him," for mice can gnaw hair. The Mouse took the scalp. It was now almost morning, and the Turtle said that as it was growing light they must hide, so they all crept under a big wooden dish. This camp stood at the edge of the timber, and close by was a pond. Early in the morning someone looked into the house and saw the man with his head cut off and scalped. As soon as the person saw this he called out, and everyone ran to the house. They all looked in, and could not think who had done this until someone moved the bowl. There they found the scalp and the war party. The Turtle called out to his warriors, "All scatter." The Mouse jumped out quickly and hid in the grass. The Rabbit hid in the brush; the Diver, the Turtle, the Frog, and the Water Snake rushed for the pond; the Skunk stayed behind and made a fight, and every time they came near him he threw his scent at them.

Then the people surrounded the pond, and said that the only way to get the four who were in it was to make the pond dry. They did not know how they should go to work to do this, when they saw coming toward them a Pelican. They told him what had taken place and asked him to drink the pond dry, so they might kill these enemies. The Pelican said he would do so, and got in the pond and filled up his pouch and emptied it out on the prairie, and then came back again. Three times he did this, and got most of the water out of the pond.

When he came back the fourth time he said, "Now I will finish it." He filled his pouch again, drying up the pool, when the Diver, who was at the bottom, thrust his sharp bill into the Pelican's pouch, making a hole through which all the water ran out again. Now the people saw that the pond could not be emptied, so they went away discouraged.

The Turtle said to the Frog, "You can call out to bring our friends together." They went to the edge of the pond and the Frog called the Mouse, the Skunk, and the Rabbit to them. When they got together they set out and reached their home, but they had lost the scalp that they had taken and the Grasshopper had lost his leg.

After that all war parties of seven were thought to be unlucky.

HOW THE TURTLE WENT TO WAR

THERE was a great camp of water turtles and, not far away, some people were living—many lodges.

The turtle sent the pipe about to all the tribes of his friends and they all smoked and all came to his camp. All the grasshoppers, frogs, snakes, butterflies, and rabbits—all the young men of these tribes—came in.

The head turtle spoke to all these people and said: "Now let us go out on the warpath. I have found many Indians camping near this place. Let us go on the warpath against them and kill their chief."

All those to whom he spoke agreed. The grasshoppers, butterflies, frogs, and rabbits all were satisfied.

These people were camped in a big circle with the opening to the east. Before they started on their warpath, they all walked around within the circle and afterward around the outside of the circle, and then they started. Some of them carried war bonnets and other war clothing, such as Indians wear. They went on all night, and toward morning, while it was still dark, they reached the Indians' camp. The turtle went into the chief's lodge and took hold of the chief's throat and choked him and he died and the turtle bit off his hair. All the different warriors went into different lodges. When daylight came the turtle leader crawled under the bed and stayed there all day.

In the morning the chief of the Indians was found dead and the old crier went about through the camp and called out, directing people to find out if there were any enemies about who might have done this thing. All the young Indians got ready and started out to look about and find out if near the camp there were any people who were on the warpath. The women acted as if they were frightened.

After the young men had gone, the chief's wife took down

the lodge, for they were going to put the chief's body in another place. While they were moving the lodge they found, under the bed, a turtle in the ground. He had not quite buried himself and someone saw the fresh earth and pushed a stick down and felt him. Soon they learned that it was this turtle that had done the injury.

They chose another chief and called upon him to say what should be done. The chief said: "Let us see what we can do to kill him. He is the one who killed our chief."

Some of the Indians said: "Let us put him in the fire"; but one said: "No, we cannot burn him, his shell is too hard. Let us cut his head off." Another said, "No, let us hang him"; and a fourth said, "No, let us drown him." To all of them this seemed the best, and they decided that the turtle should be drowned. Then, the next afternoon, they took him down to the water and a great crowd of people went with them to see him drown. The man who was going to drown him was painted up and he carried the turtle out to the center of the pond. The turtle acted as if he were very much frightened. As the man was going to let the turtle down into the water, the turtle turned his head and bit the man and the man was frightened and sank into the water with the turtle. Then everyone on the shore was afraid and no one dared to go down into the water to help the man who had sunk.

After the turtle chief had drowned the man, he bit his hair off and waited and, after night came, he crawled over to where the chief's lodge had stood and found there the hair he had bitten off the chief's head. That night all the friends of the turtle had gone away to their camp, for they supposed that he had been killed. He started on his way home, and he was glad that he had done this thing all by himself. When he got home it was daylight. He took the hair and tied it to a stick and then he had two scalps to dance over, but his friends had not done anything. So for a long time they went about the camp dancing and singing for joy. And he continued to be the chief of the turtles.

THE MOUSE'S CHILDREN

ONCE, a long time ago, when the Cheyennes lived in earth houses, their village was on a stream, and the houses stood in a row along the bank. The camp was short of food and everyone was hungry, and all the people were going out to hunt buffalo. They started, but one young man did not leave with the others; he stayed in the camp for some time after they had gone. He had determined that he would be the last person to start.

At length he set out, and as he passed the houses, he heard in one of them a woman crying. He wondered who this could be, for everyone had left the village, and he stopped and listened. After he had listened for a little while, he determined that he would go over and see who it was that was crying. As he drew near the house, the mourning grew lower and lower, and when he reached the house the woman had stopped crying. He went to the door and looked in, and saw a woman sitting at the foot of a bed, and a man at the head of the bed. When he looked in the door the man spoke to him, greeting him, and said to the woman, "Get him something to eat." The young man sat down, and presently the woman put before him some dried meat and some marrow-fat, and he ate.

After he had finished eating, the man said to the guest: "This woman, Mouse Woman, is crying and mourning because she has lost her children. They have been taken prisoner. She had her children in the arrow lodge, and they are there now and cannot get out."

The man and the woman begged this young man to help get her children back. "For," said the man, "this woman has been crying ever since she lost her children."

The young man listened to all that they said, and at length he promised to try to do all he could to get her children back for her.

At last the sun began to get low in the west, and the young man stood up and said to these people, "Now I must go on and follow up the camp." The man said again to him: "The woman's children are in the medicine bundle in the lodge that you will find in the center of the camp. Do what you can to help her."

The young man said: "I will try in every way I can to get these children. If I can get them out to-night, I will come back at once; to-night."

He started on the trail of the camp, and traveled fast, but it was after night when he reached the camp. He had been thinking hard all the time as he traveled along, to see what he could do to get this woman's children. As he went along, he prepared presents, and as he came near to the arrow lodge, he began to mourn and to cry.

The arrow keeper in his lodge heard the sound of his mourning, and as it drew nearer he said to his wife, "Someone is coming with gifts; get all things ready and then go out." The woman got things ready, and when the young man came to the door of the lodge, she went out. The medicine man spoke, asking the young man to come in. He went in, and the host asked him to come over and sit by him at the back of the lodge.

"Why have you come to see me?" said the arrow keeper; and the young man told him that he had come to make these offerings. The medicine man took them and prayed over them, performing the needed ceremonies, and then he gave them back to the young man and told him to take them out in front of the lodge and spread them over the arrow bundle where it hung over the door.

When he went out to spread his gifts over the arrow bundle, he thrust his hand into the bundle, and found there a mouse's nest with four little mice in it. After he had got the mice and put them in a fold of his robe, and had spread the gifts over the arrow bundle, he started back to the old village, and when he had come within hearing distance of it, he could hear the woman still crying for her children. He kept on, and as he drew nearer the lodge, the mourning grew lower, and when he had come to the door it stopped.

He entered and said, "Well, I have brought you your children," and he handed her the little mice, and she and the man both kissed the children. Then the man said to the young man: "You see how foolish my wife was to keep her children in the arrow lodge. They were lost and she might never have seen them again, but you have helped her and brought them back to her. Now I will give you a name which shall become great, and which everyone shall hear of. You shall become a leading man, and always when people are talking of wars and fights your name shall be mentioned first. Your name shall be Mouse's Road."

After the man had talked in this way for a little time, the young man happened to look out of the door, and as he did so he heard the sound of mice squeaking and running, and looking back he saw that the man and the woman had turned into mice and had run under the bed, and that he was there alone.

Now the young man returned to the camp, and as he followed the trail he was continually praying, for he remembered what the mouse person had told him. When he reached the camp, he went to his mother's lodge. She said to him: "Where have you been? I thought you would have been here long ago."

"No," he said, "I only just got in." Then said his mother: "A war party left while you were away. They sent for you to come with them." The young man said nothing, but the next morning he started and followed up the trail of the war party, and overtook them and went on with them.

In the first fight that they had, he, first of all, killed an enemy, and when he told what he had done, the people learned that his name was Mouse's Road. When the party got back, some old man cried out through the camp that Mouse's Road had killed the first enemy. In all fights after that he was always the first to do some great thing, and his name was always mentioned first.

After this war party had returned, they counted many coups and had many scalp dances. Also, on the hunt they got many buffalo and dried much meat, and then they returned to their village.

[A Mouse's Road was killed by the Kiowas in 1837. See the story of that brave man, *Fighting Cheyennes*, p. 10.]

THE WOODPECKER'S MOTHER-IN-LAW

BY a stream stood a lodge where people lived—a boy, a girl, a man, and a woman. The girl was very pretty. Many young men liked her and used to come to see her, to court her and try to get her to marry them. All were fine-looking men. These young men kept coming to try to get the girl to marry them, but she would take none of them. Some of them would go out and get fine fat buffalo meat and leave it at the father's lodge, so as to please the old people. They kept doing this and kept coming, but the girl would not marry any one of them.

Some of these young men who wished to marry this girl were not really persons; they were animals.

One day five young men met together and said to one another, "Everyone else has failed to get this girl; now let us go and try what we can do." They determined that they would go together and see whether the girl would not marry one of them. These young men were the Jack Rabbit, the Buffalo, the Mountain Lion, the Bear, and the Hairy Woodpecker. That evening the girl said to her mother, "I think I will go out now and get some wood."

Her mother said, "Very well; you may go." So the girl got her axe and rope, and started. She looked pretty. Her hair was long and nicely combed and braided; she wore a fine buckskin dress and a handsome, garnished robe. She had only a little way to go. Sitting in the lodge her people could hear her chopping at the wood.

While she was busy getting together her wood, these five young men came near, but stood out of sight, looking at her and whispering, each telling the other to speak to the girl, or to whistle to her, so that she would look at them.

Presently the Rabbit was persuaded, and he looked over the bank and called out, "Girl!" The girl looked up at him and said: "What are you doing here? No one would marry you; your eyes are too big, and your ears too long." The Rabbit put his head down behind the bank, feeling very much ashamed, and the others were discouraged. They talked to each other about it and said, "Rabbit is a good-looking man; if she won't look at him, it is no use for us to try."

At last the Bear looked over the bank and called out, and the girl looked up at him and said, "Ho, no one would marry you, with your long face and squint eyes." The Bear lowered his head, and the others felt still more discouraged, for they said, "Our friend Bear is a good-looking young man, and she won't have anything to do with him." The girl kept on getting wood, singing a little song as she chopped.

Next the Buffalo tried. He called to her in the same way, but the girl said to him, "No one would marry you, with your big head and your great nostrils," and she snapped her fingers at him. The Buffalo was much mortified and he went down behind the bank.

Next came the Mountain Lion. He raised up his head so that it could be seen, and called to the girl. To him she spoke as she had to the others, and talked about his round face, and, snapping her fingers at him, she went on with her work.

The others said to the Bird, "Now, you are the last; it is your turn." He said, "It is no use for me to speak; my friend Lion is a good-looking young man, and he was refused."

When the Bird called, the girl looked at him, but said nothing. She left her axe in the wood she was splitting, took off her belt and left her robe on the ground, and walked away, and the young man went with her. The axe was left there, still chopping at the wood.

Not long after this the mother said to the boy, "Go out and call your sister; she has been gone long enough." The boy went out of the lodge and called, saying, "Sister, you have been gone long enough; come back." The girl called back, saying, "I have only a few more sticks to get now." But the girl had been gone for a long time from the place where the voice came from; it was her robe that answered.

In the lodge they could still hear her axe chopping at the wood, but it was now near sundown, and her mother went out to call her. When she had called, the girl's voice called back, saying that she was nearly through now, and would soon be there. Still she did not come, and presently the mother went out to the place. When she came near it, the axe stopped chopping, and when the old woman reached it, all she found was the robe and the axe and a pile of wood. The old woman began to cry. She said: "At last they have got my daughter, but I will go after them. They will get tired and stop somewhere, and I shall overtake them at last."

After the girl had gone off with the Woodpecker, the four young men who had been refused followed on after them, and traveled together. At last they came to a patch of brush where grew many of the berries called rabbit berries. When they got there the Rabbit said, "I think I will stop here and eat." So the Rabbit stopped. The others went on further, and after they had gone a long way they came to a buffalo wallow, with nice green grass growing in it, and the Buffalo said, "Friends, I will stop here; this is a good place for me"; so he lay down there. The Mountain Lion and the Bear traveled on further, and came to a patch where many cherries and plums grew. As they were passing through this, the Bear said, "I think I will stop here"; and he stopped there in the brush and began to eat cherries. The Mountain Lion went on alone and came to a thicket where there were brush and willows, and he said to himself, "I will stop here; this is a good place to lie in wait for game."

The Woodpecker, who had the girl, went on with her, and they traveled together a long way beyond where the others had stopped. They came to a dead tree, where there were other Woodpeckers just like the one who had got the girl. The young man spoke to these birds, and said to them, "If you see a ball coming over the hill, get hold of it, and fly up high with it, and let it drop." Then he went on.

Next morning the old woman started out to find her daughter. She took the shape of a ball, and flew through the air very fast, following the trail of these people who had gone away. She first came to the Rabbit, and knocked against him, and said, "You are the one who took my daughter."

The Rabbit was frightened, and jumped to one side, and said, "It was not I." Next she came to the Buffalo. The ball struck him and said, "You are the one who has my daughter." The bull jumped up and snorted, blowing out his breath, and said, "It is not I." Then she came to the Bear. He was standing up and eating some plums, and the ball struck him in the breast, and frightened him so that he fell over backward. The ball said, "You are the one that has my daughter." The Bear scrambled to his feet, and grunted as he said, "I have not your daughter." Next she reached the Lion. The ball struck him in the ribs, saying, "You are the one that has my daughter."

The Lion gave a great bound over the willows out of sight, and said, as he was in the air, "I have not your daughter."

Soon after this the old woman saw a bird sitting on a tree, and she rushed up to it and began to say, "You have my daughter." As she said this, the bird flew out of the tree, and caught her and carried her up in the air, and let her drop, and then another bird caught her and carried her up and let her drop; and she began to beg, and at last she said, "You can keep my daughter"; but they would not listen to her, and presently they carried her very high and let her drop, and when she began to fall it was no longer the ball but the old woman.

When she struck the ground the fall did not hurt her. She still followed on foot the trail of her daughter and the young man, and went up the creek. As she was going along, she saw far ahead of her a man, wrapped in a robe, sitting on a hill. He was one of the lookouts left by the bird.

She went to him and asked him if he had seen her daughter pass. "No," he said, "no one has passed." When he said that, the old woman walked around to windward of him, and he fell over, dead.

The bird and the girl kept on going, for they could see the old woman coming, a long way off. At last they went into a butte. As the old woman went on, she came to another man, and asked him if he had seen her daughter pass. He said to her, "No, no one has passed." The old woman replied, "You do not know anything, either," and when she walked around to windward of him, he fell over, dead. The old woman went on.

She came to another man, and asked him, "Have you seen my daughter go up by here?" He said, "No." She made the same reply to him as she had done to the others, and walked around to windward of him, and he died. Then she went on. She came to a fourth man, and asked him the same questions, and received the same answer, and the same things happened.

Then she came to a fifth man, and asked him if he had seen her daughter. He said, "No," and she walked around him, but he just sat there and did not look at her. Again she asked him, and he said "No," and she walked around him again, but still he sat there. She kept doing this until she had done it four times, but still the man sat there. Then the man stood up and said to her, "You ask a great many questions." The woman did not run away, but stood there. He walked around her on the windward side, and she fell dead.

After she had fallen, the old man walked to the bluff, and pushed aside a great rock, and went in and told the girl that her mother was dead. They all stayed there.

THE FOUR SERVANTS

IN old times the Cheyennes lived in houses made of earth. In one of these a young man lived alone.

One day a very old man came to his house; he carried a bow and quiver. The young man said, "What do you want, grandfather?" He replied: "My grandson, I came here to live with you. I will make your arrows for you." The young man said, "It is good; make your bed on the other side of the lodge."

Soon after, a buffalo bull came to the house. The young man said: "Friend, what do you wish? Why have you come here?" The bull replied, "I have come to look after your house and keep it clean." The young man said, "It is good; I will make room for you." He told him to make his bed on the other side of the lodge.

Not long after this, a bear came to the house and the young man said to him, "What do you want?" The bear said, "I will keep your house supplied with firewood; I will bring it up from the timber." The young man said, "Good; make up your bed on that side with the bull."

Then came a snapping turtle, and when asked what he wanted, he said, "I have come, my grandson, to keep your house supplied with water." The young man said, "I will find a place for you; make your bed up with the old man."

Next morning when the young man arose all the four were gone and he was alone in the lodge. He went out to look for them. He found the old man sitting outside and said to him, "Grandfather, what made you leave me?" The old man said, "Oh, I just thought I would come out and sit here by myself."

Not far off lived an old woman who had a fine-looking granddaughter. The old man said, "I should like to have you marry that girl." The young man replied: "I will do as you advise, grandfather. I will go and see her." The young man went on further and came to the buffalo bull and said to him, "What are you doing here?" The buffalo bull answered him much as the old man had done, and also advised him to marry the girl, and again the young man said he would go and see her. Further on he met the bear, and afterward the turtle, and both said the same things to him. All four returned with him to his house and took their old places. After a time the young man said, "Grandfather, give me your bow and arrows and quiver, and I will go and visit that girl." They all set out together, but the old man followed him only a short distance and then stopped; the bull went on further and stopped; then the bear stayed behind, and at last the turtle. They waited for him to come back with his wife.

This girl's grandmother had some birds watching her house so that no one should take away her granddaughter. The first bird the young man met was a jacksnipe, and to him the young man gave one of the arrows from his quiver, so that he should not tell the old woman that the young man was coming. Then he met a plover and gave him an arrow, and then a heron, who also received one. Then he passed by the edge of a pond where there were many frogs. He emptied his quiver into the pond and asked the frogs to take pity on him and not to tell the old woman that he was trying to steal her granddaughter. When he had thrown the arrows into the pond he walked on up to the lodge. The young girl must have had news that he was coming, for she came out and they ran off together.

Soon after the old woman came out of the lodge and missed her granddaughter. She went back and brought out a playing ball—one of those that women play with. She hit the ball with her stick and it followed the trail the young man and girl had made. All her birds had flown away. She said: "Where are my birds? They all seem to have gone."

As she drew near where the snapping turtle had waited, she knocked the ball at him and her power was so strong that the ball struck the turtle and killed him. In this way she killed also the bear and then the buffalo bull. As the young man had passed the place where the old man was waiting, he had handed him the bow, saying: "The old woman is following us. When she comes here, shoot at the ball she rolls; it is her body, and, if you hit it, you will kill her." As the old woman struck the ball toward him, the old man shot an arrow into it and at once the woman fell to the ground.

When he knew that she had been killed, the young man went out of his house and spoke to his grandfather, saying: "Go in and wait for me. Your granddaughter is there." He went to where the buffalo bull was lying, and pushed the carcass with the foot, saying: "Get up. I have brought your granddaughter home."

The bull got up and shook himself, saying, "I did not know I had been asleep." The young man sent him back to the house and then went on to where the bear was. In the same manner he brought him back to life, and then did the same to the turtle. All went back and the young man followed them.

After that, the old man made his arrows; the bull kept his

house clean; the bear brought up wood, and the turtle brought the water. The man and his wife did not have to work.

Some time after the four helpers talked together. The old man said: "My grandson is married now. I shall make a quantity of arrows for him, and then I shall go away where I belong." The bull said that he also must go away, and the bear and turtle said they would go too. They all left him.

That cuts it off.

THE WOLF HELPER

AFTER the Sand Creek massacre was over, and the troops had gone, there were left alive two women. In 1902 these women were still living. One was named Two She-Wolf Woman, and the other, Standing in Different Places Woman. They were sisters, and each had a little daughter—one ten years old and one of six years. Their husband was badly wounded and likely to die, and he told them they must leave him and go on home to the camp, so that they might save themselves and their children. They started. They had no food, and no implements except their knives and a little short-handled axe. They had their robes.

They traveled on and on, until they reached the Smoky Hill River. Here they found many rose berries, and they pounded them up with the little axe and ate them. After they had pounded the rose berries they made flat cakes of them to give to the children, and started on. They did not know where the camp was, and did not know where to go. They just followed the river down.

One night after they had been traveling for six or seven days, they went into a little hole in the bluff for shelter, for it was very cold. They were sitting up, one robe under them, with the other in front of them, and with the children lying between them. In the middle of the night something came into the hole and lay down by them, and when this thing had come near to them, standing between them and the opening of the hole, they saw that it was a big wolf, and were afraid of it; but it lay down quietly.

Next morning they started on, and the wolf went with them, walking not far to one side of them. Their feet were sore, for their moccasins were worn out, and they often stopped to rest, and when they did so the wolf lay down near by. At one of these halts the elder woman spoke to the wolf, just as she would talk to a person. She said to him: "O Wolf, try to do something for us. We and our children are nearly starved." When she spoke to him, the wolf seemed to listen and rose up on his haunches and looked at her, and when she stopped speaking he rose to his feet and started off toward the north. It was the early part of the winter, but there was no snow on the ground.

The women still sat there resting, for they were weak and tired and footsore. They saw the wolf pass out of sight over the hill, and after a time they saw him coming back. He came toward them, and when he was close to them they could see that his mouth and jaws were covered with blood. He stepped in front of them and turned his head and looked back in the direction from whence he had come. The women were so weak and stiff they could hardly get up, but they rose to their feet. When they stood up the wolf trotted off to the top of the hill and stopped, looking back, and they followed him very slowly. When they reached the top of the hill and looked off, they saw, down in the little draw beyond, the carcass of a buffalo, and in a circle all about it sat many wolves. The wolf looked back at the women again, and then loped down toward the carcass. Now the women started to walk fast toward the carcass, for here was food. All the wolves still sat about; they were not feeding on the carcass.

WATCHING THE RETURN.

When the women reached it they drew their knives and opened it. They made no fire, but at once ate the liver and tripe, and the fat about the intestines, without cooking, and gave food to the children. Then they cut off pieces of the meat, as much as they could carry, and made up packs and started on their way. As soon as they had left the carcass, all the wolves fell upon it and began to eat it quickly, growling and snarling at each other, and soon they had eaten it all. The big wolf ate with the other wolves. The women went on over the hill and stopped; they had eaten so much that they could not go far. In the evening, when the sun was low, one of the women said to the other, "Here is our friend again"; and the wolf came trotting up to them.

Soon after he had joined them they started on to look for a hollow where they might sleep. The wolf traveled with them. When it grew dark they stopped, and the wolf lay near them. Every day they tried to find a place to camp where there were willows. They used to cut these and make a shelter of them, and cover this with grass, and make a bed of grass, and then put down their robes and cover themselves with grass. So they were well sheltered.

One morning as they were going along they looked over the hill and saw in the bottom below them some ponies feeding. They started down to see whose they were, the wolf traveling along, but off to one side. Before they had come near to the horses two persons came up over a hill, and when these persons saw the women coming they sprang on their horses and ran away fast. The women walked on to the place where the men had been. Here there was a fire, and meat that the men had left—a tongue and other food roasting. The women took the meat and ate, and they cut the tongue in two and gave the smaller end of it to the wolf, which had come up and was lying by the fire.

After they had finished eating they went on, and soon came

to a big spring with a hollow near by—a good place to camp. They were glad to find the place, for the sky looked as if it were going to snow. They made a good camp, a house of willows and grass, and covered it with bark from the trees. By this time they had become so accustomed to having the wolf with them that every night they used to make a bed near the door of the house, piling up grass for him to sleep on.

That night the women heard a noise down in the hollow— something calling like a big owl. Two She-Wolf Woman was watching; for they were afraid during the night, and used to take turns keeping watch. They could hear this thing breaking sticks as it walked about. The watcher awoke her sister, saying, "Wake up! something is coming." The wolf now stood up, and soon he began to howl with a long-drawn-out cry, which was very dismal. Soon from all directions many wolves began to come to the place. After a little while this thing that was making the noise began to come closer, and when it did so all the wolves rushed toward it and began fighting it, and the women seized their children and ran away into the night. They got far out on the level prairie and stopped there, for their feet were sore, and they were very tired. In the morning just as day was breaking they saw the big wolf coming toward them. When he reached them he lay down.

The elder woman now spoke to him again, and said, "Wolf, take pity on us; help us to find the trail of our people." When she had ceased speaking, the wolf trotted away, leaving the women, and they followed on very slowly. Before long they saw him coming back toward them fast—loping. When he got to them they saw that he had in his mouth a big piece of dried meat. He dropped the meat in front of them. They seized the meat and divided it, and gave some of it to their children and ate of it themselves. The wolf did not lie down, but stood waiting, and when they had eaten, he led them to an old camp where there were sticks standing in the ground, and on each stick hung a parfleche sack of meat. Their relations had left these things for them, knowing that they were lost and thinking that they might pass that way.

Now the women had plenty of food; they went to the water and built a shelter with a place in it for the wolf. That night it snowed. When they arose the snow was above their ankles. Again the woman spoke to the wolf, and asked him to go and find their camp, and he went away. The women stayed there. The wolf was not gone a long time; he came back the same day. They were watching for him, for now they knew that he was their friend, and that he was true; they knew that he would do something for them. The two women went to the top of the little hill near by, and before night they saw the wolf coming. He came up to them and stopped, and then began to look back. The women felt sure that he had found something, and went back to their camp and got their children, and went to the wolf, who started back as he had come, traveling ahead of them. On the point of a high hill he stopped, and when the women overtook him they looked down, and there they saw a big Cheyenne camp on the river below. This was the head of the Republican River.

They went on down to the camp, and to the lodge of Gray Beard. The wolf remained on the hill. After the women had eaten, the older woman took meat, and told the people that a wolf had led them to the camp, and she was going back to give him something to eat. She went back and gave the wolf the food, and after he had eaten she said to him, "Now, you have brought us to the camp, you can go back to your old ways." Late that evening the woman went up on the hill again to see if the wolf was there, but he was gone. She saw his tracks going back the same way that he had come. This happened in the winter of 1864 and 1865. The women and one of the children are still alive.

THE UNDER-WATER MAN

A YOUNG man who lived in a big village was courting a young woman and asked her to marry him. She told him that after he had been off on the warpath and had returned, she would marry him. Not long after this a war party left the village and the young man went with it. All were on foot, as was the custom in old times. After they had traveled for some days, he made a friend of one of the other young men and they used to walk together, apart from the rest, and tell each other stories of their sweethearts.

One day while walking along the young man said to his friend, "Let us go back to the village." His friend said, "No, we have been off some time, let us continue with the war party." The next day the young man again urged his friend to return. He did this four times and three times was refused. The fourth time his friend said, "I will go back with you if you wish," and they turned about and went back in the direction of their village. The main party kept on their warpath.

As the party had been journeying on their warpath they had passed a large lake and on their way back the two young men said, "We will stop at that lake and eat there." When they reached the lake they built a fire; they had nothing to cook, but they said, "We will build a fire anyway." While they were building the fire, a great wave from the lake swept up toward them and when the water went back they found two large fish on the bank. The young man said, "Here are two fish; now we have something to eat." His friend said, "No, we must not touch them; some great power has thrown out those fish; we must not eat them." The young man insisted, but his friend would not touch them, so he picked them up and laid them by the fire. As they sat by the fire, they heard a little noise, and, looking around, saw an antelope coming toward them. The friend picked up his bow and arrow and shot it in the breast. They skinned it and had all they wanted to eat.

When they had finished eating the meat, the young man picked up the fish and laid them on the coals to roast. When they were cooked, he said, "You eat one and I will eat the other." His friend replied, "No, I said they were mysterious; I do not wish to touch them." The young man insisted, and at last his friend said, "Eat them both if you wish; I do not care for them." So the young man ate both the fish. Then he felt like drinking, so he went to the lake and got on his hands and knees to drink; and while he was drinking another big wave came and carried him into the lake. He was drawn out into the lake until he stood up to his waist in the water. The friend knew that something must be holding him and walked to the edge of the water and asked, "My friend, what is the matter?" He called back, "Something holds me by the waist; I cannot move." His friend said, "I told you not to eat those fish, but you would not listen."

Then said the young man: "Go home and tell my people not to mourn for me; the great medicine that is here has taken me. Send for my sweetheart and tell her to ask the village to move to this lake; they must not be afraid of it. Tell her to get a fine buffalo robe and a pipe and a sack filled with smoking stuff, and when the village arrives here, let her wade into the water up to her waist. She must spread the robe on the water, and place the pipe and sack on the robe and then go back to the shore. Tell all the people when they come around here to throw entrails of animals or birds into this lake as an offering and not to be afraid to come near here."

When his friend reached the village again there was much mourning at the loss of the young man. After they had finished mourning, the friend sent for the girl to tell her what the young man had said to him. When she had come to his lodge, he said: "When we started on the war party, my friend talked much about you. When I left him in the water he said this to me: 'You are to ask the village to move to the lake and camp facing it' "; and then he went on to tell her what she must do with the robe, the pipe, and the tobacco sack. The girl said, "I will tell my father what you say." She went home and told her father the story. Her father said: "It is well; you have a fine robe and here are my pipe and tobacco sack. We will move soon." Then he called the message through the village, and everyone said it was good and that they should move at once. They made four camps on their journey, and each day the young man's friend went ahead to lead the way.

They camped by the lake, with the camp facing it as they had been told. Next morning the girl dressed herself and painted her face. Then her father announced that all must assemble, because his daughter was ready to go into the lake. All stood in line near the edge of the water and the girl stood in front. The friend was by her side. He said to her, "When you come out of the water come out backwards; do not look toward the camp." She took off her leggings, but kept her dress on. After that she began to walk in and everyone said: "Take courage. Do not be afraid." She waded out till the water reached to her armpits. She held the pipe and pouch out in front of her and spoke to the medicine man in the lake, saying: "I have come to do what you asked me to; I am sorry that the mysterious power has taken you. I wanted to marry you." Then she spread out the robe, laid the pipe and tobacco pouch on it, and went backward to the shore.

About the middle of the night a man went out of his lodge and saw sparks of fire coming out of the water, and also heard a noise in the lake. He aroused the village and all stood watching. Just as they began to get frightened and were about to run away and to leave the village, the sparks stopped rising and there was no more noise, and all the people went again to their lodges. In the morning the prairie around the lake was full of buffalo and everyone believed that the under-water man had sent the buffalo out of the lake to help the people, because they had moved over there as he had directed. They killed many buffalo close around the camp. All who killed food brought the buffalo entrails back with them and threw them into the water and offered thanks to the man in the lake. They did this four times and then they moved away, but every time the village was hungry they used to go back to the lake, and there they were always sure to find buffalo.

(Compare "The Snake Brother," *Pawnee Hero Stories and Folk Tales,* p. 171; and *The Cheyenne Indians,* vol. 2, p. 97.)

THE LITTLE GIRL AND THE GHOST

THERE was once a camp and in one of the lodges a little girl sat crying; she was angry about something. Her mother did all she could to make the child stop, but at last the mother became angry and she opened the lodge door and pushed the child out and said, "Ghost, take away this child."

A ghost must have been standing somewhere close by the door, for when the mother put the child out something picked it up. As soon as she was put out, the child stopped crying. After a time the woman went out; and when she could not find her daughter, she went about among the lodges, crying and looking for her. The one that took away the child was a young ghost, and at the place the young ghost came from there was an old ghost. The young one brought the child to the old one and said, "Here is your food."

In the morning the old ghost said to the little girl, "Go and bring in some wood." The little girl went out and gathered some dry wood. A little bird flew close to her and said, "You are getting that wood for yourself"—meaning that it was to be used to cook her. She took the wood up to the lodge and the old ghost looked at it and said, "That is not the kind I want"; and sent her to get some more. Again the little bird said to her, "You are getting that wood for yourself." She took it up to the lodge and again the old ghost found fault with it, and sent her for other wood. She went a third time and again the little bird spoke to her. She was sent back a fourth time. The bird flew close to her and said, "This is the last time; when you go back they will cook you."

The girl said: "It is useless to tell me that; the big ghost has got me and I cannot help myself. Can you help me?" The bird answered: "Yes, I can help you. Now right over here is a mountain peak. I will take you there and when you get there, you must say at the door in the rock: 'My grandfather, I have come for protection; my father, I have come for protection; my brother, I have come for protection; my husband, I have come for protection.' This must be said at the door. I will take you there. There is a big stone lying against the peak; that is the door."

The bird told her to put a hand on each of its shoulders and flying close to the ground it carried her to the peak. When they arrived the girl repeated what the bird had told her. The bird said, "Place your hand on the rock and push it to one side." She did so and went in, and saw an old man sitting there. He said, "Come in, my grandchild; I know you have come to me for protection."

When the old ghost missed the girl, he went out and followed her. He knew she had gone to the peak. As he drew near, he commenced to hoot like an owl; and when he hooted the ground shook. Four times he hooted and each time the ground shook. When the child heard the ghost, she was afraid and ran around inside the lodge, trying to hide; but her grandfather told her to keep quiet and not to be afraid. After hooting four times, the ghost came up to the rock. He stood in front of the door and said, "Bring out my meat; if you will not, I must come in after it." Four times he said that.

The old man said, "Come in and take her out." The ghost said, "Open the door that I may come in." After he had been asked four times, the old man got up and pulled the door open just far enough for the ghost to get its head in; and when the ghost had put its head in, the old man let the door fly back and cut the head off the ghost, so that it fell on the ground inside. The man picked it up and threw it outside the lodge; and said to the girl, "Get some dry wood and throw it over the head." After she had made a pile over it, the old man set it on fire; then he threw the ghost's body in the fire and handed the girl a stick and said, "Now, if anything rolls out, do not touch it with your hand, but push it back in the fire with this stick." After he had lighted the fire the head and body cracked open and pieces of flint and old-time beads rolled out. The little girl wanted to pick them up, but the old man said, "No, push them into the fire." They watched the fire until the ghost was all burned up.

When the girl was seventeen years old, the old man said she might go back to her village. He dressed her like a man; made a robe for her and painted it with Indian red paint; her leggings and moccasins were also painted red. He made her a thunder bow and put buffalo bull tails on the heels of her moccasins. Then he tied the skin of a prairie owl on her forehead. So she was dressed like a Contrary.

When she was ready to start the old man gave her a live mink and told her to put it inside her dress on her breast. He said to her: "You must pass by four villages; stop at none of them; they will call out to you, but keep on and pass by. After that, you will find a single lodge. Go in and stop there, for by that time it will be sundown. At that lodge you will find an old woman who has great power; she tries to kill everyone who comes to her lodge. When you have gone in, she will boil a kettle of brains and meal for you to eat. The brains will be those of someone she has killed. She will hand you a bowl of this with a horn spoon, but you must not eat it. Feed that to the mink. Then she will cook you some buffalo meat; eat that."

Before the girl left him the old man told her that when she stopped at this old woman's lodge she must not sleep. He said: "If you sleep, she will try to kill you; but, if you do fall asleep, keep the mink up close to your neck and it will act as a guard over you. After she thinks you are asleep, she will begin to scratch her leg and her leg will swell up; then she will use her leg as a club and will strike you on the head with it."

As the girl passed the first village she came to, on her journey, the women called out to her, "Come here, young man, and stop," but she paid no attention. When the women found that she paid no attention to them, they called out to her, "You walk like a woman." This happened at each of the four villages.

Just at sundown she got to the top of the hill and down in the valley saw a lone lodge. The old woman came out and said, "Come down, my grandchild," and took her by the hand and brought her to the lodge. She hung her thunder bow on the limb of a tree; then she went in and saw that everything in the lodge looked very fine. The old woman said, "My grandchild must be hungry; I will cook some mush for you." So she put the brains on the fire in a pot. When it was cooked she gave her a bowl full and a spoon, but the girl fed it to the mink. The old woman said, "My grandchild is still hungry," and began to boil her some buffalo meat, and the girl ate it.

After a time the old woman asked the girl if she was sleepy. She said, "Yes, I would like to go to sleep," and she lay down with the mink up close to her throat. The old woman said, "I will sit up and keep the fire burning, so that you will be warm." The girl pretended to sleep and snored, and saw the old woman get up close to the fire and begin to scratch her leg. It began to get larger and she crawled up to where the girl lay and raised

A SWEAT LODGE.

THE SACRED BUFFALO SKULL.

her leg to strike her with, but just as she held it over her head, the girl pushed the mink out. It caught hold of the woman's leg and tore off a piece of flesh. The old woman cried out, "You have killed me," and fell over; then she began to cry and said, "You have strong spiritual power."

The girl jumped up and went out; and, as she did so, picked up a burning brand and set the lodge on fire. She took up her thunder bow and started off in the direction of her camp.

She traveled all that night, and next day arrived at the big village. There she stood up on the hill with her thunder bow, and all the village came out to see the strange young man. Two young men came to her and said, "Where did you come from?" She answered, "This is my village; I have been away a long time and have come back." So they took her to the center of the camp and called an old man to announce that a young man who belonged to the village had arrived. The old man called it through the village and everyone came up to look at her. No one knew who she was. Finally they asked her who her family was. She hung her head down, for it made her ashamed to remember that her mother had put her out of her lodge. She said she was the girl thrown out of the lodge by her mother and carried off by the ghost. Then they all recognized her and her people took her to their lodge.

(A Cree story contains some of these elements.)

THE TURTLE MAN

A LONG time ago there were two brothers. One of them was married, and the two brothers and the wife lived together. The married man used to go hunting to kill food.

One day when he came back he sat about for a time, and after a while he said to his brother, "Brother, to-day I found an eagle's nest in a tree; let us go out and get the eagles, so that we may have their feathers." The younger brother was glad to do this, and he started out with the young man to get these feathers. They walked up the river for a long time, and at last came to a dead tree growing on the top of a bluff, and leaning out over the stream. In this tree was the nest of the eagles.

"There is the tree," said the married brother; "do you climb up and throw out the young birds, and we will take them home with us." The boy climbed the tree, and after he had almost reached the nest, the elder brother began to push the tree, and because it was rotten it broke out of the ground and fell over into the river, and the boy was drowned, and floated down the river.

The married brother returned to his lodge, and he and his wife quickly packed up their things and went back to the main camp. He told his mother and his relations that some enemy had killed his brother, and that he had only just been able to save himself. All the boy's relations mourned for him, crying hard.

On the river, down below where the eagle's nest had been, lived an old man—an under-water person—and his wife and two daughters. This old man had a herd of buffalo which fed about his camp all the time.

One day the two girls went down to the river to bathe, and while they were bathing they found a dead man lying on a sandbar. When they saw him they ran quickly to the camp and told their father what they had found.

"Ha," said the old man, after his daughters had told him what they had seen, "I must go after this person, and try to cure him. I will make a sweat lodge for him, and he shall be my son-in-law." He went down to the river and found the man lying as his daughters had told him, and he told them to bring the person home with them. The dead man was covered all over with sand.

After the old man had built the sweat lodge and had heated the stones, he put the dead man in the lodge and poured water on the rocks, and sang a song. Then when he took the man out of the lodge, some of the sand which had covered him had fallen off. Then the old man built another sweat lodge, and gave the boy another sweat and more sand fell from him; he repeated this until he had built four sweat houses, one after another, and after he had taken the fourth sweat all the sand was gone from his body, and the young man came out of the sweat lodge alive and well.

Now the old man said to his daughters, "My daughters, take food to this man, and if he does not like the food that you offer him, ask him what it is that he wishes to eat." The girls took down to him some of their food—a bowl of leeches—and offered them to him to eat, but when they gave him the dish the boy looked at it, and did not know what to do with it. He refused the food, saying, "I cannot eat those things."

Then the old man told his daughters to go out and gather all sorts of plants for their husband to eat. They brought him many kinds of plants, but he said to his wives, "I cannot eat those things."

The girls went back to their father, and said to him, "Our husband will not eat these plants."

The old man thought for a long time, trying to think what food he could offer his son-in-law that would please him, but he could think of nothing. At last he said to the girls, "Ask him what he wishes to eat." They did so, and when asked, the young man said, "I eat meat; buffalo is my food."

The old man killed a buffalo and brought in the meat, and the girls took some of it and offered it to the young man, but he would not eat it.

He said to his wives, "My food must be cooked; I cannot eat it uncooked." The old man made a fire and cooked the meat, and then the boy ate it.

After a time the young man had a son, who grew up until he was quite a big boy. One day his father told his wives that he was going hunting. He went up the river, looking for some food which he might kill, and as he was going along he saw a person standing on a hill. He went around behind the hills, traveling through the low places, to see who this person was, and when he had come close to her, he saw that it was his mother. For a long time she had been going out in the hills to mourn for her son who had been killed by enemies.

When the young man saw who this was, he showed himself, and went up to her; and when she saw him she was glad, and took him home with her. His elder brother, when he saw him, pretended that he too was glad. The young man told his father and mother what his elder brother had done to him. He told his people also of his father-in-law and of his family, and said that he must go back to them; but his mother would not let him go.

He wanted to go, and kept telling her that he must go, and at last his mother said to him that she herself would go to see her grandson.

So after a time the mother, the young man, and a younger brother started for the father-in-law's camp. When they had come near the place they saw two lodges standing by the stream, but as they drew near them the lodges kept growing smaller and smaller, and when they had come close to them, the lodges had disappeared; there were none there, and they saw only some turtles going toward the water as fast as they could. There were four large turtles and one little one.

When the young man saw this he was frightened, and he began to cry, mourning for his wife and his son who were in the water. He said, "I must stay here and look for my family." His mother and his younger brother tried to persuade him to go home with them, but he would not go. Finally they went off without him. For a long time the young man stayed there, mourning and crying, looking for his wife and boy, who, as he thought, were under the water. He had nothing to eat. After three days' starving, he saw a person's head come up in the middle of the lake, and when he saw the head he knew that it was the head of his son. The boy spoke to his father, saying, "Father, you must try your best to catch me in the water; if you can do this, my grandfather will let you come into the water and stay with your family; but if you cannot catch me, you cannot come to us, and we must always live apart." After this the father used to sit on the bank of the lake, watching for his boy. Sometimes the small turtle would climb up on the bank, and the father would try to get near to him, but always before he got near it, the turtle dropped into the water and sank out of sight.

The first time the turtle sank out of sight, the father dived after him into the deep water, and felt about for the turtle in the mud. At last, when his breath was almost gone, he saw the turtle and caught it in his hands, and swam hard to get to the surface; but his breath was all gone, and he came so near to drowning that he dropped the turtle.

Three times he did this, but the fourth time he kept a good hold, and reached the surface, still holding it. He kept tight hold of the turtle, and swam to the bank and got on it, still with the turtle in his hands; and he took it away from the bank and held it, and talked to it, hoping that it might answer him, for he did not know whether this was really his son or was some other turtle.

The woman (his wife), who had now lost her son, tried to persuade her father to bring her husband back, but he was angry, and said nothing, and did nothing. The man still kept the turtle, and talked to it, but it would not answer. He did not know what he should do. He was afraid to go to sleep for fear the turtle might get away from him; so he sat there holding it.

After four days the little turtle spoke to him, and said, "Father, I love you, and I do not want you to get drowned." His father answered him, "My son, I wish to stay here where you are, and I shall continue to stay around here until I die."

"I do not want you to die," said the son, "and soon I shall show you how you may find my mother."

At one side of the lake was a great wall of rock coming down to the water's edge, and under this wall, deep water; and in the wall below was a hole. The son said to his father, "Now, father, you take hold of my tail, and I will lead you to where your relations all are. All of them stay in that deep water under those rocks." The man did as his son told him to, and held on by his tail, and the turtle dived into the lake, and they went deep down into the water, and at last they reached the place where the lodges were standing; but here there was no water. At these lodges he found his father-in-law and his wives, and, besides them, a very old, gray-headed woman; very old and ugly and wearing poor clothes. All sat quiet there, except the son; he was very glad to have his father back again; he was jumping about and shouting and making a great noise.

After many years the son grew up to be a man. He learned to hunt, and kill fishes, so as to support his father. After a time the father said to his son, "Son, I should like to visit my people once more, so that I may see my father and my mother."

"It is good," said the son; "go and visit them." So the father went on his way and found the camp of his tribe, and lived with them for a time.

Sometimes, as they moved about, his relations used to camp by this water where the man's people lived, and every time when they camped there, this man disappeared. They would find that he was gone, and when they looked everywhere for him they could not find him. His relations used to mourn for him; they did not know that he was close by them in the water with his family. He stayed away from them for a long time, and at last his father and mother had almost forgotten him, for they thought of him as of one a long time dead. One day the man thought that he would again visit his relations, and went out on the prairie to where the camp used to be, to see if his relations were still living. When he reached the camp he found the circle was a large one, and when he asked where his father and mother were, someone went to his parents and told them that their son had returned. After a time they went to see him, and recognized him; and then he told them the story of how he had died and lived.

He taught them how to make a sweat lodge. This was the first sweat lodge that the Cheyennes had known. When he had died this man's name was Spotted Hawk, but when he returned the people called him the Turtle Man.

It is because the under-water people had buffalo that the buffalo's head is put before the sweat lodge. The sweat lodge is shaped like a turtle.

THE STONE BUFFALO HORN

A MAN named Listening to the Ground killed another Cheyenne and left the camp in the night, with his wife and daughter. This was when the Cheyennes lived in the Black Hills. His daughter died about 1875, and when she died she was seventy years old.

Listening to the Ground and his family went far off to the northern part of the Black Hills, and for three years they saw no one. They lived in a cave. The third year all the different animals used to come to him. When the animals began to come about, he always told his wife and daughter to keep still and not to move, so that the animals should not be frightened.

One morning while he was sitting in the cave a big gray wolf came near him and howled; next morning it came and howled again, and now Listening to the Ground understood what the wolf was saying. It spoke as follows: "All of us who are animals have taken pity on you; I have been appointed to take you home to the *Wŭ' hŭ ĭs tă' tăn*. To-night I will come here to show you the way to the village where you belong." Only Listening to the Ground understood the wolf. He told his wife what the wolf had said to him and directed her to get ready. In the night the wolf came back, as he had promised. He went first to the man and smelled of him; then he went to the woman and, after that, to the little girl. He smelled them all. He told them to get up and follow him. He started south, keeping a little ahead of them.

Before they left the Black Hills a person had come to Listening to the Ground and had put down this horn before him. He afterward said that this was some spirit who had taken pity on them. The spirit told him to take the horn back with him and showed him what to do to call the buffalo, and taught him what songs he should sing.

When Listening to the Ground and his family had been seven days on the road, the wolf told them to stop and to remain where they were until he came back. He was gone for a day or two and returned, saying: "I have found the camp where you belong. The people there are starving. The *Wŭ' hŭ ĭs tă' tăn* smell very bad"—meaning there was no smell of grease in the camp; that is, no buffalo. The wolf again took the lead and led them up on the hill near to the camp. The three people sat down, and the wolf lay beside them. The man, the woman, and the little girl were nearly naked. A man from the camp saw them and came toward them. He looked at them and said, "Is this you, Listening to the Ground?" He answered, "Yes," and said, "I have come here with a very strong medicine. Tell the people about this great medicine and tell them to come up and make an offering of presents to this wolf; tell two bands of the soldiers to put up two lodges in the center of the camp." The man went away and the three still sat on the hill.

Everybody came running up to see them and to look at the wolf, lying there with them. The only thing they had to give the wolf was a piece of red cloth, which one man tied around its neck. When the cloth had been tied to the wolf's neck, Listening to the Ground told it to return, and it went back the same way it had come. Then they went down to the camp.

Listening to the Ground told his wife and daughter that they might go to their people, but that he would go to where the two lodges were. He told the people to come to the lodge at sundown, for he was going to sing and call the buffalo. Everyone came there and as many as could entered the lodge and sat down. Listening to the Ground then sent for his wife and daughter. He sat in the back of the lodge with his wife on his right side and his daughter close in front of him.

He placed the horn on the ground with the point to the east and told everyone to watch. He said he would sing three times and asked everybody, when he sang the third time, to look at the little girl to see if her right ear moved as the buffalo calves' ears move. The words of his song said, "Buffalo, walk toward this place, and arrive here." The third time he sang all watched his daughter, and saw her right ear move. Then he sang again and she moved her left ear; she moved her right ear at the words, "Buffalo come toward this place"; and when he said, "Buffalo arrive here," she moved the left ear.

Listening to the Ground said, "Watch the stone," and the fourth time he sang, as the girl moved her left ear, the stone rolled over very slowly toward the north with its point still to the east.

Listening to the Ground at once said, "Let one man go up on top of the hill near the camp early to-morrow morning. Only one man must go." They selected a man to do this. He said also, "I want all the tongues, both large and small, brought to my lodge."

Next morning, just as the watcher was going up the hill, he

saw a herd of buffalo coming toward the camp. He ran back and called out, "Buffalo are coming."

After the hunt all the tongues were brought to the lodge of Listening to the Ground, and boiled for a feast. In the same way, he called the buffalo a second time. A third time, while he was making the ceremony, he told the people that he had made a mistake and immediately fell back and died. He died so quickly that he could not tell the secret of his power. The girl who moved her ears would never speak about the horn, but it was thought that she knew how to use it.

The second and third times Listening to the Ground used it were at the Medicine Lodge. The song is still preserved, and sung at the dance, and the stone used to be laid with the medicine, near the Thunder's Nest. When Listening to the Ground went to the Medicine Lodge, the first time he established the song, he chewed some sweet root and spit it out around him; then everybody learned the song without trouble.

Rising Bull, who died in 1865 at the age of about one hundred, declared to George Bent that he was present when the song was sung the second time—the first time that it was sung at the Medicine Lodge. It was in the afternoon and no buffalo were in sight. As the song was sung, a herd of buffalo bulls ran over the hill toward the camp. Rising Bull was a young man then. Everyone considered it a great mystery. Rising Bull said that everyone called out, "Look at the bulls." It was in June when the bulls are good and fat. The girl moved only her ears. The last time that Listening to the Ground sang at the Medicine Lodge he was so old that he had to be carried there. Everyone among the Cheyenne thinks the horn should have been buried with Listening to the Ground.

After Listening to the Ground died, his son took the horn and his father's name. The son died about 1885, and Fast Wolf, his next of kin, took the horn. Fast Wolf died in 1901 and just before his death gave the horn to Wolf Chief. Since the time of its first owner, the horn has never been used to call the buffalo, and all its owners have died suddenly.

The son of Listening to the Ground and his successors used the horn for doctoring as he had seen his father use it. It was used for curing the sick people in this way: Take the horn in the right hand and draw it up inside the right leg to the breast and rub it on the breast; change to the left hand, draw it up right arm from wrist to breast and rub; change to right hand and draw up left arm from wrist to breast and rub; change to left hand and draw up inside left leg to breast and rub; then suck the point and breathe in from it four times. It is called the buffalo horn stone and the wrinkles on it show that it came from a very old bull. It is a great mystery.

[The object is a much worn specimen of the horn coral, *Streptelasma rusticum*, common in the late Ordovician shales of the Cincinnati region. It also occurs in Michigan and in Stony Mountain, Manitoba.]

THE POWER OF STANDS IN THE TIMBER

THERE was once a man whose name was Stands in the Timber. He was a great medicine man, one of the greatest we have ever had. He always carried about with him two buffalo horns, and it was with these that he made his medicine. These two horns had been taken from a berdash—hermaphrodite—buffalo. They were wrapped in wads of the long hair of the buffalo, such as are rubbed off in the wallows, and outside of this hair the horns were wrapped about with feathers.

The people were starving. The buffalo had all gone away. None were to be found. A number of the old head men got together and talked among themselves, to determine what they might do to persuade this man to call the buffalo. He had done so before, and they knew he had the power to do it. They decided that they would fill four pipes and offer them to Stands in the Timber to smoke, asking him if he would not call the buffalo.

When the pipes had been filled, they called four little boys, each about ten years old. To each boy they gave a pipe, and told the boys to take the four pipes to this man's lodge, and to enter it. One boy at a time should go to Stands in the Timber, and place the pipe on the ground before him, with the bowl standing upright and the stem pointing toward him, and as he placed the pipe on the ground, the first boy should say, "Grandfather, I am hungry." As the second boy put down his pipe, he should say, "Uncle, I am hungry." The third boy should say, "Father, I am hungry." And the fourth, as he put down his pipe, should say, as the first had said, "Grandfather, I am hungry." Then the boys should go out of the lodge and to their homes. As the boys had been directed, so they did.

A little while after this, Stands in the Timber sent out and called to his lodge many people, men, women, and children; and they came. After the lodge was full of people, those who could not get inside stood about without the lodge. The pipes still lay where they had been placed, and at the end of the stems lay the two buffalo horns. In the lodge were two young men, painted, and sitting one on each side of the door. The man to the south of the door was painted with a wide black stripe all around his face—across his forehead, and passing down outside his eyes, over his cheeks, meeting under his mouth. The one to the north of the door was painted red, in the same manner that the other was painted black. Before he had called the people, Stands in the Timber had built, or caused to be built, on a high hill back of the camp, a pile of buffalo chips that looked like a man standing there.

When all the people had come to the lodge, and those in it were seated, Stands in the Timber unwrapped a bundle of small sticks, three feet long and as thick as a man's finger.

There were forty-seven of these sticks. He drew a coal from the fire and placed it between himself and the pipes, and on it sprinkled sweet grass. Then he took the sticks, one at a time, and passed them lengthwise through the smoke which rose from the burning sweet grass. After doing this he wiped them on his robe, and one by one passed them to the people sitting near, until he had given out the forty-seven sticks. Then he picked up the two horns, and holding one in each hand above his head, he sang—the song is still sung in the Medicine Lodge. Before he began to sing he told all the people to join in the song and to beat time to it with these sticks, either on the lodge or on the ground. Everyone sang, those outside as well as those within, and all beat with the sticks in time to the song. Those who did not have the sticks that he had given out used other sticks. As they were singing, Stands in the Timber shook the horns in time to the song. Then he held the horns to the heavens, praying to the Above Spirits, saying in the song: "Spirits, take pity on me. Send me something for the people to eat." When he spoke these words in the song, he held the horns toward the hill where the pile of chips stood, and said, "Call the buffalo to this camp to-night." Then he put the horns down on the ground, and stopped singing.

He took up the first pipe and lit it, and passed it around, and everybody smoked until it was smoked out. After this he sang again and made the same prayers, and lit the second pipe and passed it around. And so with every pipe, until the four had been smoked out. Then he spoke to the young man painted in black, saying to him, "Do you go up to the hill where the pile of chips stands, and sit down there and stay until morning." To the man painted in red he said, "You stay here until daylight, and when daylight comes, do you go up to that pile of chips and see if there are any buffalo."

The next morning the red-painted young man went up to the hill to look for buffalo, and when he had reached the top, and looked off away from the camp, the whole land was full of buffalo, hundreds and hundreds of them. He called out to the camp, and told the people that there were many buffalo close by. They all rushed out and killed many and brought them into the camp, and ate and were filled.

HERO MYTHS

Hero Myths.

THE Cheyennes, like other Indians, conceive of the existence of certain hostile powers and influences that injure the people, and believe too that there are other powers and influences that possess the ability to overcome and destroy these harmful forces. Many Indian tribes give accounts of the achievements of heroes who overcome and put an end to the evil powers, and some of these stories are given here. The power for good possessed by the hero may have come to him through some peculiarity of his origin, but quite as often the reason for it is unexplained.

Where the hero is a boy, he is often described as a poor boy, perhaps without relatives; at all events, without wealth or influence. Such boy heroes are often called merely *Makos, Mahkos,* or *Mahkuts,* terms which signify "the little one," a name often applied to the youngest child in a family, whether it be male or female. Another nickname often applied to young children is *Mŏk' sŏ ĭs,* usually translated "potbelly."

I give here only a single example of the so-called "Found in Grass Story," of which there are a multitude of variants. They are common to many Algonquian peoples. Some of the stories suggest the well-known account of the destruction by Nana boshu of the Manidos who killed his brother.

While the narratives about the mysterious arrows taken away by the wounded bird carry suggestions that they may have grown up in recent times and may have some relation to the medicine arrows, I am inclined to believe that they are actually old stories.

STONE AND HIS UNCLES

ONCE there were seven young men, brothers, and their sister, living together by themselves. The young men hunted, and killed buffalo. They had plenty to eat and were happy. The main village was camped somewhere else.

One day the oldest brother said to his sister, "Sister, make me some moccasins; I am going off to look for the people."

When the moccasins were finished the young man started on his journey. He traveled and traveled, and at last one day he saw far off a lonely lodge. When he came near it he saw that it was standing in a bend of the river, and to reach it he was obliged to wade the stream. He supposed that now he had found the people.

When he came to the lodge he passed on by it to look for the camp, but just then an old woman came out and said: "Grandson, where are you going? Come in and eat; everyone who passes by stops and eats with me. The people are camped on the river just below."

The young man entered and sat down, and after he had eaten he rose to go on his journey. The old woman said to him, "After people have eaten, I always ask them to pound my back; my back hurts me." So just before he left the lodge the old woman stood before him, and he hit her on the back as she had asked him to, and the jar of the blow paralyzed him and he fell down dead.

After many days, when the brother did not return, the sister said to the next oldest brother: "You had better go and look for your brother. Something may have happened to him."

The young man started, and followed the same trail that his brother had taken, and at length saw the same lodge. He was passing by when the old woman came out and said: "Where are you going, grandson? Come in and eat; your brother stopped here and ate the other day, and then went on." She spoke to him as she had to his brother, and when he struck her, he too fell down dead.

When the second brother did not come back, the sister said to the next oldest: "I do not see why our brothers do not come back; they are the ones who get the most game, and soon now we shall be out of meat. You had better go and look for them." He started, and it happened to him as it had to the others.

Then the girl sent out the next brother, and the same thing happened, and she sent the next one. None of them came back. The woman killed each one in the same way. The girl was getting very uneasy.

At last the girl sent out the seventh to look for his brothers. He was the youngest, only a boy. As he was going, she said to him, "We shall starve if you do not find your brothers and bring them home."

He went on his way, but the old woman killed him as she had killed the others.

Now the sister was left alone. She had no food, was crying and mourning all the time, and starving. One day she went to the top of a high hill, to look over the country and see whether she could see anything of her brothers. As she was climbing the hill she saw on the ground a sun arrow.* She picked it up and put it to her mouth, to touch her tongue to it, and it slipped out of her hand and into her mouth, and she swallowed it.

When she had reached the top of the hill, she looked all over the country for a long time, but could see no one moving. Then she lay down there and slept for a long time, and at last she went back to her lodge. Soon after this a little boy was born to her. The woman used to mourn and cry a great deal. The little boy grew very fast, and one day he said to his mother, "Why do you mourn and cry all the time?"

* A sparkling stone fragment—selenite.

The woman answered him: "Son, your uncles went away and never returned again. It is for this that I am mourning."

One day the boy said to his mother, "Mother, make me some moccasins, and I will start out to look for my uncles."

She made him some moccasins and a little pack, and pointed out to him the trail that his uncles had followed, and he set out. He traveled for a long time, and at last he came to the same lodge that his uncles had found, and waded the stream, and was going by when the old woman came out. She seemed to know him, and said to him, "Grandson, come in and eat; your uncles stopped here and ate." So he went in and sat down. When the little boy had finished eating, he said: "Grandmother, I cannot stop long with you; I am in a hurry; I am looking for my uncles, and my mother is all alone and has nothing to eat. I must go on."

Then the old woman said to him, "Grandson, my back always hurts me, and whenever anyone eats here I always ask him to pound my back." She stood up before him, and he struck her back, and the old woman fell down dead. He dragged her outside of the lodge and burned her body with her own wood. After this he went back into the lodge, and found in it many skulls. Then he gathered willow branches and built a sweat lodge, and took down the old woman's lodge, and with this and her robes he covered the big sweat house. He put all the skulls in the sweat house, and built a fire and heated the stones, and then went in to take a sweat. He poured water on the hot stones, and sang a song; then he poured the water on the stones again, and sang another song, and so a third time and a fourth; and the fourth time he poured the water on the rocks he could hear all these people begin to talk to one another.

After he had finished taking his sweat, he raised the covering and went out, and all the people came out after him, alive and well. After they had come out, he said to them: "Friends, I have uncles here—seven of them. My mother sent me to look for them, and I should like to know if they are here."

Then his uncles stepped forward and told him who they were, and they were all glad to see him, and loved their little nephew. After this he told the people that they could all go to their homes. He took his uncles home, and they found there his mother, nearly starved; but they hunted and soon had plenty of food.

This boy's name was Stone.

After this Stone asked his oldest uncle to make for him and for his youngest uncle each a bow and arrow, so that they might hunt little birds and rabbits. He made them these arms, and they used to go out hunting.

One day in the winter, when there was snow on the ground, Stone and his uncle were going along, when they saw two people sliding down hill. These people called to them, saying, "Hello, friends; come and slide with us."

"Yes," said Stone, "we will come." The two went to them, and the strangers said, "Get on in front."

"No," said Stone, "we will ride behind." The two strangers got on in front, and then Stone next to them, and his uncle behind him. They slid down the hill, and when they got to the bottom they ran into a bank, and Stone was thrown against the two people in front of him, and crushed and killed them.

When they reached home and told what they had done, they learned that these two people were really two white buffalo, sons of double-teethed buffalo.* Stone's uncles told them that they had done a bad thing, for the double-teethed buffalo would kill them.

After the two double-teethed buffalo found that their young ones had been killed, they started for the camp, and with them all the other buffalo. When they got near to the lodge, all the buffalo stopped except those two, who went on down to the

* *Cheyenne Indians,* vol. 2, p. 99.

camp. But Stone took a little pebble and threw it into the air, and where it went up there was a great high cliff.

"Now," said Stone to his mother and uncles, "do you climb up there, high up." He climbed a little way, but stopped on a low ledge where the buffalo could reach him. One of the double-teethed buffalo stood up on his hind legs to hook him, and Stone reached down and caught the buffalo by its horn and threw it away as if it had been a little, light stick, and it struck the ground and turned over and over, and was dead. Presently the other double-teethed buffalo made a rush at him, and the boy threw this one in the same way.

After this they came down, and lived well, and roamed the prairie.

FALLING STAR*

ONCE, a long time ago, two girls were lying outside the lodge at night. They were looking up at the sky, and one said to the other, "That star is pretty; I like that one." The other answered, "I like that other one better." One of them pointed to a very bright star and said, "I like that one best of all; I would marry that star."

That night as they lay down in the lodge, going to bed, they said, "To-morrow we will go out and gather wood." Next day they went out together for wood, and as they were going along in the timber they saw a porcupine in a tree, and the girl who had chosen the bright star said, "I will climb up and pull him down." She climbed up into the tree toward the porcupine, but could not quite reach him. As she stretched out her hand to seize his foot, he always moved up a little, so that she could not grasp it. Meantime, the tree seemed to be growing taller. The girl below called to her friend, "You had better

* *Journal of American Folklore*, vol. 34, p. 308, July-Sept., 1921.

182

WOMAN'S WORK.

come down, this tree is growing taller." "No," said the other, "I can almost reach him now"; and she kept on climbing. When the girl below saw the tree growing so high, and the other girl so far above her that she could hardly see her, she ran back to the camp and told the people. They rushed out to the tree, but the girl had gone; she could not be seen.

The tree grew and grew, and at last the girl reached another land, and there she stepped off the branches of the tree and walked away from it. Before she had gone far she met there a middle-aged man, who spoke to her and told her to come with him. When he said this, she was frightened and began to cry. He said to her: "Why, what is the matter with you? Only last night you were wishing to marry me." He was the bright star.

He married the girl, and they lived together. He told her that she could go out and dig roots and *pommes blanches* with the other women, but that there was a certain kind of *pomme blanche* with a great green top that she must not dig; to dig this was against the medicine. Every day the girl went out to dig roots, and one day after she had been doing this for some time she began to wonder why it was against the medicine to dig one of these strange *pommes blanches*. She thought much about this and at length made up her mind that she would dig one and find out about it. Next day she dug one up. It took her a long time, and when she pulled up the root she saw that it made a hole through the ground on which she was standing. She looked down through this hole, and far below saw the great camp from which she had come.

When she looked down and saw the lodges, and the people walking about, very small, she was homesick; she wanted to get back to her people, and kept wondering how she could get down. Near by there grew long grass, and after she had thought for a time about getting away, she wondered if she could not make a rope of this grass. She began to try to do so, and for many days she worked, braiding a great long rope. Her husband used to wonder why she was out of doors so much, and what she was doing, and one day he asked her. "Oh," she said, "I walk about a great deal, and that makes me tired, and then I sit down and rest." He did not understand it.

At last the woman had finished her rope, and let it down through the hole in the ground and thought she could see it touch the earth below. She got a strong stick and laid it across the hole, and tied the rope to it, and began to let herself down. For a long time she went down safely, but when she reached the end of the rope she found it was not long enough, and that she was still far above the earth. For a long time she held on there, crying, but at last she had to let go; and she fell, and the fall broke her all to pieces. Although the fall killed her, her unborn child did not die; he was made of stone, and the fall did not kill him.

A meadow lark, flying about, found him, and took pity on him and took him to his nest. The lark kept him there like one of its young ones, and when the boy got big enough, he used to creep out of the nest with the young birds. The stronger the birds grew, the stronger he became. He got so after a time that he could crawl about very fast. After the birds had grown big enough to fly a little way, the boy was able to run about. When the birds became strong and could fly about anywhere, he could follow them. He was growing to be a big boy.

When the time came for the birds to go south, the meadow lark said to the boy, "Son, you would better go home now; before long it is going to be very hard weather here; we are all going to the south country." The boy said, "Father, why do you want me to go home? I want to go with you." "No," said his father, "it will be too hard; you would better go home. Your people live down the stream; go home to them." "Well, father," said the boy, "I will go home, if you will make me a bow and arrows." The meadow lark did so, and pulled out some of his own quills to feather the arrows. He made him four arrows and a bow; and after they were finished the meadow lark pointed out to him which way to go, and the boy started in that direction.

He traveled along for some time, and when he reached the camp he went into the nearest lodge, where an old woman lived. The boy said to her, "Grandmother, I want a drink of water." She said: "Grandson, water is very hard to get. Only those who can run the fastest can have water."

"Why is it hard to get water, grandmother?" he asked.

"Why, grandson," said she, "only the young men go for water —the fastest runners. There is a fearful animal there, a *mĭh′n′** that draws in [to himself] people who go near it."

The boy said: "Grandmother, give me your buffalo paunch bucket and your buffalo horn ladle. I will go for water."

"Grandson," she said, "many young men have been killed by going there for water. I fear you will be killed too." Nevertheless, she gave him the things he asked for, and he went to the stream and began to dip up water. While he was doing this, he kept looking about for this animal.

When his bucket was full, the *mĭh′n′* raised its head above the water. It had a great mouth, and as it drew in its breath the suction from the mouth drew in the boy and the water and the bucket and the spoon. Now when he was sucked in the boy had his knife, and when he found himself inside the *mĭh′n′*, he saw there all the people that had ever been swallowed by it. With his knife he cut a hole in the animal's side and let out all the people. Then he brought the water to his grandmother.

"Why," said his grandmother, "my son, who are you? What are you?"

"Grandmother," said he, "I am Falling Star; I have killed

* A mythical water monster described as a very large lizard partly covered with hair and with one or two horns on the head. The Thunderbirds have been known to kill these monsters. One or two writers have inferred that *mĭh′n′* is an alligator, but this is not true. *The Cheyenne Indians*, vol. 2, p. 97.

the great thing that has been starving you for water." The woman told an old man of this, and he cried it through the camp that Falling Star had killed the great animal that had so long deprived them of water.

After he had saved that camp he said to his grandmother, "Grandmother, are there any other camps of people near here?" The old woman said, "Yes, there is one down below, on this stream." Then Falling Star left the camp, taking with him his bow and arrows.

It was now the fall of the year. The boy traveled and traveled, and at length he reached the camp below. When he got there he went into an old woman's lodge. She was sitting there alone, with her head hanging down, and only one stick of wood. He said to her, "Grandmother, I am very cold; why don't you have a larger fire?"

"Why, grandson," she said, "we cannot get any wood; there is a great owl* in the timber, that kills people when they go for wood."

"Give me your rope and axe," said Falling Star; "I will go and get wood."

"Ah, no, grandson, do not go; he is a great and terrible owl. He takes people up and sticks them into his ear," said the old woman.

Falling Star took the rope and axe, and started out for wood. As he was chopping wood in the timber, he kept looking all about him for the owl. After his wood was cut and tied up, suddenly this great owl appeared, and took the boy up and put him into his ear. After the boy had been put in the ear, with his bow and one of his arrows he shot the thing in the brain, and it fell down dead.

The boy crept out of the ear, and took up his wood and carried it back to his grandmother's lodge. "Now," he said, "grandmother, we will have a big fire and get warm. I have killed this

* *Mis tai*—owl or ghost.

great thing that kept you from getting wood." The grandmother told of this, and an old man called it through the camp, that Falling Star had killed the great owl that lived in the timber.

Some time after this Falling Star asked his grandmother if there were any other camps near by, and she told him that on beyond there were others. So he left that camp. By this time it was winter, and snow lay on the ground. Falling Star came to the camp, and went into an old woman's lodge, and sat down. The old woman did not set food before him, and at length he said to her, "Grandmother, I am hungry."

"Oh, my son," said she, "we have no food; we cannot get any buffalo. Whenever we go for buffalo, a great white crow comes about and drives them away."

Falling Star said: "That is bad, that is very bad; I will see what I can do. Do you go out and look about the camp for an old wornout robe, with but little hair on it, and tell the old chief to choose two of the swiftest runners in the camp, and send them to me."

The old woman went out to look for such a robe, and found one, and then went to the chief's lodge and told him that she wanted him to choose two of the swiftest men on foot in the camp, and that when he had found them he should send them to Falling Star at her lodge. She took the robe back to the lodge.

The two swift young men were sent to Falling Star, and he told them that when any buffalo came near the camp he would go out to a certain place, and when the buffalo ran, he would follow them, and that these young men must chase them, following him far, and not giving up, and that when they overtook him they must shoot at and kill him, and that after they had killed him they must cut him open and leave him lying there.

Not long after this buffalo were seen and came close to the camp, and the men started out to try to kill some. When they started, the white crow flew over the buffalo, and called out,

"They are coming! they are after you! run! run!" The buffalo started and ran, and behind them ran an old scabby bull, with little hair on its body, which could not catch up with the herd. The two swift young men chased this bull, and did not give up, and at last they caught him and shot him, and killed him, and then opened him and left him there and returned to the camp, as Falling Star had told them. After they had cut him open and left him, as they were going back to the camp, the young men looked back and saw birds of all kinds, and wolves and coyotes gathering about the carcass. Among the birds was the white crow. He would fly over the carcass and alight and say, "I wonder if this is not Falling Star." Then he would fly over the bull again and alight and say, "I wonder if this is not Falling Star." He kept getting closer and closer to the carcass, and called out to the other birds: "Leave the eyes for me; do not touch the eyes! I wonder if this is Falling Star!" He kept getting still closer, and just as he was about to peck at the eyes, Falling Star reached out and caught him by the legs. As soon as he did so, all the birds flew away, and the coyotes and wolves scattered all over the hills. Falling Star brought the crow to his grandmother's lodge, and sent for one of the soldier bands and the chief, to decide what should be done with the crow. The chief said, "I will take him to my lodge and tie him in the smoke hole, and smoke him to death." He took him to his lodge, and tied him over the fire in the smoke hole; but one day the crow twisted loose and got away.

Falling Star sent some of his young men out to gather flax weeds, and from the bark he made a long string, and to the end of the string he tied a slender thread, and to the thread he tied a small feather. He blew this feather out of the top of the lodge, and told the people to watch the string, and whenever it stopped going out to pull it back quickly, and at the end of it they would find the crow. When the string stopped, they drew it in, and soon the crow came fluttering down through the smoke hole.

Then they killed it. After this they caught many many buffalo. The people said: "Now we are saved! Now we can have plenty to eat."

Falling Star left that camp and traveled on to another. He went into an old woman's lodge and said, "Grandmother, I am hungry, I want something to eat."

"Son," she said, "it is bad here, we have nothing to eat. When we go to chase buffalo the Winter Man sends a big snowstorm, and we can get nothing."

Falling Star said to his grandmother: "The next time that buffalo come, you and I will go out and get some meat. So fix up your dog travois."

When the buffalo came, he said to her, "Get ready now, we will go." They all went out and killed some buffalo. There was one nice fat cow, and Falling Star said, "Come, grandmother, we will cut up this one."

As they were butchering, the Winter Man appeared on the hill, with a great club in his hand. He started down toward them, and the grandmother wanted to run. Falling Star said, "Do not run away, grandmother," and as he said this he cut out the kidney from the cow, and handed it to his grandmother. By this time the Winter Man was close to them. He said to Falling Star, "Why do you give the kidney to that old woman?" The Winter Man lifted his foot and kicked the old woman, and his leg flew off. He raised his hand and struck at her, and his arm flew off. He opened his mouth to speak to her, and his head flew off, and he fell down. They butchered the cow quickly, and went away and left the Winter Man lying there.

After they got to the lodge with the meat they had something to eat, and Falling Star said, "I think I will go over and see the Winter Man." "No," said his grandmother, "do not go, you have treated him badly and he may kill you."

"I think I will go," said Falling Star. "Where does he live?"

His grandmother said, "He lives over there in that cut bank."

Falling Star went over to the cut bank, and went in; and the Winter Man, who had been brought in and cured by his wife, said, "Why do you come here after the way you have treated me?"

"Why, uncle," said Falling Star, "I only wanted to talk to you, and to see your bow." He took up the bow, which was made of a great tree, and bent and broke it.

The Winter Man said: "Why do you do this? Get out of my lodge. Why do you stay here when I order you out? Have you no feeling? Have you no shame?"

"Oh," said Falling Star, "I want to see your club." He picked up the club and struck the Winter Man over the head with it, and killed him with his own club. Then he killed his wife and children, all except one little one who got away and crept into a crevice in the ground. After he had done this he went back to the lodge and told his grandmother that he had killed the Winter Man and all his family except one. He said to her, "Tell everyone in the camp to heat water and pour it into that crevice, and try to scald that child to death." The people did this for a long time, but whenever they stopped they could see frost still rising out of the crack, and at last they stopped. If he had killed that one we should have had no more snow.

Falling Star left that camp and traveled on. It was now the middle of winter. The days were short, and it became dark early. One night he came to a stream and saw a light on it. When he had come close to this light he saw near him a man, wearing a necklace made of many ears of people strung together, standing looking at the camp. Falling Star said to himself, "That is Double Eyes." He crept back and went to where some box elders grew, and from the fungus which grew on them he cut out many pieces shaped like ears, and strung them about his neck. He walked back and went up to Double Eyes, who said to him: "Hello, friend, where do you come from? Why, you look just like me!"

"Yes," said Falling Star, "I am the same kind of medicine man. Suppose now the people wanted to kill you, how could they do it?"

"Why," said Double Eyes, "if the people knew it, and caught me and threw some grease in the fire, and rattled on a medicine rattle, I would fall down dead. I go around biting people's ears off, and making necklaces of them. There is one lodge here that I have not been into. After it is quiet, and these people all get to sleep, I am going into that lodge."

Falling Star said, "We are just alike; that is the only way I can be killed." Of the lodge he was talking about, Falling Star said, "I will go in and see if all are asleep, and will come back and tell you."

"It is well," said Double Eyes.

Falling Star went to the lodge, and when he got there he said, "Are all here asleep?" Someone answered, "No." Falling Star said: "That person who goes about biting off ears is coming here. You must all pretend to be asleep, and snore, and then you can kill him. The only way he can be killed is to build a big fire and throw some grease in the fire, and shake a medicine rattle. If you do that he will fall down and die."

The people in the lodge were glad when they heard this, and they said they would do as Falling Star had told them. Then Falling Star went back to Double Eyes and said to him: "All are asleep and snoring. Let us go. I will go in first."

"No," said Double Eyes, "I will go in first."

"Very well," said Falling Star. They went to the lodge, and when they got close to it they listened, and all were snoring.

Falling Star said again to Double Eyes, "I will go in first."

"No," said Double Eyes, "I will go in first." He entered, and when he was inside, Falling Star closed the door and put his weight against it, and called out, "He has gone in." The people arose quickly and built up a big fire. Double Eyes was trying to get out everywhere, but Falling Star was like a rock against the door. The people threw some grease in the fire and shook a medicine rattle, and Double Eyes fell down dead. Next morning the people threw Double Eyes out of doors. All those in the camp came about him, and recognized their own ears and took them. Falling Star made a big sweat house, and told the people to get into it and take a sweat and to hold their ears against the sides of their heads. They did so, and when they came out all had their ears on as natural as ever.

While he was in this camp he was told that they needed him at the next camp; that a lodge had been built for him, and a girl was waiting to marry him. Those people were worse off than any. An old woman lived there who scalped the people. Falling Star reached the place and found it just as he had been told. His lodge was up, and the girl he was to marry was waiting for him. All the people had been scalped and had their heads tied up.

The old woman heard of his coming, and went over to see him. She said: "Why, grandson, I heard that you had arrived, and have come over to see you. I need two scalps to use on the robe I am fixing."

"Yes, grandmother," said Falling Star, "we heard you needed scalps, and that is why we came." The girl had not been scalped; she had long hair, and so had Falling Star. After a while he went over to the old woman's lodge, taking his wife with him. She did not want to go into the lodge, she was afraid; but he coaxed her to go; yet it was a long time before she would go in.

When they entered the old woman said: "I am glad to see you. You have nice hair."

"Yes," said Falling Star, "we came here for that reason, because we heard you needed good scalps." He told his wife to sit on the side away from the old woman, saying, "I will let her take my hair first." The old woman made ready her knife, and walked over to Falling Star to cut off his hair. As she came close to him he struck her, and because he was made of stone he knocked her down and killed her at the first blow.

When the people heard that Falling Star had killed this old woman, they all rushed into the lodge, and after they had seen that she was really dead, when they looked about the lodge, each man knew his own scalp hanging there. Now Falling Star made a big sweat house, and he told all the people to go in it and take a sweat, and while they were sweating to hold their scalps on their heads. They did this, and when they came out of the sweat house their heads were perfect.

Falling Star married the girl and lived always with these people.

THE BAD HEARTED MAN

I

LONG before this there was a man who was very poor. He had a wife and a child. In those days the people had nothing to pack their things on; they carried them on their backs. One day the people moved off and left this poor man. And while they moved on westward he stayed where he was, and built for himself a lodge made of poles.

After the people had moved away, they found no buffalo. They hunted everywhere, but could find none. They had disappeared. So all became hungry, and at last they were starving. Finally they thought that if they could find this poor man again, they might get buffalo. They kept looking for the man, and sending out young men to look for him and for buffalo. One day two young men found the place where he was living in his lodge of poles, and saw that all about this place the whole land was covered with buffalo. The poor man said to the young men: "Go back to your camp and tell the people to move here to me. I will take pity on them and will give you buffalo." The young men went and gave this message, and the village moved to where he was, and camped. There they killed buffalo, and had plenty to eat. Close to this man's lodge was a hole in the ground in which water was always bubbling up. It was a hot spring—the water in it was boiling.

By this time the poor man's child had grown up and was a handsome girl. Soon after the camp had returned to him he called all the people to a feast, and said to them that he was going to choose a son-in-law, and that next morning all the unmarried young men should come to his lodge. Next day the young men gathered there, and he said to them: "Sit all about me in a circle. I want to choose some young man to whom I can give my daughter for a wife." After they had formed the circle the man walked around among them for some time, looking for the handsomest young man for a son-in-law. At last he chose one, and said to him, "Get up." He led him over to where his daughter was, and said to him: "Sit down by her. I give her to you for your wife."

Then he chose four men to make arrows for him; men who understood how to make good arrows, and said to them, "Stay here with my son-in-law." A little while after this, he said to his daughter: "Now, tell your husband to go out and cut me forty-four arrow shafts. They must be cut from a thorny bush —somewhat like a bullberry bush—must be straight, and the branches must have no twigs on them. After he has cut these, let him give them to these four men, so that they can make arrows." The girl told this to her husband.

The next day the young man started out to go and cut these branches. He went on looking for these arrow shafts, but it took him a long time to find them. When he brought them in on his back, his father-in-law began to look them over. He looked at the sticks, one at a time, and as he looked at each, he said, "This is not good," and put it down. At last he had looked at them all, and had laid all aside, and said, "They are not good."

Then he arose and said to his son-in-law, "Stand up." He took him by the arm and led him over to the spring of boiling water, and lifted him up and threw him into the hot water. In a short time the people saw his bones rise to the top of the water. The flesh was boiled off them. When the people saw this they were frightened, and moved their camp and ran away and left him.

They were gone a long time, and again began to starve. Then, because they were so hungry, they moved back to look for the person, and found him still in the same place. Here again they killed buffalo. Again the person called them to a feast and said that he was going to choose a son-in-law, a handsome young man. He chose one, and married his daughter to him, and said to him the same things that he had told the other, but this time he said that he wished his arrow shafts made of currant bush shoots, straight, without a twig on them. The young man tied up his robe to go and look for these arrow shafts. He traveled and looked, and looked and traveled, but he could not find the bushes he wanted. Still, he brought in forty-four shoots of currant bush, nice ones, and the four arrow makers worked on them, but they could not satisfy the father-in-law. He found fault with everything. He took this son-in-law to the boiling spring and threw him in.

Again the people were frightened, and moved their camp and went away, and could find no buffalo, and once more were starving.

Again they returned and got food, and again he called them together so that he might choose a son-in-law. By this time some of the young men were afraid of him, and when he walked around among them they covered up their heads, so that he could not see them. But he made them uncover, and at last chose a son-in-law. He told this one to go out and bring in some arrow shafts of cherry brush, and he brought in forty-four.

When the four arrow makers began to work on these, *Hĭ vāv'sts*, the father-in-law, kept stopping them and finding fault with the shafts, saying, "This one is crooked; that one has a knot." He was not satisfied with anything. Again he threw his son-in-law into the boiling spring, and again after a little while the people saw the bones rise to the top. The people were frightened and went away, and they starved a long time before they came back.

When they had returned the fourth time, he chose a fourth son-in-law. His name was Red Tracks. He again chose four men to make the arrows, and told Red Tracks to cut forty-four shoots of sarvice bush, without a twig on them. That night after Red Tracks and his wife lay down to sleep, the girl said to him: "If you have any power, try to help yourself. This old man, my father, is making me very unhappy."

Next morning Red Tracks tied up his robe and started out to look for shafts without a twig on them. He was not long gone, and brought back just what he had been sent for, but he had not cut them from sarvice bushes; instead, he had cut forty-four smooth cane stems, but they looked like sarvice berry shoots. After the shafts had been brought, the old man began to find fault, but the arrow makers said to him, "These are good; you cannot find fault with them." After the shafts were ready, the old man said, "*Ĭ ho' hoh*"; perhaps he thought now he had come to his end. Then he said, "I want these arrows feathered with feathers from a gray eagle."

Red Tracks started out, crying and mourning for help. He had not been gone very long when he returned with a gray eagle on his back.

The old man said, "I want to have these feathers tied on with young sinews from a two-year-old buffalo." Red Tracks went out, and soon returned with four sinews from a two-year-

old buffalo. When the old man saw them he said again, "*Ī ho'
hoh.*" After the arrows were feathered, he said, "I wish to have
the points for these arrows with the corners toward the shafts
rounded." Red Tracks started again, crying. His wife said to
him as he was going: "Take courage. You will find what you
are looking for." Soon Red Tracks returned with the arrow-
points. The spirits had helped him; for, as he was going along,
he had come to the face of a cut bluff, and along the foot of
this bluff grew bushes that had nice smooth leaves coming to
a point at the end. He took forty-four of these leaves and
brought them in to the old man, and to him they looked like
stone points. After all these things had been given to the arrow makers, his father-in-law said to Red Tracks, "I need the
skin of a little wolf, to make a quiver to put these arrows in."
The young man went away again, crying and praying for help.
Before he had gone very far he found a coyote, lying dead.
He skinned it and brought the skin back to his father-in-law,
who gave it to the four men, and they made the quiver.

When the arrows were finished, the old man looked them
over one at a time, very carefully. With some of them he found
a little fault, but at last he said, "They are good." He spoke
to Red Tracks, and said to him: "I want you now to go out
and find buffalo, and pick one out and drive it in to me here;
choose a bull that has long, slim, smooth black horns; he must
be fat, and with long hair on his hump and neck. Drive him in
here in front of my lodge to me, so that I may kill him with
these arrows."

The young man started away, crying and mourning. He went
toward the setting sun to look for the buffalo. He traveled a
long way, always praying for help from *Hē' ămmă wih'io* and
all the animals. He climbed upon a big hill; but he did not
know where to go to find the bull, nor how to bring it if he
found it. As he was going along he came to some buffalo, and
he went in among them. The buffalo when they heard him

crying and mourning asked him what he wanted. He said, "I need a four-year-old bull." The buffalo said: "Well, we will give you what you want. Go on your way over the next hill, and you will find it." The young man climbed up over the next hill, and there he saw seven bulls lying down asleep with their noses on the ground. When he reached the top of the hill, crying and mourning, the bulls awoke. His power was so great that when he appeared over the hill, all the bulls stood up and said, "Here is our son-in-law."

Red Tracks stood on the hill, looking and thinking, wondering—if he should choose one out of this bunch of bulls—how he could ever drive him in to the camp. Between the man and the bulls there was a great black flint rock on the prairie. One of the bulls put down his head and charged toward Red Tracks, and when he reached the rock he struck it with his head, and knocked both his horns off. Then the bull said, "That will not do"; and he stood aside and waited. Five others of the bulls charged toward the man, and each, when he hit the rock, broke his horns, and some of them flew high in the air. The seventh bull stood for a long time looking at the man, and pawing up the dust, thrusting his horns into the ground, and at last getting so angry that he threw himself down on the ground and rolled there.

Red Tracks looked at the bull, and said to himself: "This is the bull I want. He has long horns, is fat, and has long hair."

When the young man said this the bull charged the rock, and when he struck it with his head he broke it in many pieces, and passed on and went by the young man, and toward the camp. The young man followed him and drove him in, and the bull ran so fast that when Red Tracks reached the camp he was almost tired out.

The bull walked up to the door of the old man's lodge. He seemed very tired, and his tongue was hanging out. He stopped with his head toward the door of the lodge, and the old man called out to Red Tracks, "Turn him around with his side to the door." The young man did so, and his father-in-law began to shoot at the bull, but he could not kill him. Some arrows went over him and some under him, and some seemed to glance off. Sometimes he would not hit, and when he did hit, the arrows would not go into the flesh, for they were light and had no points.

When his father-in-law found that he could not kill the bull, he grew angry and shot at Red Tracks, but he did not hit him either. He used up all the arrows in the quiver, and then called for more arrows, and used up all those. Soon only a few arrows were left. He was getting still more angry. Sometimes he would shoot at the bull, and sometimes at his son-in-law, but he could kill neither. Several times he said to himself, "This man must be a friend to those I have put in the boiling spring." Almost the last arrows that he had he shot at Red Tracks, but they were made of light reeds, and were pointed with leaves, and would not fly straight nor pierce anything.

The bull kept moving a little, all the time getting farther from the lodge, and the old man kept following, trying to get close so that he might kill him. At length he shot his last arrow at the bull, and the bull turned and charged on him, and caught him on his horns, and threw him up into the air, and each time he fell the bull caught him and threw him up again, until at last he had torn him all to pieces; but all this time the old man kept talking, even after he had been tossed many times. At last he fell to the ground, dead, all torn to pieces by the bull's horns. The bull stepped up close to him, and stood looking at him for a little while, and then turned about and walked away in the direction from which he had come. Then Red Tracks called his wife and mother-in-law, and the four men who had made the arrows, and told them to gather wood and pile it on the old man, and set it on fire; and so they burned him up. As the fire was burning, beads of all sorts began to fly out of it, but Red Tracks told the people not to touch any of them, and they made another big fire over where the beads were.

Then these seven people went away and found the village. When they found the village they had plenty of buffalo, and they have had them ever since.

This young man had great power. He could call a wolf or a bird or an animal to him, and make it fall dead. In this way he got the wolf and the eagle and called the buffalo. He made the leaves seem to be stone arrow-points. He got this power from his father, *Hē′ ămmă wih′io,* and it was to him that he cried and prayed for help. The old person was also a man who had great power and could do many things; but when he threw the first man into the boiling spring his power was taken from him.

THE RED EAGLES

THERE was once a big Cheyenne village—a very large one. A young man from this village, the son of the chief, went up on top of a high hill and made a pit for catching eagles. After the young man had finished it he went out to the pit one day very early in the morning, and that day he caught some eagles. After he had caught several, he saw four eagles flying over the pit. When he looked up he always saw these eagles flying above him. They were fine-looking birds with red feathers, and once when flying over him they called down to him from the air over his head, and said that he would never be able to catch them unless he put out his father's body as a bait. After night had come he went back to the village, and when he arrived at the lodge he refused to speak or eat.

Next morning, before day, he went back to the pit, and again the red eagles came close to him. They were very handsome birds. Again they told him that he would not be able to catch them unless he used his father's body as a bait.

He went home in the evening, feeling very sad, for he wanted very much to catch these eagles, and again he would neither speak nor eat. Four times in all he went up to the pit and each time the eagles circled close to him and told him to use his father for bait, so that he might catch them. At last on the fifth day his father asked his son what was the matter, and why he refused to speak or eat. The old chief said: "I think the eagles must have told you something. Now, whatever it is they have asked you for, let it be done." When his father spoke to him in this way, the young man said, "Well, I will tell you"; and he told him about the four red eagles, and that they had told him that they could not be caught by him unless he used his father for bait. The old chief said that this was good and that he ought to do as the eagles had advised him. After the chief had said that he should do what the eagles directed, the young man began to eat.

His father told him to go up to the pit the first thing in the morning. During the night the man's father did not sleep, for he was afraid, because he was going to be used for the bait for the eagles. Early next morning they went up to the pit together. When they reached it the father said: "Go to work now and kill me just as if I were an animal. Do not hesitate about it." So the young man shot his father down and dragged him to where he put his bait, cut him open and laid him down. Then he went inside the pit with his father lying above him as a bait. After sitting there a few minutes, he heard a noise far up in the air over his head. He could hear eagles flying down. He looked up and saw the four red eagles all flying down together. They alighted, two on the arms and two on the legs of his father's body, and before he could seize one of them, the four eagles flew up in the air with the body, till quite out of sight. When he saw them going, he leaped out of the pit and began to mourn for his father. The people in the village could see the four eagles carrying off the old man till at last he was out of sight.

The young man returned to the village weeping and the whole camp began to mourn for their chief. No one ate anything. They were sorrowing for their chief.

Next morning a small boy was out playing—hunting little birds. He was a poor orphan and lived with his grandmother. When the poor boy came in at evening, he said, "Grandmother, what is everybody crying about?" And she said, for the boy was ignorant: "Why, don't you know? Our great chief has been carried off by the eagles." The boy said: "Is that possible? Did the eagles carry him off? Now you had better go at once and tell his people that I will follow him." This was as much as to say that he knew where he had been taken. His grandmother said, "How are you going to be able to follow him?" He said: "That is something that I must do. Do you go and tell them that I will follow him. Go on. Go and see his son."

The old woman went to see the son of the chief who had been carried away. When she had found him she said, "My grandson, *Mŏk' sŏ ĭs*, may be telling the truth or perhaps he may not, but he wants to follow the chief who has been carried off by the four red eagles."

The young man who had killed his father said, "Is that true, old woman?" The old woman answered: "That is what he says. Why do you not go down and have a talk with him yourself?" The young man arose and said, "I will go and see him." He went into the lodge where the boy was, took him on his lap, and asked him if it was true that he wished to follow his father, and *Mŏk' sŏ ĭs* said, "Yes, it is true." The young chief said, "If you can do what you say you can, I have a very good-looking sister, and I will give her to you for your wife." *Mŏk' sŏ ĭs* said: "The first thing we must do in the morning is to go up to the top of the hill where the pit is. I want four heart bladders [the skin that covers the heart of an animal, the pericardium] filled with air and tied to each heart bladder one small down feather." He told his grandmother to pound up a little meat, as he would carry that also. Then he made a basket of willow twigs like those they used on a travois to carry children in when moving, and to each corner of the basket he tied one of the bladders. They carried this up to where the pit was and many people went up with them. They put their basket right over the top of the pit where the bait had been. *Mŏk′ sŏ ĭs* got in the basket and the young man who had killed his father got in with him. Then *Mŏk′ sŏ ĭs* said to the people who were looking on: "Come, get around the basket and make a motion as if to lift it up. Do this four times, and the fourth time lift the basket and throw it up and let go. We will be back with the chief in five days." The people gathered around the basket and all who could took hold of it, raised it four times, and the fourth time let it go.

The basket went up slowly, swaying from side to side just as the eagles had done. All the people watched it till it went completely out of sight.

When the basket had risen very far up indeed, those who were in it felt it striking against something. They looked up and saw that they were touching the sky. There was a hole there—perhaps the hole had been made by the basket striking the sky. *Mŏk′ sŏ ĭs* said, "Now we had better get out and go on foot and leave the basket here," and they got out and started, walking on the ground.

All that day they followed the trail, and that evening came to a big village. *Mŏk′ sŏ ĭs* told his friend to wait where he was; and left him and went on toward the camp. On the edge of the camp he came to a very small old lodge. He went inside and found an old woman sitting there. He said, "Grandmother, I want something to eat," and asked the old woman what the news was. She said: "Why, haven't you heard? Four red eagles went by here with some chief that they were carrying away. They went right past this way." After he had finished eating *Mŏk' sŏ ĭs* said, "Well, I think I'll go out and play around a while." He went back to where the other man was and said, "They carried your father along past here."

Next morning they traveled all day till they came to another camp. It took them the whole day and they arrived about sunset. Here the same things happened.

At the third village they reached *Mŏk' sŏ ĭs* went into an old woman's lodge. She said that the four red eagles had passed near her lodge carrying the chief, that he was not dead, but that the next day the eagles were going to have a feast on him.

When they arrived at the fourth village, *Mŏk' sŏ ĭs* went into an old woman's lodge and talked with her. This old woman said: "Do you see that large lodge in front of and toward the center of the circle of lodges? That is old Red Eagle's lodge, and to-night he is going to have a feast on that chief. The four red eagles are his four sons." The old woman also told him that they were going to sing four songs, and the fifth time they sang they were going to cook the old chief in a big kettle, so that old Red Eagle could have a feast. Then *Mŏk' sŏ ĭs* went back to his friend and said, "Let us go over to that lodge and see what they are doing." When they got there they found that the singing had not yet begun. *Mŏk' sŏ ĭs* and his friend went to the lodge and looked in. There they saw sitting many people who were eagles, and in the back part sat old Red Eagle. He was so old that nearly all his feathers had fallen off from him. They looked around and saw the old chief—the young man's father—building a fire and heating water in a kettle. It was very warm in there. *Mŏk' sŏ ĭs* said to his friend: "Come, it will be some time before all is ready. Let us go round to the different lodges and fasten the doors." They went around and against the door of every lodge put up a barrier so that the peo-

ple could not rush out quickly. When the old chief came out of
the lodge to bring in more wood for the fire, *Mŏk′ sŏ ĭs* spoke
to him, telling him that they were there to help him. Then *Mŏk′
sŏ ĭs* and his friend went out into the center of the village and
made three big clubs with knotty heads. Soon they heard them
singing in the lodge. They sang three times and as the fourth
song was to be the last one, *Mŏk′ sŏ ĭs* and his friend went back
and entered the lodge.

When *Mŏk′ sŏ ĭs* went in, he was carrying the three clubs.
He handed one to the old chief and one to the son. The three
men killed Red Eagle's four sons and everybody inside; all were
eagles. The four red eagles were so surprised that they could
not do anything. Then the young men picked up old Red Eagle
and threw him into the pot. *Mŏk′ sŏ ĭs* then turned to his friend
and said: "See here, you wanted these four eagles. Now take
their feathers." Afterward they went to the different lodges and
killed all the other eagles and came back loaded with eagle tail
feathers. Then they went back to the place where the basket
had been left, went in through the hole, and found the basket
there still. When they got to their basket, they found a cedar
limb sticking through it. *Mŏk′ sŏ ĭs* took the air out of the
bladders and tied them onto the cedar limb. Then he told the
father and son to get on the cedar limb and they also tied their
bundles of feathers to it. Then they slipped down through the
same hole and sank down to the eagle trap.

It was the fifth day and all their people were waiting for
them. When *Mŏk′ sŏ ĭs* got down to the earth the people spread
a buffalo robe and carried him down the hill in it. They had
already put up a lodge for him, and they carried him down to
it in the robe. He was married to the chief's daughter and never
afterward had to lift a wooden bowl of water to his lips when
he was thirsty. Some woman always held the wooden bowl to
his lips.

BOW-FAST-TO-HIS-BODY

THIS was a long time ago, in the very beginning of people. There was a camp of people on a stream, and near it a big white raven always stayed. The Winter Man, who makes cold weather and brings the storm, was camped close by, and a camp of bears was near. Whenever any buffalo came close to the camp and the people started out to kill food, the raven would fly out and make a great noise and scare the buffalo away. So they starved a great deal and had a hard time.

When the buffalo came close to the camp and the raven did not frighten them, the Winter Man used to create a big storm, with snow and hard cold, so that the people could not go out, and would have to get back into their lodges to keep from freezing.

Once in a while, when they did manage to kill some buffalo, the bears would go out to the killing ground and take all the best of the meat away from them. So these people suffered.

In the camp was an old man who had starved much, and who was always troubled because the people could get nothing to eat. He was always thinking of their sufferings, and wondering whether he could not do something to help them. One day he went out and cut a stick, and flattened it on one side, and on the flat part cut marks which looked like a bow with an arrow lying by it. That night he made up a bed in the back of the lodge, and put the stick in the bed and covered it with a robe, as if it were a person.

Next morning, when the people in the lodge arose, a young man, holding in his arms a bow and arrows, got up from the bed in the back of the lodge.

"Ah," said the old man, "my son has come. My son has arrived at last."

"Yes, father," said the young man, "I have just got in."

After a time the young man said: "Father, in which direction do you go to look for buffalo? I wish to go out to see if I can find any."

The old man pointed to a high hill and said, "When the young men go out to look for buffalo, they generally go up on that hill."

The young man left the lodge and went up on the hill. He had not been gone long, when he came back. He said: "Father, do you go out and tell the people to make ready to kill buffalo. Not far beyond that hill there are buffalo. Tell them that your son, Bow-Fast-to-his-Body, brought the news. That is my name." This young man never put down his bow or his arrows. When he went to bed, he kept his bow in his arms.

The people all made ready, and started to make a charge on the buffalo. The raven came up and made a great noise, but the buffalo were not frightened. They did not move. This young man killed many buffalo with his arrows. The people were all glad and happy, singing as they butchered. Soon the bears came up on the hill, and stood on their hind legs looking at them, but they did not dare to come down to where this young man was. They suspected something. They were afraid. Even the storm did not come up.

After all had brought in their meat to camp, the young man spoke to his father, saying, "Father, how have you people been getting along; how have you been living?"

"Son," said his father, "we have not been living well. A big white raven stays about here and frightens the buffalo away, and the Winter Man makes storms, so that we cannot go out of the lodges; or when we do succeed in killing any buffalo, the bears come out and take the meat from us. We have often tried to kill these two bears, but we can do nothing to them. We cannot hurt them."

The young man said, "I will destroy all these."

That day Bow-Fast-to-his-Body got a great many sinews

from the buffalo that had been killed, and worked all day making a great long string from them. At night the string was finished, and he went to bed. No one knows when he went out, but he came back early in the morning, and again told his father to tell the people that there were many buffalo over beyond the hill, and that they should go out and get food. All went out, and they made a chase and killed some buffalo. The white raven was there, and made a noise, but he could do nothing. While the people were butchering, the young man told them that on the prairie beyond there was lying a young bull, the farthest off of all the buffalo. "Open this bull," he said, "and spread it out and leave it there, but do not take a single thing from it." Then he went away. Afterward they found the young bull, as he had said, and opened it and spread it out, but took nothing from it.

After they had finished cutting up the animals they packed home their meat, leaving the young bull lying there spread out. Birds—magpies and crows and eagles—gathered about it, and began to feed on it, but the white raven did not come to eat of it. He kept at a distance. He feared something. He kept calling out, "He is playing a trick, he is playing a trick." He saw the magpies feeding at the meat, and began to come closer. As he came closer and closer, he lost his fear, and called out to the magpies, "Do not eat the eyes; leave them for me." For ravens like to pick out the eyes of animals. He came hopping along to the head to pick at the eyes, and just as he bent over to do this, the young bull reached out and caught him by both feet, and stood up, holding the raven in his hands. It was Bow-Fast-to-his-Body.

He walked toward the camp with the raven, which was screaming and crying as he held it. It said: "Take pity on me, Bow-Fast-to-his-Body, and let me go. If you will let me go, I will make a great medicine man of you, and will teach you all I know. I will go far away from here, and do this to some other tribe. I will not trouble your people any more; only take pity on me and let me go."

Bow-Fast-to-his-Body held the raven tightly by the legs, and walked along, as if considering. At last he said, "I was angry at you, and was going to kill you; but for the promises you have made I will let you go." But as he talked he was tying his long string to the raven's feet, and the raven did not know it was there. The young man let him go, and the raven flew up in the air; but as soon as he flew he laughed and said: "Ha! Bow-Fast-to-his-Body thought he was smart, but I am smarter than he. I fooled him. I hate him." Bow-Fast-to-his-Body said, "I took pity on you once and let you go, but now I know you"; and he began to pull in the string. As the raven fluttered down, he screamed: "Ah, I did not mean it. I was just pretending. Give me one more chance. Take pity on me this once."

After he had brought him down, and had him again, the raven kept begging, begging. Bow-Fast-to-his-Body said: "I will take you home with me and have you for my friend. You shall live in my lodge." He took him to the lodge, and tied him over the fire in the smoke. The raven stayed there until he got all black from the smoke, and at last he died. Ever since that all ravens have been black.

The next morning the young man went out to the same hill, and when he came back he said: "Father, tell the people that Bow-Fast-to-his-Body has brought word that there are again buffalo in the same place. Let them sharpen their knives and start out." That morning nothing came to frighten the buffalo, and they killed. While they were butchering, the two bears came up on the hill, and stood up on their hind legs and looked at them and called out: "Here, what are you doing down there? Go away from that meat." The people were afraid, for they had often tried to kill these bears, but could do nothing against them, for each of these bears carried its life in the first toe of the hind foot, and the people did not know it.

Bow-Fast-to-his-Body told his people not to go away, to stay where they were; and when the bears came down to attack the people, he shot each bear in the first toe of its hind foot and so killed them both. He told the people to butcher the bears, for now there was nothing to fear. He went to the cave where the bear's children were, and found there two little cunning bears. They said, "Friend, take pity on us, and do not kill us." The young man replied, "I came here to kill you all, but I will take pity on you." He took hold of the two little bears and cut the muscle from the calves of their legs. "Now," he said, "you can live. Go away. Go farther north. You will find there plenty of food to eat." If he had not saved these two, there would have been no bears now. This is why the bear's foot is so long and queerly shaped.

After he had returned to the lodge, he asked his father, "Where does the Winter Man live?"

"He lives right out here," the old man answered. "There is his lodge," and he pointed to it from the doorway.

Bow-Fast-to-his-Body went to the Winter Man's lodge, and when he came to it he spoke and said, "I have come to visit the people, and have a talk with them." He lifted the door and went in, and when the Winter Man saw him, he said, "Ha, I have heard of you already." Then he caused a great storm in the lodge, and called out, "Help me, my children, help me," for he was afraid. It grew very cold, and the snow flew so thickly that they could not see across the lodge. The young man was carrying a fan made of an eagle's wing, and he began to fan himself, as if he were in a sweat house, and as he fanned himself the snow ceased falling, and that which lay deep on the floor of the lodge quickly melted.

The Winter Man cried out: "Run, my children, run. He is stronger than we are. He has the greater power." They all ran, but Bow-Fast-to-his-Body caught up a club and ran after them, and killed them as they ran, all except one little one that crept into a crevice in the rock and escaped. Afterward, when the people used to go to look into this crevice, in the morning, they would find frost there. They used to bring hot water and pour it into the crevice, trying to scald this child to death, but every morning the frost was there. They say that if this one had been killed, there would have been no more winter. After that the tribe lived well and happily for a long time.

THE RED DUCK

THERE was a man who camped alone. He liked to hunt buffalo alone. He had a wife and two children—four persons in all. The boy was large enough to go about and his father had made him a bow and four arrows.

The man had two medicine arrows.

A red duck lived on the creek and the boy often tried to kill this duck, shooting his arrows at him. The duck had come there on purpose to get one of the two medicine arrows that the man had.

When the man went hunting he often said to his wife, "After the day is partly gone, do you come out and help me carry back the meat." The two children stayed at home, playing about the camp.

One day the boy was hunting along the creek and he saw the red duck and shot at it until he had shot away all four of his arrows. The boy's sister was older than he, and when his four arrows were gone, she said to him, "Go and get one of those two arrows that our father has, and shoot that at the duck."

"You stay here and watch the duck," he replied, "and I will go and get one of the arrows." He ran to the lodge and took the arrows down from their place and carried one of them down to the stream. When he had come to where his sister was watching, she said, "There is the duck, right there." It was sitting among the other ducks. The boy shot at it and hit it on the thin part of the wing and the arrow pierced its breast a little way. This was the fifth arrow he had shot at the duck. When he hit the duck it flew away, carrying with it the medicine arrow. The children noticed that it flew straight toward the sunset.

When the children saw that the arrow was gone they were frightened, and stayed there crying and looking in the direction in which the duck had flown. They were afraid their father would scold them. The boy knew how it was that his father had come to own those arrows, for the boy used to dream about them. The two children cried and cried there, until they became very hoarse. At last the father and mother came back over the hill, each carrying a load of meat.

When the father reached the camp he saw that the children had been crying until they were hoarse. He asked the two children what they were crying for. The boy said, "Father, I shot all my four arrows at the red duck and lost them, so I took one of those two arrows you keep, and shot the red duck and he flew off with the arrow." When the man and his wife heard this they too began to cry.

The boy said to his parents, "Father and mother, do not cry any more; I know that arrow and I shall follow it, and try to get it again." The boy painted himself all over the body with red paint and went out of the lodge and started in the direction the duck had taken.

He traveled until he had crossed four ridges, and between each two ridges was a creek. When he had come to the fourth ridge he looked down on the stream, and saw the circle of a big camp; on the side toward where he was, was a little old black lodge, an old woman's lodge.

The boy went down to the camp and opened the door of this lodge and looked in. The old woman was alone in the lodge and he entered and sat down. He said to her, "Grandmother, there is not anything being talked about here, is there?" "Yes," replied the old woman, "the red duck flew by here carrying a medicine arrow. It was a terrible thing to have happened." She stopped speaking for a moment and then said, "Here, grandchild, take this pounded meat and grease and eat it." The boy took the food and ate fast, very fast. Then he said, "Grandmother, have you any red paint?" The old woman gave him some red paint and again he painted himself with red paint. "Where are you going, grandson?" said the old woman. "Oh," replied the boy, "I am only traveling about."

He went on and traveled a long distance, crossing four ridges. From the top of the fourth ridge he looked down on a big camp. At one side stood a little old lodge. After night had fallen he went down to this lodge and looked in and saw there an old woman alone. The boy went in and asked the old woman, "Grandmother, is there any news to hear?" The old woman said to him, "Eat this," and she gave him food, and while he was eating she told him the news. "People say that the red duck went by here, flying away with one of the medicine arrows." He said to her, "Grandmother, have you any red paint?" She said, "Yes, grandchild," and gave him some. He dressed himself with the red paint and after he had painted himself the old woman was going to touch him, but he said to her, "Grandmother, do not touch me."

The boy got up and started on again and traveled across four ridges and saw a camp. It was just as the camps had been before. He entered an old woman's lodge and found her alone, and said to her, "Grandmother, what is the news?" "Dreadful news," she replied, "terrible news. To-day the red duck flew by here with one of the medicine arrows, but the people say that the duck was flying very slowly—he was weak from his wound."

The old woman gave the boy something to eat and when he had finished he asked her for some red paint, and after she had given it to him and he had finished painting himself, he said, "I am on a visit and must be going," and he went out of the lodge.

Again he traveled and crossed four ridges, and looked down on the circle of a big camp. He went down into it and entered an old woman's lodge, and at once she gave him something to eat. When he had finished he said to her, "Grandmother, what is the news?" "Terrible news," answered the old woman, "it was said in camp to-day that the red duck flew by here with the medicine arrow. It was said that it was the medicine arrow that we live by, that keeps our lives. You go outside of the lodge and listen; you will see a light in the lodge. The Ree Medicine Men are doctoring him. I understand that the arrow is still in him. It has not yet been taken out. I heard that the duck went after this arrow on purpose to bring it."

The boy said, "Well, I am just on a visit traveling about," and went out of the lodge. It was late in the night and the camp was all silent. Everybody was in bed. Inside the circle, by itself, stood the lodge in which they were doctoring. There was a light in it. The boy was trying to think how he might come close to this lodge and look into it without anyone hearing him. He crept up very slowly and silently and looked into the lodge. Those who had been doctoring had stopped and had leaned back and gone to sleep, but at the back of the lodge lay the wounded one, still groaning. The boy slipped quietly into the lodge, without waking anyone, and picked up the duck and carried it through the door and outside. When he was outside of the lodge he wrung off the duck's head, took the arrow from the body, covered the body with earth near the door, and started back toward his home with the arrow.

As he went along he picked white sage and wiped the blood off the arrow and off the flint point. Then he placed the arrow across his arm and kept on his way back to his home.

Now, he did not go to any of the camps he had visited, but went straight on. Near the first camp near his home he stopped and again fixed the arrow. He wrapped it in white sage so that he could carry it easily. He still had the duck's head.

When he came in sight of his camp, he could see his mother and father and sister sitting on a little knoll near the camp. They were still mourning, but they had wailed so much that they were hoarse and seemed to be crying way down in their throats.

As he came closer to them, his mother and father ceased mourning. He walked up to them and said, as he held up the arrow: "Father, from now on, this shall be our life, the life of the whole tribe. Here is the way they shall paint." Then he pointed to his face. When he had gone away from the camp his face was painted red, now it was still red, but over his forehead and on both cheeks and under his mouth was a broad line of black. "When we meet any people," he continued, "we shall conquer them easily. We shall have good luck in fighting them. We have saved our lives and our lives will be to go to war and to take horses. We shall have no trouble in taking horses—as many as we need. We shall easily strike our enemies. We shall never be sick and we shall live well and happily."

When the boy finished telling his father this, the father threw up both hands and said, *"Ha ho', ha ho'!"* He felt glad. Then they all went to the lodge.

"The head of the duck brought back," said the boy, "means that when we meet the enemy we must take heads." The little red feathers tied over the medicine arrows below the arrow feathers are those of the red duck. A little later the boy said, "Father, we must have a war dance, but this dance will be made only when we kill enemies and bring in scalps."

They had the war dance. The boy was the maker of the war dance and he it was who made up all the war dance songs. These are the songs which the people have to-day. The whole tribe learned these songs.

"Father," said the boy, "you have only two arrows, but I

am going to put two more with those so that you may have four arrows." Those arrows were given to the boy by the Great Spirit. The boy said: "Father, whenever these arrows are to be renewed, the people must paint themselves red over their whole bodies. If anyone in the tribe is killed by another of the tribe, the people must paint themselves red and must renew the arrows."

The arrows were painted red with buffalo blood and charcoal mixed with the blood. That is the reason that from that time on people used red paint in all of the making of medicine —of ceremonial performances.

"It is struck; there is no one to tie one to it."

MAKOS' STORY

THERE were seven brothers; Makos was the youngest. They lived by themselves in their own camp. No one else was with them. One day six of the brothers went out to hunt, leaving Makos behind to take care of the camp. Near the camp there was a pond. Makos took his bow and arrows and went down to the pond, and there he saw a little speckled bird, which he tried to kill. He shot away all the arrows from his quiver, and then he shot all the arrows that were in his brothers' quivers.

The bird always stood in the water when Makos shot at it, so that the arrows that missed the bird were lost.

On their return from the hunt his brothers made more arrows.

His oldest brother pointed out to him certain arrows and told him that, even if he needed arrows while they were on the hunt, he must not use these.

After his brothers had again started on the hunt the speckled bird came to the same place by the pond, and Makos saw it.

He took his arrows and began to shoot at it, but while he was doing this his brothers returned, and the bird flew away. Makos had shot away all the arrows except those his brothers had told him not to use.

When he saw his brothers come back from the hunt Makos went out to meet them and told them that the bird had come back again. "It came back," he said, "and I have shot away at it all the arrows, except those you told me not to touch." His brother said, "That is well, you must not touch those arrows."

All this happened a third time. The fourth time that his brothers were getting ready to go hunting, one of them said to him: "We are now going out hunting again. Be sure to try to kill that bird."

This fourth time Makos shot away all his arrows, and then went back to the lodge and took one of the arrows that his brothers had told him not to touch. He got as close to the bird as he could and shot it. The bird struggled round on the edge of the water, and kept running away over the prairie. Makos kept following it, hoping that he might catch it. After he had followed it for a long distance the bird took wing and flew away. Makos marked the direction of its flight and followed.

Meantime his brothers returned from the hunt, and when they found that Makos was gone they all cried. On looking up they saw their quivers empty, and that one of the arrows they had told him not to touch was missing.

About dusk that night Makos came to a village, and saw on the edge of the village a small lodge. He went into it and saw an old woman sitting there. He said to her, "Grandmother, give me something to eat; I am hungry." She said, "Why, where have you been, my grandchild?" Makos said, "Oh, I have been home."

The old woman said, "I have very bad news." "What is it?" said Makos. She said, "I have heard that the speckled bird went by with one of the medicine arrows that belonged to the seven brothers that live away over yonder." Makos said to her, "Which way did the bird go, grandmother?" She said to him, "It flew that way," pointing. So Makos followed in that direction.

The next day he went on and traveled all day, and about dusk came to another village, and again entered an old woman's lodge and said, "Grandmother, give me something to eat; I am hungry."

As the other old woman had said, so this one asked him, "Where have you been, grandchild?" He said, "I have been playing around." The woman gave him some dried meat and said, "There is bad news in the camp." "What is it, grandmother?" "Why," she said, "the speckled bird is carrying away the medicine arrow that belongs to the seven brothers. He is taking it off with him." Makos asked, "Which way did it go?" and when the old woman told him he followed on in the same direction.

The next night the same things happened, but the grandmother told him that she had heard that the speckled bird was wounded, and was carrying the arrow to the next camp, where he expected to be doctored. Makos asked her, "How far is that, grandmother?" and the old woman said, "It is not very far; that is where the bird belongs."

Next morning Makos went on again, and about dark came to this village. He went into a little old lodge and asked for food. The old women seemed always to take him for some boy about the camp that they knew, and said, "Where have you been?" This one added, "I have something here for you to eat." Makos asked, "Grandmother, what is the news?" The old woman replied: "The speckled bird has returned to the camp, wounded. One of the seven brothers has hurt him. There is big excitement in the camp. In a lodge at the back of the circle they are doctoring him. The Otter man is doctoring him.

He lives over at the side of the circle, and when he goes over to the lodge where the sick man is he sings." Makos said: "What does he do? How does he doctor the speckled bird?" The old woman said: "When he gets to the lodge, from the outside he kicks the lodge pole next to the door to the south of it, and then the lodge pole on the south side of the lodge, and then the one at the back, and then the one at the north side of the door, and then goes around to the back and strikes the important pole at the back; then he goes in to doctor. All the chiefs are there, and Wihio also. They make Wihio carry the wood for the fire. As the Otter man goes to the lodge he sings *Nai i no, Nai i no* [a doctor's song, meaning *doctor* and also *otter*, and also *I am doctoring*]. He sings that until he goes into the lodge."

Makos said, "Grandmother, I will go out for a little while." Makos went out, and he had not been out long before the doctor came by singing. Makos caught the doctor and twisted his neck, took off his clothing and dressed himself in it, and then went up to the lodge singing. He did just as the old woman had told him to do, and went into the lodge among the chiefs. Wihio was sitting there making the fire, and he spoke and said, "This man's face is too young."

The chiefs said: "What do you know? Don't be joking the old man"; but Wihio kept on saying it. Makos began to shake a rattle and to sing, and gradually everyone went to sleep. Wihio lay right across the door. He was the last one to go to sleep. As soon as Wihio fell asleep Makos took hold of the speckled bird and choked him. Then he looked under the bed and found the medicine arrow wrapped up in a bladder. He took it, put the speckled bird on his back and went out of the lodge without waking anyone. Makos took off the doctor's clothes and left them and went back with the body of the speckled bird and the arrow to the last camp he had left, and asked for food. The old woman said to him, "Where have you been?" He said, "I have just been playing with the boys." His grandmother said, "Ah, there is bad news." Makos asked, "What is it?" "Why," said the old woman, "someone has killed the doctor and carried off the speckled bird."

At each camp this happened, but Makos returned to his brothers, who were glad to see him and the medicine arrow again.

POSSIBLE SACK AND HER BROTHERS

ONCE there was a great camp—a very large circle of lodges. In this village was a girl who wanted to go to a certain place where there lived seven brothers, six young men and a little boy. For a long time the girl had been ornamenting with quills seven robes and making seven pairs of moccasins. At length she finished making these things, and hung them out on a line. Then she changed her name, and called herself Possible Sack. After a little while she took the robes down from the line, folded them up and packed them away. Her mother saw her doing this, and said: "Why do you put these robes away? Why do you not give them to someone?"

Possible Sack answered: "I want to go to the place we hear of, where those seven young men are living. I have no relations here, and I want to have these young men for my brothers."

Her mother thought for a little while, and then said: "Yes, you may go. I will go with you. You can fix your travois on the dog, and in that way can carry your sacks which hold the robes." The girl did as she was told, and they started. The mother went part way, and then turned back, but before she left her daughter she said to her: "When you come in sight of where these young men live, take the pack off your travois and carry it on your back. Fasten up the rope and throw it in the travois, and tell the dog to go home, and he will do so."

After the mother left her, the girl traveled on all night, and just at daylight she came to where she could see the lodge where the brothers lived. She stopped, took the sacks off the travois, did the rope up and threw it into the travois, and told the dog to go home, at the same time making motions to him to do so. The dog trotted off, and after she had sent him away, she took her pack on her back and started down the hill toward the lodge. Before she reached it, while she was yet a long way off, the six young men came out, carrying their bows and arrows and with their robes tied up, and started off to hunt buffalo. When she reached the lodge and looked in, only the little boy was there. His name was *Mŏk' sŏ ĭs*. When he saw her he asked her where she was going, and she said to him: "I came here to claim you as a brother, and also your brothers. I am a lonely child in my family and I want brothers. That is why I came. In my sack I have a robe for you."

When *Mŏk' sŏ ĭs* heard her say this, he was glad; he wanted her for a sister, and he told her so. Possible Sack said to him: "I am glad that you want me for your sister. Now when your brothers come back, do you go to meet them and tell them that a girl has come who wants to claim them as brothers. Tell your eldest brother that you want her for a sister, and tell them that she has a robe for each one of them."

Mŏk' sŏ ĭs said: "Yes, I will tell them all. I will go to meet them when they come in with their meat."

So Possible Sack and the little boy stayed in the lodge. She was unpacking her sacks, and fixing a robe on each of the seven beds, and putting a pair of moccasins on each robe. Every little while *Mŏk' sŏ ĭs* would run out to look to see if his brothers were coming, and at last he told the girl it was about time for them to come, and soon they would be in. The fourth time that he went out to look, he saw the young men coming. He ran back and said to her: "Sister, they are coming. Quick, give me my robe and my moccasins, so that I may run to meet them." She took the robe and the moccasins from his bed and gave them to him, and while he was putting them on he said: "Sister, they are bringing in plenty of liver and nose of the buffalo. We shall eat together. I want you as a sister. When I meet them I will tell them so. They all love me, and all will be willing to own you as a sister."

Mŏk' sŏ ĭs started out dressed in his new robe and moccasins, and he kept looking at himself and felt proud. Before he got to his brothers he threw himself on the ground and held his feet up, so that they might see what he had on. The young men saw the moccasins, and were wondering where he got them, and if perhaps a woman had come to their camp. They said to one another, "Maybe a woman has come, and wants to marry one of us."

When *Mŏk' sŏ ĭs* had come close to his brothers, they called out to him, "Hallo, friend, where did you get your new robe and moccasins?" The little boy was out of breath from running, and was breathing fast as he said to them: "A girl has come who wants to be our sister, and she told me to come and tell you. I told her that you all loved me, and all would be willing to own her as a sister."

"No, friend," said his eldest brother, "you must not say that. I shall have to marry that girl. Then you will always have a home, and someone to sew your moccasins for you. I have been going to see that girl for a long time. I have been sticking close to the camp where she lives." When *Mŏk' sŏ ĭs* heard that, he dropped his robe, and threw himself down on the ground and burst out crying, saying, "I told my sister that you would all be willing to do as I said." His next eldest brother said to him: "Get up, do not cry; your brother is only teasing you; he is only joking. Wipe your tears off, so that your sister will not know that you have been crying, and go down to the lodge and tell your sister to get ready to hang up the meat." *Mŏk' sŏ ĭs* jumped up quickly, and wiped away his tears, and started to go to the lodge. He ran down there and told his sister what to do, and she fixed a place for the meat; and then he ran back and told his brothers that she had done so. She had taken off his robe and put it away, telling him to take care of it and save it.

The brothers went in and found that she had prepared a place for the meat. She made ready some food and got some marrow from the bones, and they began to eat. She was happy. She hung up some ribs before the fire, and when they were roasted took them down and cut them up, and had *Mŏk' sŏ ĭs* carry them round to his brothers.

Next morning the six oldest brothers again went out to hunt. Possible Sack had with her some lodge skins, and she began to cut them into moccasins. The next day the young men went hunting again. Each day they told *Mŏk' sŏ ĭs* to stay close to the camp. They said to him: "You must not leave our sister alone. Some young man might come along and try to carry her away. If anyone should come, you must take your sharp arrows and shoot him." His sister had spoken to him about this, and had said: "*Mŏk' sŏ ĭs*, it may be that someone will try to take me away from you. Now, I have some porcupine quills, stained red and yellow. If anyone should take me, and you cannot find my trail, look for these porcupine quills. You can follow me by them."

Mŏk' sŏ ĭs stayed pretty close to the camp, as he had been told; but on the fourth day, when he was out hunting little birds, he wounded one and followed it quite a long way from the lodge. The bird kept flying a little way, and seemed badly hurt, and every time he would decide to leave it to go back to the lodge, it would fall; but when he went to pick it up it would fly a little farther. At last he left it and went back.

II

While *Mŏk' sŏ ĭs* was away a great big buffalo bull came to the door of the lodge and spoke to the girl, saying, "Come out, Possible Sack." When she heard him speak, she sprang to the back of the lodge, where hung the medicine sacks of the brothers. These were all made of the skins of birds and animals that eat flesh. One was a coyote, one a raven, another a magpie, a blackbird—all birds and animals that eat flesh. Only the medicine sack of *Mŏk' sŏ ĭs* was made of tanned buffalo hide, in the shape of a half moon, and in it there was only the skin of a gopher. Near this were the only arrows that he had; one made of cottonwood, one of large willow, one of small willow, one of bullberry, and one of cherry. The first three had points on them, but those of bullberry and cherry had no heads. He had chewed the ends of these to fine splinters.

When the girl jumped to the back of the lodge the bull called again to her to come out. He spoke four times, and the fourth time he said to her, "If you do not come out, I will come in." Now this lodge was a strong one, built of logs, like a war lodge, and in front of the door there was a passage, also built of logs, for a wind break. The girl thought the bull could not get into the lodge, and she said to him, "You can come in." When she said that, he started in through the passage, and the logs fell down on either side of him; and when he came to the door, he lowered his head and raised it, and the logs flew in all directions. He was a monster bull. When he stood in the door he stopped and said: "I suppose you have never heard of me. You have never heard of the Double-Teethed Bull.* Take your robe and come."

When he said that she picked up her robe, and at the same time her bundle of red and yellow quills, and put them under her arm and went out of the lodge; and the bull followed her.

* Mysterious buffalo with upper as well as lower incisor teeth.

He told her to walk fast, and made her walk close by his head. She was crying all the time. As she walked she kept dropping the quills on the ground.

They traveled and traveled, and at last they came near to great herds of buffalo lying down, and the bull said to her: "Now you will see your mother-in-law. She will come out to meet you." Just before they reached the great herd of buffalo they stopped. All the bull's relations came out to meet them—his mother, his father, his uncles, his aunts, his brothers-in-law, and his sisters-in-law—and after these had met her, all the buffalo stood up and came out and crowded about her.

III

When *Mŏk′ sŏ ĭs* reached the lodge again, he found it partly torn down, but all the beds with the robes and the moccasins on them in back of the lodge were just as he had left them. In the earth of the floor he could see the tracks of a big bull. When he saw this he was very much frightened and began to cry. He ran about everywhere calling to his sister, but no one answered.

Soon he saw his brothers come up over the hill, returning from hunting, and ran to meet them. When they saw him coming, crying, one said to another, "I wonder if his sister has been taken away." When *Mŏk′ sŏ ĭs* reached his brothers he began to call out to them: "Oh, my sister is gone. There is a great bull track in the lodge, and the tracks went off together." One of his brothers said: "Why, this is terrible. That bull cannot be killed. We cannot do anything against him." They added, "It is useless to take our meat to the camp, for there is no one now to take care of it for us." They threw the meat down on the ground and went on without it. When they reached the house, and saw how it was torn down, and saw all the things in it just as the girl had left them, they all began to mourn and cry.

After all had finished mourning, they began to talk together, and to say: "What can we do to get our sister back? And if we get her back, how can we keep her from the power of this bull?" They thought for a long time, and at length they said: "We will make four big corrals each in a circle and one outside the other. Then we will go and try to get our sister." While they were building these pens with logs green and dry, *Mŏk′ sŏ ĭs* was going out and getting ant hills, and bringing them back in his robe, and strewing a line of the sand and ants all around inside the inner and smallest corral. He told his brothers always to step over this line of sand, not to step on it. He talked very brave, saying, "I am going to get my sister. I will get her. Even if the Double-Teethed Bull takes her under the ground, I shall bring her back."

After they had finished all this, the brothers made ready to start, and put on their medicine sacks. Those of the four eldest were made, one from the skin of a blackbird, one from a magpie, one from a raven, and one from a coyote. *Mŏk′ sŏ ĭs* put on his medicine sack too; the half moon with the gopher skin in it. When they were ready to start, *Mŏk′ sŏ ĭs* said, "Come this way," and he started on ahead, following the quills that the girl had dropped. For a little while he kept ahead, but after a long travel he fell behind, and at last was a long way behind. They traveled for a long time, and at last reached the top of a high hill, from which they saw on the other side of a broad river a great mass of buffalo, and in the center of this big herd was an open space, and in this they could see the great bull and the woman sitting by him.

As they sat there on this hill, they were wondering how they could get their sister back, and how they could let her know that they had come after her. They determined that they would send the blackbird down to her with a message. The brother who wore this medicine sack took off from it the blackbird's skin that was tied to it, and as he held the skin in his hand it became a living blackbird. They told the blackbird to go down to the buffalo, and to hop about, and if he could get close to their sister to tell her to hold her robe open so that he could creep under it and talk to her. The blackbird went down to the buffalo, and when he got near, the bull suspected him and said to him: "What are you doing here, blackbird? Go away, or I shall look at you, and you will fall down dead. I think you are a spy. You have come here to say something to Possible Sack." The blackbird went back and told the brothers that the bull suspected him, and had warned him to go or he would look at him.

Then the brothers sent the coyote. He went far around behind the hills and came in from the other side of the buffalo. He pretended to be poor and sick, and limped along very pitifully, but the bull suspected him and said: "You are here as a spy. You have come to tell Possible Sack something. Go away, or I shall look at you." The coyote returned to the brothers, and told them the same thing that the blackbird had told.

Next they sent the raven. He went away round the lower end of the buffalo. He kept flying about and alighting, and flying again, and at last he flew up over where the bull was lying, but the bull suspected him. "Raven," he said, "you must go away. You are here to do something bad." The raven went back and told the brothers that he had gone far around and had flown over the bull, who had told him to go away, but he said: "I could see the girl there, leaning over against a root digger. I had a good look at her. I think she was asleep."

Now the brothers sent a little yellow bird. He was very small and crept along from one buffalo to another, and through the grass, and was not seen, and at last he slipped under the girl's robe and spoke to her. He said: "Possible Sack, wake up. Your brothers are right out here. *Mŏk' sŏ ĭs* sends word to you that you must not sit on any part of your robe, but must put it up over your head and over your root digger, and must sit with your robe spread out." Then the yellow bird crept out through the grass, and then flew back to the brothers, and told them that he had given their message to Possible Sack.

When he had told them this, *Mŏk′ sŏ ĭs* said, "Now, I must try to put that great bull to sleep." He spread his robe on the ground, and lay down on it, and put his medicine sack—his half moon—at his head. He had lain there only a short time when he arose, and sent the blackbird down to see if the bull were sleeping. Soon the blackbird returned and said: "He is asleep. His nose is on the ground." "Ha," said *Mŏk′ sŏ ĭs,* "I have said that I would get my sister back even if the bull should take her under the ground. I will get her." As he said this, he opened his medicine sack and took out the skin of a gopher, to put it on the ground. As he reached his hand toward the ground, the skin looked more and more like a gopher, and began to move its paws, and as he placed it on the ground it began to dig, and soon *Mŏk′ sŏ ĭs* and the gopher both disappeared together under the ground.

After they had gone under the ground they went toward the buffalo. They had to go under the great river, but they passed along under the ground to the place where the girl was, and came up under her robe. *Mŏk′ sŏ ĭs* said to her: "Sister, you must shut your eyes. Do not open them." He took hold of the girl's arm and drew her under the ground, leaving her robe hanging over the root digger, and they went back the way they had come, and soon appeared by the brothers, just where *Mŏk′ sŏ ĭs* had gone under the earth.

IV

When they appeared there, Possible Sack opened her eyes, and began to cry. She said: "Brothers, you had better save yourselves. He is great. He will kill us all." *Mŏk′ sŏ ĭs* said to her, "Do not cry, do not be afraid; I shall kill him." To the others he said: "Go on now; go on home. I will stay here. I am not afraid of that bull. He can look at me. He cannot kill me. I will wait here." They went on, running toward their home, and *Mŏk' sŏ ĭs* waited there alone and watched the buffalo.

Soon they began to get up and start for water, and at last the bull stood up and began to paw the dirt. He raised a great dust, pawing. Pretty soon he went up to the robe and touched it with his nose, thinking that the girl was there. When he touched it, he pushed it over and found that she was gone. Then he was angry, and he hooked the robe and threw it into the air until it was torn in small pieces. He smelt where the hole was, and seemed to follow the underground trail by smelling it, for where they had made a turn he missed it, and then he became still more angry, and tore up the ground. He followed them to the river, and went into the water with his head down, till nothing but the top of his back could be seen above the water. Then he turned and went back to where the robe was. When he came to deep water he seemed to lose the trail. At last the bull crossed the water and came near to where *Mŏk' sŏ ĭs* was. Then the little boy arose, and shot one of his arrows as far as he could toward his home, and when the arrow touched the ground, *Mŏk' sŏ ĭs* stood beside it. He kept doing this until he had reached home. When he had come to the lodge he told them all to make ready, that the bull was coming. They went into the corral and kept watch, and soon they saw it as if the prairie were on fire—a big smoke—the dust raised by the buffalo. Soon they saw all the buffalo coming, and at the head of them all was the big bull.

They came to the top of the hill, and there all stopped. Pretty soon an old buffalo cow came down the hill and said to the girl: "Come back with me, Possible Sack. The Double-Teethed Bull wants you. If you do not go back with me, he will come after you himself."

Mŏk' sŏ ĭs answered her: "Go back and tell him to come. I am angry with him already, because he took away my sister when I was not at home." But when the old cow started back up the hill, *Mŏk′ sŏ ĭs* shot her, and after she had gone a few steps she fell dead.

An old bull came down next and said to the girl: "Daughter-in-law, come with me. The great Double-Teethed Bull himself will come if I do not bring you."

Mŏk′ sŏ ĭs replied, "Let him come"; and when the old bull started back, the boy shot him and he dropped dead a little beyond the first one. Two more buffalo came down, and each one received the message from *Mŏk′ sŏ ĭs*, and was shot, and fell a little farther off than the one before. The fourth got close enough to the big bull to give him the message before it fell dead. When this one gave the message and fell dead, the Double-Teethed Bull rolled over and over, and jumped up and hooked the ground, and made fearful noises, for he was very angry. Soon he started down the hill on a gallop, and all the buffalo followed him, and they got around the pens in a dense mass. The big bull came up to the corral and said to the girl: "Come out; come out. Have you never heard of me? Do you not know who I am?" The girl was crying, and said to her brothers: "Let me go out anyhow. It may save you." *Mŏk′ sŏ ĭs* said to her: "Do not cry. What are you afraid of? Do not fear him. I will kill him."

When he heard *Mŏk′ sŏ ĭs* say this, the bull dashed at the outer corral and put his head under a great log and threw it high in the air When he had done this, all the buffalo made a rush for the corral, and broke down first the outer one, and then the next, and then the third, and then the fourth. By this time they had reached the place where *Mŏk′ sŏ ĭs* had strewn the sand from the ant hills, and now each grain of sand was a great rock, making a big stout rock corral.

Every time they broke down a corral the bull would shout, "Come out; come out," and the girl would say to her brothers, "Oh, let me go; let me go. He will kill us all." The buffalo charged the rock corral, and the big bull dashed himself against it and threw the rocks in all directions. One of the brothers soon called out: "He almost got in that time. He will be inside soon." The girl kept saying, "Let me go out to him, or he will kill you all." *Mŏk′ sŏ ĭs* said: "No, stay here. Wait." He took his arrow made from the large willow, and shot it in the air as high as he could, and as high as it went there stood a great willow tree.

"Now," said *Mŏk′ sŏ ĭs,* "climb up there." The girl climbed up, and after she had reached a certain height he called to her: "There, that is high enough. I will take the lowest limb." The brothers climbed the tree, and then *Mŏk′ sŏ ĭs.* Just as they climbed into the tree the bull broke through the rocks. He rushed around the tree and rubbed against it, trying to push it over, and at last he charged the tree and ran his horns through it. When he struck the tree with his head, the girl screamed again, "Let me go, and save yourselves." When the bull ran his horns through the tree he tore off a great sliver from the trunk which he carried off on his horns, but before he had gone far, the piece flew off his horns and back against the tree, and joined to it, and the tree was natural again.

When the bull charged the tree a second time, *Mŏk′ sŏ ĭs* fitted to his bow the arrow made of bullberry, and shot the bull in the head, and he fell down dead; and *Mŏk′ sŏ ĭs* jumped down from the tree and ran to the bull, and jumped on him and stamped on him until every bone of his body was broken in fine pieces. When the bull fell, all the buffalo ran away in every direction. They raised a fearful dust.

Now they all came down from the tree, and *Mŏk′ sŏ ĭs* said to his brothers, "Now we must go up above." They did so. You can see them yet. These are the seven stars. There are really eight, but you can only see seven. The girl is at the head. *Mŏk′ sŏ ĭs* is the little one, off to one side.

FOUND IN THE GRASS

ONE day *Mŏk' sŏ ĭs* was playing with a number of boys when he said to them, "Look here, my friends; I am going to make a hoop and we will have races after it." He made one, and all the others said, "The weather is perfectly still; it cannot go"; for when the wind is blowing, the hoop is sent with the wind and so often travels a long distance. The boys talked to one another and said, "We do not see how he is going to make it run."

Mŏk' sŏ ĭs held the hoop in his hand and said, "Now, which one of you will chase it first?" Because there was no wind, several said, "I will do it." After he had made four motions as if throwing it, *Mŏk' sŏ ĭs* let it go and said to one of them, "Now follow it." As it left his hand, there came a little puff of wind. The first boy chased it a little way. Then the hoop fell over, and he brought it back to *Mŏk' sŏ ĭs*. The second time he threw it he made the same motions, and it ran a little farther, and a second boy brought it back. *Mŏk' sŏ ĭs* took it in his hand a third time, and threw it, and another boy chased it, and it went still farther before falling. The third boy came back saying: "That hoop runs pretty fast. I am all out of breath."

Before he threw it the fourth time, *Mŏk' sŏ ĭs* said, "This time I will run after it myself." He said to the boys: "I am going to find another place to live in. Here I am poor and have no mother to take care of me. You will not see me again for a long time." While he was talking the wind blew still harder. He threw the hoop and ran after it, keeping close to it, and it went far, rolling along till it went over a big divide. They all watched for him, but he did not come back; they saw him no more.

The hoop led him to a big village. The lodges were planted in a circle and the hoop fell near one of the smallest in the circle. As *Mŏk' sŏ ĭs* was tired, he lay down among the tall grass. A very old man and an old woman came out of this little lodge to cut some grass, and began to work near *Mŏk' sŏ ĭs*. He called to the old woman, saying, "Grandmother, do not hit me." The old woman took him by the hand, saying, "Why, I might have hit my grandson!" He said, "What is the news, grandmother?" and she said: "It is very bad. Everybody is starving, for we have nothing to eat in the village." *Mŏk' sŏ ĭs* said, "I will go with you to your lodge." The old woman's lodge was little and old—nearly worn out.

When she took *Mŏk' sŏ ĭs* into the lodge, she said: "I do not know what I can give you to eat. I have nothing for you." *Mŏk' sŏ ĭs* said, "Put a kettle on the fire and cook me some pounded—pulverized—roots." The old woman put on the kettle and said, "I do not see where I am to get you that mush." He said, "Go on; it will be well." He took a handful of ashes and put them in the kettle and said, "Now cook it." When she commenced stirring it, the old woman saw the mush begin to thicken. The old man was delighted to see *Mŏk' sŏ ĭs* do such a thing. When the mush was cooked, the old woman put it in three wooden bowls and they all had as much as they could eat. After eating, *Mŏk' sŏ ĭs* said, "Grandmother, is there any news at all in the village?"

The old woman said: "Well, I will tell you. The chief of this village has a handsome younger daughter. He is anxious to get a real red fox [of a species said now to be extinct] and he says that anyone who can trap one for him shall have his daughter in marriage." *Mŏk' sŏ ĭs* said: "Is that true, grandmother? I think I am the one who will catch one. I will make one or two dead falls." His grandmother said: "My grandson, I do not think you can catch it. Everybody has tried," but *Mŏk' sŏ ĭs* said, "Well, I shall try my luck."

The other young men had their traps scattered all about outside the camp. *Mŏk' sŏ ĭs* went out and fixed his trap not far from some of these. One of the young men said to him: "What are you doing? You will not be able to catch the red fox."

Wihio was living in this camp. He said to *Mŏk' sŏ ĭs,* "You are too ugly to catch the red fox, anyway." *Mŏk' sŏ ĭs* had a fine piece of fat meat for his bait, and early next morning when he went out to look at his traps he found the red fox in one of them, and brought it to the village and everybody ran to see it. Wihio said, "Oh, I caught that and *Mŏk' sŏ ĭs* took it from one of my traps." The chief called out and said: "I believe that Wihio caught that fox. I wouldn't have *Mŏk' sŏ ĭs* for my son-in-law anyway. He is too ugly." He said to his soldiers, "Go and take that fox away from *Mŏk' sŏ ĭs.*" A party of them went to take the fox away. *Mŏk' sŏ ĭs* pulled some of the hair from the fox skin and hid it, and gave up the fox, and they took it back and the chief hung it as a token on the top of his lodge. As soon as it was hung up, it turned white, and was not a red fox any more. When *Mŏk' sŏ ĭs* looked under the robe where he had hidden the hair, there was another red fox skin.

Mŏk' sŏ ĭs said to the old man he lived with: "Grandfather, make me a bow and arrows. The camp has nothing to eat and I want to get something." His grandfather said, "What are you going to do with them?" *Mŏk' sŏ ĭs* said: "Go on and make them. I will show you." The old man made them, and *Mŏk' sŏ ĭs* told him to paint two of the arrows black. After they were finished *Mŏk' sŏ ĭs* said, "Grandmother, make me a wheel [*hōhk tsĭm'*] for the game of wheel and stick." The old woman said, "I have no rawhide to make it of." *Mŏk' sŏ ĭs* said, "Go around among some of the lodges, and see if you can't find some." She went out and found some pieces, and when she returned said to *Mŏk' sŏ ĭs,* "Now that I have got it, see what you can do." He said: "Go ahead and make it. Cut the hide into strips and make the wheel." The old woman began it, and soon it was finished. Then *Mŏk' sŏ ĭs* said, "Hand that to the old man." *Mŏk' sŏ ĭs* had the bow and arrows in his hand, and was pulling on the bow to see if it was good, well made, and strong.

All three were in the little lodge alone; no one else knew anything about it. *Mŏk' sŏ ĭs* said to the old man: "You and grandmother are old, and if I were to make a big buffalo you could not chew it. It would be too tough for you." Then he told the old man to roll the wheel, and said, "Grandfather, make the motion to throw the wheel four times, and as you let it go the fourth time, say, 'Grandson, here comes a two-year-old heifer.' " When he rolled the wheel, the old man said, "My grandson, here comes a two-year-old heifer." As the wheel passed, *Mŏk' sŏ ĭs* shot it and it turned into a two-year-old heifer, and fell down inside the lodge. Then he said, "Go ahead now and cut it up." He stepped out of the lodge, and there near the door was a pile of ashes. He kicked the ashes up into the air, and at once a big snowstorm began. He did that so that nobody would know about the buffalo in the lodge. They cut up the meat, and the little lodge was filled with the cut up meat drying. No one outside knew anything about it. It snowed hard for four days.

Somehow *Mŏk' sŏ ĭs* must have exercised his power, for the chief's daughter came to the lodge to visit. When she came in, she was surprised to see the little old lodge full of meat. *Mŏk' sŏ ĭs* said, "Grandmother, give her all she wants to eat." He spat toward the fire, and there dropped from his mouth an *ar ri cas*—a sort of shell highly prized by the Indians and found by the big lakes. She picked it up and was very much pleased with it. She said, "*Mŏk' sŏ ĭs,* spit again." He did so and another shell fell. *Mŏk' sŏ ĭs* was so ugly that nobody thought he could do such things. He kept spitting till she had a whole handful, and she said, "I will wear them in my ears." She tied them up and when she looked at the boy he had turned into a handsome young man. She hung her head and looked down, and when she raised her eyes again he had changed again, and was very ugly.

Mŏk′ sŏ ĭs told his grandmother to give the girl some meat to take home to her people—for he liked her. He told his grandmother to go over to the lodge where the girl lived, taking with her a small piece of buffalo fat. The old woman said, "Oh, I am so old, ugly, and poor, they will order me out of the lodge." But he said, "Go ahead." He also said to her: "Now, when you come out of the chief's lodge drop the bit of fat. When they see you drop it, they will tell you you have dropped something. Then you must tell them it is the fat that *Mŏk′ sŏ ĭs* uses to grease his face and eyes with"

The old woman went to the chief's lodge as he had told her, and when she dropped the fat all cried out, saying: "Give me that. Let me have it."

When the old woman returned to the lodge, *Mŏk′ sŏ ĭs* said to her, "Now take some of this buffalo meat to them, and also this red fox, and give it to the chief." Then the old woman took the meat on her back and also the red fox skin on top, so that everybody could see it. She went to the lodge and went in with the red fox skin on top of the meat, and said: "My grandson has sent you this. Now he wants to marry your daughter." When the old woman came back she told *Mŏk′ sŏ ĭs* that everything was well.

They had the lodge put up for him, and when night came *Mŏk′ sŏ ĭs* said, "Now I will go over and take possession." He went over to the lodge, and when he entered the girl was in there by herself sitting on the bed. He had become a fine-looking man, and she recognized him, for she had seen him look like that once before.

Mŏk′ sŏ ĭs said, "You go and tell your father to come over to this lodge." When his father-in-law arrived, he told him to go out and cry through the village that *Mŏk′ sŏ ĭs* was going out to look for food.

When daylight came *Mŏk′ sŏ ĭs* started out to look for buffalo and went over a big hill. The snow had melted from the ground except in a few spots. He set to work to collect a large pile of buffalo chips and piled them together in one place; then he took two of the chips and set them at some distance on one side of the pile.

When he returned to his lodge, he said to his wife, "Go and tell your father that there is a big herd of buffalo on the other side of that hill." His father-in-law went out and cried through the camp that there was a big herd of buffalo on the other side of the hill. Wihio said: "Why I went up on that hill and saw the buffalo. This boy saw them after I did."

Everybody went out after the buffalo. After all had left the camp, *Mŏk′ sŏ ĭs* started with his wife. He said, "They will kill all those buffalo, but let us go this way." He said to his wife, "We will go this way"—meaning to the place where he had laid the two chips. They found two big fat cows lying there, and he killed them and his wife began to cut them up. Wihio got nothing but an old bull, which he had killed because it looked so large. Everybody else got good meat. *Mŏk′ sŏ ĭs* and his wife returned among the last to camp. He and his wife had each a red bird skin tied on the head and looked very fine.

Wihio went up to *Mŏk′ sŏ ĭs* and said he wanted to be his friend, and *Mŏk′ sŏ ĭs* said this would please him. Wihio then said, "I want to come over with my wife to your lodge." *Mŏk′ sŏ ĭs* said, "It is good; you just come over and we will live in the same lodge." So Wihio and his wife moved in with *Mŏk′ sŏ ĭs* and placed their bed on the opposite side of the lodge.

One night *Mŏk′ sŏ ĭs* said: "I am going over to see my grandfather and grandmother. Do not be uneasy or frightened when I come back late to-night." When he returned his steps sounded very loud, and sparks of fire flashed all around him, and when

237

he went to bed they could see the sparks flying out all over him.

Next morning *Mŏk′ sŏ ĭs* said, "I am going out again to look for buffalo." Wihio said, "I also will go." He started out ahead of *Mŏk′ sŏ ĭs,* but went too far. *Mŏk′ sŏ ĭs* went out soon after, picked up buffalo chips as before, and went back to his lodge and told his wife to tell her father that another herd of buffalo was in pretty nearly the same place as before. His father-in-law again called out through the village that there was a big herd of buffalo there again, and that everyone should get ready and go out. Everybody went out to the herd, and *Mŏk′ sŏ ĭs* and his wife went to the same place to which they had gone before. When he started he tied the two red birds on his and his wife's head again. Meantime, Wihio, who had returned, went out and caught two woodpeckers and tied one on his head and one on his wife's head, just as *Mŏk′ sŏ ĭs* had done with the red birds. He and his wife rushed out with the woodpeckers tied to their heads. *Mŏk′ sŏ ĭs* and his wife came back loaded with meat, and the red birds came to life and flew around over their heads. Wihio's woodpeckers also came to life and pecked his wife's head till her scalp was all torn to pieces.

That night Wihio said, "I am going out, so do not be alarmed if I come in late." The morning after *Mŏk′ sŏ ĭs* had gone out at night, Wihio had seen the tracks of a buffalo bull coming toward the lodge, so this night when he came back, he tied buffalo hoofs on his hands and feet and put coals of fire around so that they would sparkle when he moved or lay down.

Some time after that *Mŏk′ sŏ ĭs* announced that he was going back where he came from, and said his name would be "Found in the Grass"—*Mio in ihko.*

THE EARLIEST STORIES

The Very Earliest Stories*

B ECAUSE the Cheyennes are made up of two different tribes, Tsistsistas and Suhtai, the tribe has two culture heroes and two special sacred objects, the buffalo cap and the medicine arrows. The medicine arrows were brought to the tribe by the' Cheyenne culture hero, who is variously known as Sweet Medicine, or Sweet Root Standing, or Rustling Corn Leaf, while the Suhtai hero, called Red Tassel (of corn), Straight Horns, or Standing on the Ground, brought to that tribe the buffalo cap, which was its special medicine.

The union of the two tribes took place so long ago and the absorption of one by the other has been so complete, that the young people of the present day hardly know that these different objects were brought to the tribe by two different persons. The two culture heroes named above are reported to have brought food to the people in ancient days, and to have ended a long period of starvation.

The arrows and the sacred hat are mysterious and are greatly reverenced, and a generation ago the men and women who knew the secrets about them were not willing to talk of them to any stranger. Some of the ceremonies in connection with them have never been seen by a white man.

Long before the time of these culture heroes, human beings existed on the earth and some stories are told of those earlier days. But before human beings came is the story of the making of the land we live on.

* Compare *Journal American Folklore*, vol. 20, p. 171, July-Sept., 1907.

CREATION TALE

THE creation story of the Cheyennes tells of a being who was floating on the surface of the water. Water birds, swans, geese, ducks, and other birds that swim already existed, and these were all about him. The person called to these birds and asked them to bring him some earth. They were glad to do so, and agreed one after another to dive down through the water and see if they could find earth at the bottom. The larger birds dived in vain. They came up without anything, for they could not reach the bottom, but at last one small duck came to the surface with a little mud in its bill. The bird swam to the being and put the mud in his hand, and he took it and worked it with his fingers until it was dry, when he placed it in little piles on the surface of the water, and each little pile became land, and grew and grew and spread, until, as far as one could see, solid land was everywhere. Thus was created the earth we walk on.

After there was firm ground the creator took from his right side a rib and from it made a man. From the man's left side he took a rib and from that made a woman. These two persons were made at the same place, but after they had been made they were separated, and the woman was put far in the north, and the man in the south.

Another creation story told me long ago by Ben Clark, who had married a Cheyenne woman and lived long with the tribe, says that once the Cheyennes were all under the ground, living in darkness. One day a man saw far off a little spot of white. He approached it, and gradually it grew larger, and presently he found himself surrounded by the light, which blinded and frightened him. After a little time, however, he became used to this, and going back below the ground, as he had come, told his fellows, and a part of them also came out from under the ground, and thereafter lived on the earth's surface. This suggests a tale told of the beginnings of the Mandan Indians.

After the creator had made the two people, whom he placed far apart in the north and in the south, he stood between them with his back toward the rising sun. He said to them, "In that direction," pointing to the south, "you will find many sorts of animals and birds different from those which you will find in that direction," pointing to the north where the woman stood. "The birds that live in the south will go to the north in summer. Where the woman is it will be cold and the grass and trees will not grow well. There will be hardly any of them, but where the man is everything will grow; trees, bushes, grass."

The woman in the north, though she was gray-haired, was not old. She never seemed to grow any older. The man in the south was young. He did not grow older.

In the north lives *Ho ĭm' a ha,* the Winter Man, the power that brings cold and snow, and also brings sickness and death. He obeys the woman in the north. He is often spoken of in the stories and is said to have declared at a meeting of the supernatural beings that he would "take pity on no one." When at this meeting he spoke in this way, the Thunder, who represents the power of the south, declared that it would not do to let *Ho ĭm' a ha* have everything to say; so, with the help of the buffalo, the Thunder made fire, and taught one of the culture heroes how to do the same thing.

He said to Sweet Medicine, "Get a stick and I will teach you something by which your people can warm themselves, can cook food, and with which they can burn things." He showed Sweet Medicine how to rest the point of the stick in the middle of a dried buffalo chip, and then to rub it between his hands and twirl it fast. The young man did so, and after a time the chip caught fire. Thus, by the help of the Thunder the people were given something to use against the cold, something that would warm them.

The man and woman in the south and in the north appear to typify summer and winter, the man representing the sun or the Thunder, while the woman represents the power that wars against the sun.

Twice a year there is a conflict between the Thunder and the Winter Man. At the end of summer when the streams get low and the grass becomes yellow and dry, *Ho ĭm' a ha* comes down from the north and says to the Thunder: "Move back, move back, to the place from which you came. I want to spread all over the earth and freeze things and cover everything with snow." Then the Thunder moves back. Toward spring, when the days begin to grow longer, the Thunder comes back from the south and says to *Ho ĭm' a ha,* "Go back, go back, to the place from which you came; I wish to warm the earth and to make the grass grow, and all things to turn green." Then the Winter Man moves back and the Thunder comes, bringing the rain; the grass grows and all the earth is green. So there is a struggle between these two powers. They follow each other back and forth.

The two first people, the man in the south and the woman in the north, never came together, but later other people were created and from them the earth was populated.

E HYOPH' STA

BEFORE the appearance of the two culture heroes the people, according to the later stories, knew nothing of large food animals, and lived on fishes, turtles, the eggs or young of birds, and small animals, such as ground squirrels, skunks, and the like. A sacred story said to be much more ancient than those of the culture heroes is that of the Yellow Haired Woman, through whose influence the people first learned of the buffalo. Later the buffalo disappeared, were long absent and were forgotten, returning only when they were brought back by the two culture heroes. This story of the Yellow Haired Woman is sacred and might be told only at night. Before it was related a prayer was made asking pardon for telling it. This is the story.

This story is told of the very beginning of the people far off on the other side of the Missouri River.

There was a big camp and the people had nothing to eat. Everyone was hungry. They were depending for food on the fish, geese, and ducks in the little lakes, for where the people were camped there was almost nothing to eat. Early one morning the old crier went through the village calling for two young men who were fast runners. They were told to go to all the small lakes round about and see if they could find anything to eat. They were told not to come back until they had found something. The camp was in great need of food; the children were starving. These two men traveled far in different directions, and in four days they came back, but they had found nothing. Then it was ordered that the people should pack their dogs and travois; they must move somewhere, for here there was no food.

After they had made camp that night the chiefs gathered in the center of the village and sent for two young men, the sons of chiefs, and the old men told them to go on ahead of the camp and not to return until they had found something. They said to these young men: "You must try hard. You hear the old people and the children crying for food. Be sure to find something. Do not come back until you do so." When these two young men set out, the older of these two said to his young companion, "Now we must find something before we come back or the people will starve." They started, going straight north.

After they had been gone for eight days they saw before them a high peak, and nearer to them something that looked blue. They had eaten nothing since they had left the camp. One said to the other: "I am weak and nearly dead. I fear I cannot travel much farther." The other said: "You see that peak over there; let us go over there and die. It will be a mark for us. It will show our burying place." The other replied, "We will go there and die together."

They walked toward the peak and when they were near it they saw that at its foot a large stream ran, and that they must cross this stream to reach it. They sat down on the bank and looked at it. The peak came right down to the river's edge, and off to one side of the peak a high bluff ran out. The elder said, "Take off your leggings and let us cross to the peak." He entered the water first and then the other followed him. The water came up to mid thigh and then higher. Presently the one that was following called out and said: "My friend, I cannot move, something is holding me. Tell my people what has happened to me. Tell them not to cry for me. Some mysterious power holds me." As the young man stood there and could not move, he said, "Friend, come back and shake hands with me for the last time." The elder boy turned back weeping, and went to his friend and shook hands with him, and then left him. The younger shouted his war cry, and the elder went on weeping toward the bank. He walked out of the water and then up and down the bank crying.

Presently he saw a man come out of the peak and down toward him, carrying in his hand a large knife, and wearing a coyote skin on his back, the head coming up over his head. The boy ran to him and said, "Something is holding my friend." The coyote man said, "Stand where you are," and went into the water toward the boy standing there. Just before he reached him he dived under the water and with his knife cut off the head of the great serpent which was holding the boy. The one on shore saw the serpent, after its head had been cut off, rise and splash the water in every direction. Then the coyote man came to the top of the water and called to the boy on the shore: "Go to the peak; you will see there a big rock, which is a door;

there you will find an old woman. Tell her that grandfather has killed the serpent he has so long been trying to get, and that she must bring some ropes."

When the boy reached the place the rock flew open like a door, and an old, old woman came out. He said to her, "Grandfather has killed the serpent he has been so long trying to get." "That is true," the old woman answered, "he has been trying to kill it for a long time." The boy went back to where the coyote man was standing and he said to him, "Go and get your friend and bring him out to the shore." When the elder boy reached him, the younger said, "I can walk no further; I cannot move." The elder turned his back to him and took him on his shoulders, and carried him to the bank and laid him there. Then the coyote man said: "Let him lie there awhile. Help me to drag out this serpent." The two went into the water and cut the serpent to pieces and dragged them to shore. When they had brought all the pieces to the bank the coyote man said to the elder boy, "Put your friend on your shoulders and I will lift his feet, and we will carry him up to the peak." Meantime the old woman had begun to carry up the meat.

The two men carried the younger boy up to the peak, and when they were close to the rock the coyote man threw open the door, and they went inside, and the boy saw that the peak was a lodge and that at one side they had a sweat house. The coyote man told the elder boy to carry his friend into the sweat house and to start a fire. They put the boy in the sweat house and the older young man started a fire and heated the stones. When the stones had been put in the sweat lodge the coyote man sprinkled water on them four times and sang four songs. Four times he sprinkled water on the stones and sang, and after he had done it the fourth time he told the boy that he was cured, and he arose and came out of the sweat house.

The old woman called them to come and eat, for she knew that they were nearly starved. Standing by the fire were two jars in which she was cooking. She said to them, "I know that you are very hungry." She put before each one of them a white bowl made of stone. These bowls were as white as snow, and in each dish she put meat. To each one she gave a white flint knife to cut with, and told them to eat all they wanted.

After they had finished eating, the coyote man, who was sitting at one side of the lodge with the old woman, said, "Look over there," pointing. They looked, and saw a very handsome young woman sitting on the other side of the lodge. The coyote man said, "Now, my grandsons, I want to ask you two things; do you want to take that woman for your sister, or does either of you want to marry her?" The elder boy said, "My friend here is poorer (less fortunate) than I, let him take her for his wife." The coyote man said, "*Ha ho'* (thank you), that is good; I am glad to hear that." After the younger had chosen the young woman for his wife, the coyote man told them to look to the north. They did so, and saw a big field of corn. He told them to look to the east, and there they saw a country covered with buffalo. He told them to look to the south, and they saw elk, deer, and all kinds of game. A little to one side of where the elk were, as they looked again, they saw herds of horses, and to the west they saw all kinds of birds.

The coyote man said to them: "Now you shall go to your home. Take this woman with you back to your camp. It is very good that one of you selected her for his wife. She is to be a great helping power to your people. She will take everything I have shown you to your people. All these things will follow her." They went out of the lodge and stood looking toward the south, the direction whence the two young men had come. The old woman stood on the east side, then the coyote man, then the young woman, then her husband, and then his friend.

Now for the first time the two young men knew that this young woman was the daughter of these two old people, for the coyote man said, "My daughter, rest four times on your way."

THE STICK GAME.

He meant stop four times, not rest for four nights. He said they would arrive that night at their village, and that the next morning they would see all these animals around their camp. He said to his daughter: "If ever a little buffalo calf is brought into the camp do not say to it, 'My poor animal.' If ever they bring in any kind of fowl, never say to it, 'My poor animal.' Do not express pity for any suffering creature." The coyote man said to the girl: "I send you there for a special purpose. These poor people now have only fish and a few birds to eat, but when you are there, there will be plenty of game of all kinds. The skins of all these animals will be useful for clothing."

The three young people started for home and rested four times, and as they started the fifth time they passed the crest of the hill and saw the village below them. When the people saw that there were three persons coming back instead of two, the whole village came running toward them. They came close and looked at the handsome woman. Then they spread down a robe and carried her in it to her father-in-law's lodge. He was one of the head chiefs. They all three sat together and the elder boy told the story. All crowded close about them to hear the news they had brought. He said, "Old men, old women and chiefs, societies of soldiers, and children, we have brought this woman down here from far up north, and she has brought great power with her. You people are suffering from hunger. Now, when the sun goes down and comes up again, you will see many animals around you."

That night as the village went to sleep they heard noises all around them. Early the next morning an old man called out, "Make ready, make ready," and when they rose from their beds they saw buffalo all about the village. The wind was blowing toward the east, and in front of the village there was just a little open space. Except for that the buffalo were all around. The Indians ran out with their bows and arrows and killed many buffalo. The buffalo were so near that they shot them even from the lodge doors. The elder boy said to the people, "You must kill only what you need, and then must leave the others alone." The buffalo came right up to the lodge in which lived the woman they had brought down, and rubbed against it. She sat there and laughed.

One of the chiefs went into the lodge where this woman lived, and said to her father-in-law: "All the chiefs will come here in the morning to hold a council and arrange some plan, deciding what to do. We want to talk about returning favors to the girl and her people, because they have been kind to us and brought us these animals." The woman said nothing, but her father-in-law answered, "Come together here in the morning, and we will smoke and talk."

When the morning came, all the chiefs came to the lodge to talk with the woman. Each in turn thanked her for what she had done and what she had brought, and asked if they could do any favor for her or her father in return for all that she had done for them. She said her father had not told her to accept favors, and she must do only what her father told her.

Four years after that, this woman's husband said to her, "Let us go back and visit your father and tell him what the chiefs told you, for they asked if they might do you some favor." She said again, "No, my father did not say I was to accept any favors." But after a while she said, "You are anxious to go there with me, let us go." So her husband went to his friend, and said they were planning to go to the peak again. The woman told her husband to tell his friend not to come to the lodge until late at night; and he came after all the village had gone to sleep. The woman said: "Everything is arranged. We will start now." It was then late in the night. They walked outside the circle of lodges. There they stood and the woman said, "Shut your eyes." They did so, and when she spoke again and said to them, "Open your eyes," they were standing in front of the door of the peak.

The woman said, "Father, we have come back; open the door." The stone moved back and they went in. The coyote man and his wife got up and hugged all three.

After they had eaten, the coyote man said to his daughter: "I did not expect you back, as I did not tell you to return, and I do not ask for any favors. After you have rested, return to your village." The coyote man also said: "None of you must return here again. The only favor I ask is that no one shall ever say 'Poor animal' in speaking of a bird or a beast; do not disobey me in that." They all stepped out, and as before stood in front of the lodge. The three shut their eyes, and when they opened them they were standing in their own village.

Four years after they returned, some boys were dragging a little buffalo calf into camp; they were abusing it by throwing dirt into its eyes. The woman went out and said, "My poor calf"—then she said, "I forgot," and went in and lay down in her lodge. When her husband came in, he saw that she was sorrowful and said, "What is it, my wife?" She answered, "I have done what I was told not to do; I said, 'My poor calf,' and my father told me not to."

That day the buffalo all disappeared.

Next morning the woman said to her husband, "Go and call your friend." So he came. She said to both of them, "I am going back; if you wish to come back with me I am glad; but if I must leave you here, you will have a hard time." They both spoke and said, "We love you and will go with you; let us go to the center of the camp and have it announced that we are going to where your father and mother live, so that all the village may know what becomes of us." So it was announced, and all the people came running to where they were. She told them all that she had disobeyed her father in spite of his many cautions, and that they must go away. When she said that the whole village began to cry. Her friend then stood up and said that he and her husband were going also; he told his father and mother and all his people not to sorrow for him. Her husband also stood up and said the same, and that they now must work for his wife's father and mother. After that, they announced that they would start that evening for the peak. All their relations wept because they were going to leave them forever. That night all three disappeared, and no one ever knew what became of them.

The name of the woman was $\bar{E}$ *hyōph' stā* or Yellow-top-to-head, for she had light-colored hair.

The buffalo never came back till they were brought from the spring by the two young men. This happened long before that.

THE RACE

IN the beginning the creator made first the earth, then the trees and the grass, and afterward he made the animals and the people and put them on the earth. At that time the animals and the people lived together as friends.

Yet after this, as you all know, the buffalo used to eat us people, and the animals as well. The Great Power thought that it would be a good thing to have a race of all the animals, to decide whether the buffalo should eat the people, or they the buffalo.

So at that time all creatures living upon the earth, Indians, buffalo, birds, and all animals, were called together at a place east of the Black Hills, which we call the Race Track. It is near what white men now call the Buffalo Gap.

All these creatures were going to run in this great race, and when they prepared for the race all painted themselves different colors. What paints they used we do not know, but as they painted themselves then, so they are to-day. The coot, for example, rubbed a little white paint on his nose, and it is white to-day. It is the same with all the other animals, antelope, deer, birds, and all. In this race the people had the birds on their side, and the race was run to decide whether the people should eat the buffalo and other animals, or the animals the people. When they were talking about this race, all thought that the buffalo cow or the coyote would win it.

After they had finished painting themselves, they all formed in a line. The buffalo formed in one line, and all the other animals formed in a line by themselves. While they were all getting into line there was the greatest noise you could imagine—all the birds and animals were talking, uttering each its own cry.

The buffalo chose a cow, named Slim Walking Woman, to run for them, and placed her next to the other animals. They said to her, "We do not have to tell you to run, but you must push hard." This implied that she had never been beaten.

After all was ready two animals, a coyote and a big wolf, howled at the same time, and when they howled all the people and animals began to run, starting toward the east over a track that had been marked out. They were to run clear around it. When they started, Slim Walking Woman shot ahead, and a little bird kept close to her.* These two were soon far ahead. The other animals were running hard but a long way behind these two.

At last the little bird became tired out; he flew off to one side away from the track, and stopped to rest. Then the swift hawk went ahead, and flew hard, but at last he too grew tired. After a time Slim Walking Woman began to get tired, and the buffalo began to shout to encourage her. All the time the magpie was flying along slowly and steadily.

They ran a long way eastward and then turned, and the wolves which were behind them said to them, "Now you must run hard back to the place you started from." Long before they had got back there most of the animals became tired out, and

* From the description inferred to be *Rhyncophanes maccowni.*

some of them bled at the mouth. The ground there is still red with this blood.

By this time almost all the birds, even the swift hawk, had become exhausted, but the magpie kept on, and at last he got ahead. He was now ahead of everyone. As each animal gave out, it stepped off to one side. The magpie kept on, and came back to where they started, far ahead of all. He had won the race. He is the slowest flying of all birds, but he can endure a very long time, and he got there first. That is why, to this day, though the people eat most birds and everything that goes on four legs, they never eat a magpie, because he won the race for them, nor a swift hawk, for he tried hard.

This was the beginning of the eating of flesh by the people.

When they got back from the race, they all scattered out, going their different ways, and after this the land was full of people and animals and birds, and all kept the same colors with which they had painted themselves for this race.

In old times before this, when the people went to try to kill a buffalo, it would run toward them and fight, but after that race the buffalo always ran away. This beating made the buffalo afraid of everything. From that time the people began to have bows and arrows; and after they had beaten the buffalo in the race, they began killing them with bows and arrows.

CULTURE HERO STORIES

OLD WOMAN'S WATER AND THE BUFFALO CAP*

THE two culture heroes of the tribe make their first appearance as two similarly dressed young men, previously unknown. These heroes are called by various names, but are best known as Standing on the Ground for the Suhtai, and Sweet Medicine for the Tsistsistas. Accounts of how they were first seen and what they did differ in detail, but all are essentially similar. I have chosen here one of the oldest.

The people were having a "medicine" hunt; they knew nothing then about the buffalo. Before making a "medicine" hunt, the medicine men all came together and pledged themselves to make a hunt; they appointed a man to be leader and also his wife, so that, when they caught animals they would get the females as well as the males. After these had pledged themselves, they sent out runners to see what they could find. This was when the Cheyennes were far on the other side of the Missouri River where there are many lakes.

This time they chose two men to go out to look for ducks, geese, and other birds. The men came back and reported that a certain lake was covered with water-fowl of all kinds; so the whole camp moved over to it, the dogs hauling the travois. The lake was not large, and the men, women, children, and dogs surrounded it, and made a great slaughter of birds, for they had called on the spiritual powers to aid them so that the birds should not fly away.

When they moved again, they sent two more runners ahead to see what they could find. These two went toward a high grassy table-land and climbed up on it. They reached it toward sunset, and, as they stood there, they saw the grass

* Journal of American Folklore, vol. 20, no. 78, July-Sept., 1907.

moving and found quantities of skunks all around, so they went back to the camp and told what they had seen. Next morning everybody started for the table-land. They all got around it early in the morning and killed great numbers of skunks; everybody was loaded down with them. The next day they again sent two men to the same place, and many more skunks were seen, so that on this day more were killed than the day before. They sent them again the next day, and when they had finished killing they could hardly carry away the meat. Again a fourth time the two men reported skunks there, and many were caught and killed.

The next day they camped near a little knoll, where a spring came out of the rock. This spring is called "Old Woman's Water" (*Mā' tā mā Hĕh'k ā ĭt*). They camped near this spring with the opening of the camp toward it.

In the morning two sets of hoops and sticks were taken to the center of the camp, and they rolled them there and gambled on the game. Two games were going on. They selected the head of the hunting party as one of the men to keep the count. While they were gambling, a man came from the right side of the camp to the center, where they were playing. He was naked except for his breechcloth, and was painted yellow all over and striped down with the fingers; on his breast was a small circle, in red, and on the back a half moon of the same color. His face under his eyes was painted black, and there was a red stripe around his wrists and ankles; he had a yellow down feather on his scalplock and wore his robe hair side out. He stood for a time and watched them playing. While he stood there, a man came from the left side of the camp, whose paint and dress were just the same as his. While they were rolling the wheel, the man who had come from the right said to the players, "My friends, stop for a moment." He walked toward the other and asked him to come toward him, so they met in the center of the camp and stopped a short distance apart. They stood facing each other, and the first one said to the other: "Why do you imitate me? This is spiritual paint." The second said, "Mine also is spiritual paint." The game had stopped and all the players were listening.

The first man said, "Who gave you your spiritual paint, and where did you get it?" The other replied, "Who gave you yours?" The first man pointed to the spring and said, "My paint came from there" (meaning that at the spring he was instructed to paint himself in that way). The other said, "Mine also came from the spring." Then the first man said, "Let us do something for the hunters, the old men, old women, young women, girls and boys." And the second said, "Yes, let us do so." By this time everyone in the camp was listening. So the first man said again, "Soldiers of all societies, every one of you shall feel happy this day," and the other said, "Yes, you shall all feel happy this very day." The first speaker walked toward the spring, and the other followed close behind him. When he came to the spring, he covered his head with his robe and plunged under the water into the opening out of which the spring came. His friend followed him closely and did the same thing. All the people in the camp saw them go in.

The first man came up under the spring, and there under the knoll sat a very old woman. As he stepped in, she said to him, "Come in, my grandchild." She took him in her arms; held him for a few minutes and made him sit down at her left side. As the other man came in, she said again, "Come in, my grandchild." She took him in her arms, held him for a minute, and set him on her right side. Then she said to them: "Why have you not come sooner? why have you gone hungry so long? now that you have come here, I must do something for your people." She had near her two old-fashioned earthen jars. She brought them out and set them down before her and also brought out two earthen dishes; one was filled with buffalo meat and one with corn. She said, "Come, my children; eat the meat first." They ate it very fast, for it was very good;

but when they had eaten all they could, the dish was still full; it was the same way with the corn. They could not empty the dishes; they were full when the men stopped. They were both satisfied, but the dishes did not show that they had been touched.

The old woman untied the feathers they had on their heads, and threw them in the fire. She painted each man with red paint; striped him, and repainted his wrists and ankles, and the sun and moon, yellow; then she stretched her hand out over the fire and brought out two down feathers painted red and tied them to their scalplocks. After that she pointed to her left and said, "Look that way." They looked and could see the earth covered with buffalo. The dust was flying up in clouds where the bulls were fighting. Then she said, "Look this way" (pointing partly behind her), and they saw wide cornfields. She said, "Look that way" (pointing to the right), and they saw the prairie covered with horses. The stallions were fighting and there was much movement. She said, "Look that way again," and they saw Indians fighting. They looked closely, and among the fighters recognized themselves, painted just as they were then. She said: "You shall always be victorious in your fights; you will have good fortune, and make many captives. When you go away from here, go to the center of your village; call for two big bowls and have them wiped out clean. Say to your people, women and children, and all the bands of the societies, 'We have come out to make you happy; we have brought out something wonderful to give you.' Tell your people that when the sun goes down I will send out buffalo." To each of the young men she gave some corn tied up in sacks and told them to divide this seed among the people. She told them to take some of the meat from the dish with one hand and some corn with the other, and sent them away. So they passed out of her lodge and came out of the water of the spring.

All the people of the village were sitting in a circle watching the spring. The two young men walked on together to the center of the village, where the one who had first appeared said: "Old men, old women, young men, young girls, I have brought out something that is wonderful. Soldiers, I have brought out something wonderful for you. When the sun goes down, the buffalo will come out." The other young man repeated these words. The first man stood ahead, and the other right behind him. The first man said, "I want two wooden bowls, but they must be clean." A young man ran to the right and another to the left to get the bowls. They set one down on each side of him, and with his right hand he put the meat in the right-hand bowl, and with his left hand he put the corn into the left-hand bowl. The bowls became half full. The other man did the same, and the bowls were filled.

The old woman had told them that the oldest men and women were to eat first. They all ate, first of the meat and then of the corn; then the young men, young women, and the children ate, but the pile in each dish remained nearly the same. After that the people in the camp ate all they could, and after all had eaten there was but little left. At the last came two orphans, a boy and a girl; they both ate, and when they had finished, the meat was all gone and also the corn. It was just as the young men had said, everyone was happy, for now they had plenty to eat.

As the sun went down, all the village began to look toward the spring. After a time, as they watched, they saw a four-year-old bull leap out. He ran a little distance and began to paw the ground, and then turned about and ran back and plunged into the spring. After he had gone back, a great herd of buffalo came pouring out of the spring and all night long they could hear them. No one went to sleep that night, for the buffalo made too much noise. Next morning at sunrise the earth, as far as they could see, was covered with buffalo. That day the medicine hunters went out and brought in all the meat they could eat.

The village camped there all winter and never lacked food. Toward spring they sent out two young men to look for moist ground to plant the seed in, for the old woman had told them that it must be planted in a damp place. They divided the corn seed; everyone got some, for there was enough for all. They made big caches in the earth to hold the meat they had dried, and then went to the place the young men had found and planted the seed. They made holes with sticks and put the seed in the ground. Sometimes when they were planting the corn they would go back to get their dried meat, for the buffalo had moved to another place. Once, when they returned with their dried meat, they found that some of the seed had been stolen, and they thought that it was the Pawnees or the Arickarees—and that this was the way these tribes got their corn.

It was Standing on the Ground who had brought the corn. He said: "I told you to watch this corn, but I can see that someone has been stealing it. That takes from you the power of raising corn. I am going away now, but will be back in four days. I will bring you something new that will give you the power again."

He went to the Old Woman's Water; went in and brought out the buffalo cap. They saw him coming to the center of the village, carrying something in his hands. Standing on the Ground said, "Now we will begin a new life again." He selected a young man of his own age, and put him in charge of the cap to take care of it, and said, "Put up a lodge for the cap." Then Standing on the Ground unwrapped the cap in the center of the camp, so that everybody, men, women, and children, could look at it. They first put down white sage, then four buffalo chips on the sage, and on the chips placed the cap. All the village stood in a circle around it.

After all had finished looking at it, he carried it over to the lodge he had had put up for it. When he entered, he asked for a buffalo rawhide and made a sack of it, and in this put the cap.

The Cheyennes declare that the sack they still have is the same that Standing on the Ground made.

Standing on the Ground began to teach the young man he had selected to take charge of the cap. He told him how to put it in the sack, and how to take it out. He told him that at times he must take the cap out, set it in the back of the lodge, and let the people see it, and that this would drive away disease and sickness of all kinds.

Standing on the Ground told him to teach the people that they must never have bad feelings against anybody; that they must never quarrel or do harm to anyone. He said: "There will be many who will own this cap; its owner will die, but it will never wear out. You must tell whoever you pass it over to that he must take great care of it, and never injure it in any way. If, in any manner, the cap is abused, or hurt, the buffalo will disappear, because the cap is the head chief of the buffalo."

SWEET MEDICINE AND THE ARROWS

THE accounts of the adventures of Sweet Medicine are longer than those related about Standing on the Ground. They have many forms. The one given here is lacking in detail, but the whole long story is told in another place.*

This woman was married. Her second child was called Sweet Medicine. When the boy was a baby he appeared to know what people were saying about him, and when he had grown to be five years old he seemed very smart. After he learned to talk he said, "Father, on your next hunt kill for me a yellow calf; and skin it, taking the whole skin, head and all; I want a robe to wear."

His father brought him in the whole skin of a calf and the boy was glad. He asked his mother to dress it, and he wore it

* *Journal of American Folklore*, vol. 22, Oct.-Dec., 1908, pp. 3-54.

with the hair side out. He wore it always until he outgrew it, and the next year he asked his father to kill for him a larger calf, a yearling, and to skin it in the same way. His mother dressed it with the head on. A few years later he asked his father to kill for him a two-year-old coal-black buffalo, for he wished a black robe. The boy had the power to make his father find the kind of robe he wished.

Some time after this, when Sweet Medicine was about seventeen years old, the people who had spiritual power were about to have a medicine dance, and when all had been made ready Sweet Medicine said, "Father, I am going to this dance, to dance, myself."

His father said to him: "Son, those who make these dances have power and must show what they can do. You are only a boy; you can do nothing." Sweet Medicine said, "I shall go anyway, and shall wear my new buffalo robe." He said also, "I shall carry your bow and its string shall be about my neck." His father said, "What are you going to do with a bowstring about your neck?" and the boy answered: "I am going to break my neck. I must have my buffalo robe painted red. I wish you to paint me just as I tell you."

His father painted him all over from head to foot with red paint, and Sweet Medicine took the bowstring and himself painted it red. His father asked him, "Son, what am I to do if you break your neck?" Sweet Medicine replied: "After I have pulled my head from my body, my head will fall to the ground, but my body will stand up. Then you must take my body and lay it down with my head toward where the sun rises; then put my head next to my body in its place, with the head toward where the sun rises; then cover me with my robe."

When his father took Sweet Medicine to the door of the lodge where the dance was to be held, a number of people were standing there looking on. The boy had an eagle feather in his hair. The people all called out, "Sweet Medicine is coming!"

When they had come to the door of the lodge, the father said to the spiritual men there, "My son wishes to dance." Some of the men inside called out, "Yes, come in!" and asked him on which side of the lodge he would sit. He chose the right-hand side.

After a little the sacred dance began. Sweet Medicine stood up on his feet, and danced the first dance. Some of the men with great power, who were looking on, said to one another, "Sweet Medicine is one of the greatest dancers that we have." They had a smoke and another dance. While Sweet Medicine was dancing, he kept time with his bowstring in both hands. Then they all sat down. At the third dance they all rose and began to dance. Sweet Medicine kept time with his bowstring around his neck; and the first thing they knew, his head fell to the ground. His eyes were open, and he was looking about at the people. His body was standing up, his bowstring still in his hands.

All the people outside, men and women, were frightened; and they called out to one another, "Sweet Medicine has broken his neck!" All those in the lodge sat down, and the dancing stopped.

Sweet Medicine's father took the boy's body and placed it on the ground, and put back the head in its place, lying toward where the sun rises, and covered him with his robe.

After a little time, Sweet Medicine raised the buffalo robe off his body, and stood up and faced the sunrise, and took his robe in both hands and shook it lightly four times toward the sunrise; and when he stopped, a light wind came from the north— a cool wind. The people said, "Sweet Medicine has called that wind from the north." Then Sweet Medicine went over and sat down on the right of the door, and rubbed his bowstring down four times. They all feasted.

Sweet Medicine always dressed in the same way. He wore a two-year-old buffalo robe. At that time the tribe seems to have been moving constantly, and Sweet Medicine seems to have had the power to keep them moving. Once a party of young men came in, and said that over where they had come from there were many buffalo. The camp moved over there; but when they got to the place, no buffalo could be found. Then the people began to say, "Sweet Medicine is doing this; he has the power to keep the buffalo away."

One day they had surrounded the buffalo, and this young man had killed a fat two-year-old bull, with a robe as black as charcoal. He skinned the bull, and left the head, legs, and even the hoofs, on the hide. After he had done this, he spread it out, hair side up, and stood with his friend, looking at it and thinking how pretty it was. While they were looking at it, a great chief came up to them. "Ha!" he said, "that is just the kind of a robe I have been looking for. It is just what I want. I will take it."

"No," said Sweet Medicine, "I need the robe, and that is why I killed him; but he is nice and fat, and you can have the meat."

"No," said the chief, "I want the robe."

"That is what I want," said the boy. "Many other buffalo have been killed. Go take a robe from one of those. I want this for my own use. But you can have the meat."

The chief grew angry, and said, "How dare you talk back to me!" He drew his knife and ran to the hide, and cut it into small pieces. Then the young man was angry; and he caught up the bone of the buffalo's hind leg, and struck the chief on the head, and killed him. Then he went back to the camp.

By the time he had reached his lodge, everyone knew that he had killed the chief. The soldiers were angry. They said: "We will kill him. We will beat him to death." His grandmother ran to the lodge where he was sitting, and said to him, "Run, run! the soldiers are coming." Sweet Medicine said to her: "Go away! You trouble me." The soldiers gathered about the lodge;

and when they entered to take him, he upset a pot of water that was standing on the fire, and rose out of the smoke-hole with the steam and ashes. The soldiers tore down the lodge, but could not find him; and while they were looking for him, one of them saw him sitting on a little hill not far from camp. They rushed over there to catch him; but when they had come to the hill, he was not there. Still they kept watching for him.

One day a man was out looking over the country, and near a great cut bluff he saw a little smoke; and looking down below, he saw Sweet Medicine among the thick bushes about the foot of the bluff, roasting meat over a little fire. When they learned of this, the soldiers went out and surrounded the place; and when they had done so, they ran into the bushes, calling out, "Rush on him and kill him!" A coyote ran out of the bushes by them; and they said, "Why, a coyote was in there too!" They looked everywhere for Sweet Medicine, but could not find him. They found his meat on a stick where it was roasting.

Another time he was found in a similar place. A man saw him and told of it. They surrounded the place and rushed in to seize him, and a magpie flew out and alighted on a hill, and made a great chattering; but Sweet Medicine was gone.

Again a man saw him in a canyon with high bluffs all about. Again he was roasting meat. They surrounded the place, and began to come together and to shout that they now had him. A crow flew out and alighted on the bank, but the young man was gone. They thought that he might have hidden himself among the thick overhanging willows, and searched for him; but he was not there.

A fourth time they found him in a similar place, and he looked up and smiled at them. They surrounded the place, and again began to shout and say, "Now we will beat him to death." When they rushed in, a blackbird flew out and lighted on the bluff, and looked down, chirping at the crowd. They could not find Sweet Medicine; and some said: "Look carefully among those matted vines and that thick grass. Perhaps he is there." They did not find him.

Again he was seen, and they surrounded the place with a double line; and when they rushed in, an owl flew out and alighted on the ground above, and watched them.

One day, after all this had happened, Sweet Medicine was seen standing close to the camp. He was finely dressed, with feathers in his head, a rattle in his hand, and wearing a long shoulder belt that looked as if it were ornamented with porcupine quills,—a dog rope. The soldiers ran to catch him and he ran away. While they could see him, he ran slowly, and they almost caught him; but when he passed over the hill, he ran very fast; and when they next saw him, he was a long way ahead. They could not catch him.

The next day he was seen again, dressed differently. He wore a bonnet of buffalo hide, and a belt strung with buffalo tails hanging down, and rattles on his moccasins, and carried in his hand a lance that he used as a cane. When he was first seen, he was walking about outside the circle. When they saw him, they called out, "There is Sweet Medicine!" and rushed toward him. He did as he had done before. While they could see him, he ran as if exhausted; but when hidden from sight, he ran fast. At last they became tired out, and left him.

The next day he came in a different dress. He wore a war-bonnet, and carried a crooked lance in his hand,—the dress of the *Hĭm' ō wē yŭh' kĭs.* All happened as before.

The fourth day he was painted black all over. He carried a lance like that now used in the Fox dance. All things happened as before.

On the fifth day he wore an owl headdress and bullhide moccasins, with the long beard of a bull attached to the heels and dragging behind, and carried a Contrary lance. The same things took place that had happened on previous days.

The next day he came differently dressed. His face was painted. He carried a pipe and tobacco sack, and was acting like a chief. He sat down on a hill, and they rushed on him. Before they reached him, he walked over the hill; and when they came in sight of him, he was on the next hill. They gave him up then, and decided that they would try a different plan to catch him.

One day they heard a great rumbling sound beyond a hill near the camp; and as they looked, they saw an animal come over the hill. As it drew nearer, it was a different animal from what they had thought at first; and then it changed to another animal; and at last it was Sweet Medicine, playing the wheel game, and running close to the camp, as if to tempt them to pursue him. The people were all afraid, and said to one another, "Do not trouble him." When he saw that they did not try to take him, he went back the way he had come, and disappeared over the hill; and the rumbling grew fainter as he moved away. They think that he came, intending to have destroyed the people if they had tried to take him.

One day they went to his brother and said to him: "Your brother may come back now; we will not harm him. He may come back; we will not hurt him. But when he comes back, you must take him out hunting, and kill a buffalo, and pile up the meat, and leave Sweet Medicine there to keep the flies off it, while you return to camp to get the dogs. Then we will all move off and leave him."

One night Sweet Medicine decided to go to his home, and he went to his brother's lodge and entered. His brother said to him: "Is that you, brother? Come in and sit down." He said to his wife, "Give him food." She did so, and Sweet Medicine ate. A number of men had seen him come in, and went to the lodge and told him that no one would harm him. After he had eaten, he went to bed.

The next morning his brother asked him to go hunting. They started and while they were gone the camp moved. The brother killed a buffalo, cut up the meat nicely and heaped it together in a pile, and told Sweet Medicine to walk about the meat and keep the flies off while he went home for the dogs, so they could pack in the meat. The brother went to where the camp had been, and followed it. Sweet Medicine stayed by the meat, keeping the flies away; and at night he lay down by the pile and slept.

The tribe moved and moved; but they could find no game, and came near starving. They could get no food, but were obliged to eat whatever they could,—roots, and the bark of trees, even mushrooms. It was a hard time. Everyone was hungry. After they had been gone for one winter, they thought they would move back to the place that they had come from. They thought that perhaps there they might find some buffalo, at least some old bulls. When they had come to the place, Sweet Medicine's brother went out to see if he could find him. He was still walking about the pile of white bones where the meat had been, and about them he had worn a trail so deep that only the top of his head could be seen. His brother felt very sorry, and cried and mourned for Sweet Medicine, but Sweet Medicine did not speak to him.

The brother went back to the village and told the people that his brother was yet alive, but would not speak to him. The next day others of Sweet Medicine's relations went out to see him, but they did not find him; he was gone.

Now, when Sweet Medicine went away, he went to some great place where he got his power, and remained for four years. The buffalo and all the animals disappeared, and the people continued to starve. All that they had to live on were such things as they could gather from the ground,—roots, berries, grass,—anything that they could pick up. As time went on, they grew more and more hungry; and at last all were becoming so weak that they could hardly travel,—the people mere skin and bone; and children helpless from starvation, and unable to walk.

One day, as the camp was moving along, seven little boys—two of them small, and the others larger—were traveling along off to one side of the camp. They were all hungry. As they went along they found some large white mushrooms, and they began to pull and eat them. While they were sitting there, eating the mushrooms, a man walked up to them; and they looked around, and suddenly saw him standing close to them. He was tall and good-looking, and had long hair, hanging loose way down his back.

He looked at the little boys and said to them: "Why, little boys, you seem to be very hungry. Are you starving?" The little boys answered, "Yes, it is a long time since we have had any meat, anything real to eat."

"Ah," he said, "poor little boys! you are starving. Those things that you have are not fit to eat. Throw them away; we shall find plenty of food."

The boys did not like to throw away these things, which were all they had to eat, but again he told them to do so, and they threw them away.

Buffalo chips were lying all about where formerly buffalo had been; and the young man said to the boys, "You little boys go off now, and let each one find a buffalo chip and bring it to me." While they were gone he took a stick in his hand and broke it in two, and put it on the ground, and immediately it began to burn—he had a fire. The boys soon brought him seven chips. He spread his robe on the ground, and placed the chips brought him by the five large boys on the robe in a square, with one in the middle. The two brought by the two smallest boys he placed, one to the east, and one to the west, of the corners of the square. The four chips at the corners of the square represented the four cardinal points, and the middle one the sun. The two to the east and the west represented, one the rising sun, and one the setting sun.

Then he folded the four corners of his robe over, so that the chips were in a bunch in the middle of the robe, and covered, and with his hand he broke up the chips and crumbled them to powder. He unfolded and opened out his robe, and there lying in it was pounded meat and fat.

Then he said: "Now, you little boys come up here and eat. Eat as much as you want." They ate all they wanted, until all were satisfied. After they had finished, he said to them, "Now grease yourselves all over with fat,—grease your faces, your hands, and your whole bodies. You look all dried up, as if you had been out in the sun. If you cannot eat all this food, take what is left back to the camp with you. Now, do you seven boys go to your camp, and tell the people to put up their lodges in a circle, and to leave an opening in the circle toward the rising sun. In the middle of this circle they must pitch a big lodge; and if they have no big one, tell them to take two or three lodges and make a large one from them. Tell them to have all the head men come together in that lodge; and if they have anything in the camp to smoke, let them have the pipe there, filled. Say to them that I am he who has come back to them."

The boys went into the camp, tired and full, and went to sleep without telling the people what Sweet Medicine had said. In the morning the smallest of the boys remembered, and said, "O father, Sweet Medicine has come back, and gave us plenty to eat yesterday"; and then he gave the message. His father did not quite believe him, and sent a messenger to ask the older boys if this was true. They said: "Yes, that is true. We forgot to tell it."

The people sent for the chiefs, and told them what the little boys had said; and the chiefs went over to the lodge of Sweet Medicine's brother, to ask if he had heard of Sweet Medicine, who had sent good news to the camp. The brother said, "No, I have not seen him." At the head of the brother's bed, covered up with robes, a man was lying who had come in during the night. "Who is that person?" the chief asked. "I do not know," said the brother. "He came in during the night." They awoke the man; and when he sat up and took the robe from his head, it was Sweet Medicine. The chiefs asked him about the message that he had sent in; and he said: "Yes, that is what I told the little boys. Now, put up a big double lodge, and level the ground off nicely inside; and when it is ready, send for me. Let the lodge face the rising sun." They did this, and he entered the lodge.

When he went to it, all the people were mourning and crying, asking him to take pity on them, and help them to food. After he had gone in and sat down, he said, "Go and get an old buffalo skull, and put it in the opening in the circle." They did so, and he began to sing; and as he sang, the head began to move toward them; and when it got pretty close to them, it grunted. After it had grunted, he told some of the men to bring it in, and have it put at the back of the lodge, near the fire.

To those sitting there he said: "I have been gone four years. I know that you people are hungry, and are starving because there are no buffalo. I want you all to stay in this lodge for four days and four nights. I shall sing for four days and four nights. After I have sung two days and two nights, on the third night you will hear buffalo coming. On the third morning there will be buffalo in sight, a few to be seen here and there. The fourth night they will come closer; and on the fourth day, in the morning, they will come into the camp, and be all around this lodge."

It happened as he had said. He sang; and on the third night, while he was singing, singing, singing, they began to hear noises all about the camp,—the blowing and grunting of buffalo. Early in the morning of the fourth day the buffalo were all through the camp and about this lodge. He said to the people, "Now go out and kill food for yourselves, as much as you need. I will sit here and sing, and the buffalo will not run away. You can kill all you want here in the camp." They did as he had said, and killed many buffalo. After he saw that they had enough, he called to them to stop, saying that they had enough; and those buffalo that were alive all walked out through the gap in the circle.

After Sweet Medicine had come back to the camp, the people lived better and had more to eat. When he told them the whole story of where he had been and what he had done, the chief of the tribe gave him his daughter, a very pretty girl, for his wife; but they were not yet married. The people fixed up a dog with a travois, and he and the girl started back for the great place. When he went back to this place,—a big lodge within a hill,— he entered; and the people in the lodge said: "Ah! here is our grandson come back again. Come in, and sit down at the back of the lodge."

The people who were in this lodge were all the things and beings that belong to this earth. There were persons and buffalo and antelope; all animals and birds, rocks, trees, bushes, and grass; all things that grow or exist upon the earth.

When Sweet Medicine entered the lodge, a number of people were sitting there, of whom four seemed to be principal men. And besides, at the right of the door as he went in, sat a black man; at the left of the door, a brown man, very handsome; at the back of the lodge, to the left, was a white, good-looking man; to the right, at the back of the lodge, was a brown, well-built man. All these men were handsomer than any he had ever seen.

After Sweet Medicine had been in the lodge for some time, the chief person there spoke to him, saying, "Now choose one of these four men to be yourself" (that is to say, choose the one you would like to resemble). Sweet Medicine looked about and thought. When he had entered the lodge, the man at the left of the door had caught his eye, and he had liked him; but still, before choosing, he looked about at all the others. All were handsome; all were men that he would have been glad to resemble. The chief person seemed to be making signs to him with his lips that he should choose a particular man. But at last Sweet Medicine pointed to the man at the left of the door, and said, "I will be like that one."

There was a moment's pause, and then all who were sitting in the lodge gave a low groan saying, "*Ē hē hēh'!*" showing that they were sorry for him,—that he had made a mistake. When they said this, he looked around quickly, and saw that the handsome white man was not there; but a great white, smooth stone stood in his place. He looked for the next man, and he was gone; but where he had sat, a tall slender weed-stalk was growing. The black man had changed to a smooth black stone, while the man whom he had chosen was a nice pretty weed as high as a man's knee, with green leaves and pretty flowers on it.

The chief person pointed to one of the stones and said: "You ought to have chosen that one. Then you would have lived to old age; and after you had grown old, you would have become young again always. You would not have died. That man there is a mere fish-bladder. If you had chosen either of those persons," pointing to the stones, "you would have lived forever."

The chief spirit had placed these stones so that they might be the first things Sweet Medicine would see, hoping that he would choose one of them and live forever.

When Sweet Medicine made his choice, one of the people sitting in the lodge said, "That man is a fool," and rose and went out. The chief person said, "Follow him; he has great power." Sweet Medicine and another went out, and followed the man for a long, long time. It seemed as if they went all over the world, and at last they came back to the same place.

Then they gave Sweet Medicine advice, and gave him the medicine arrows, and told him that he should take them back to the tribe.

Then said the chief person: "Take these arrows with you, and guard them carefully. They will be a great help to you for a long time; but you will keep them until they will cease to be a help, and will be of no more use to you." With the arrows was given him a coyote's skin to wrap the arrows in. The arrows were feathered with eagle feathers, and he brought them out, wrapped in the coyote's skin. The feather that he wore in his head was from the eagle that had given the feathers for the arrows.

After they had left the sacred place, the girl carried the arrows on her back, and they led the dog. As they drew near the camp, they met some people out hunting; and he sent them back to the camp to tell the people there to camp in a large circle, and to put up his lodge in the center. He waited until he thought the camp was all arranged, and then went into it. The people in the village supposed that those who brought the word were mistaken about its being Sweet Medicine, but they said they were sure. When they reached the camp, all was arranged as he had ordered. He went to the lodge, and hung the arrows in front of it, over the door.

In the morning he unrolled his bundle, and took from it the four arrows. He said to them: "Here are four arrows for you to keep. Make your arrows to kill the buffalo like these." Afterward he hung the bundle of arrows on the door of his brother's lodge. Then he moved about and lived with them, and himself made arrows. He and his brother lived with the people for a long time, and taught them how to live, how to tan skins, to make clothing, and to dress robes. He taught them to take the leg bone of the deer or antelope, and cut it off, and make a pipe of it; and he gathered a certain weed, and told them to dry it, and to smoke it in their pipes.

THE CEREMONIAL FIRE.

He lived with these people for four or five generations of people,—four long, long lives. Young people would grow up, get old, and die; other young people would be born, grow up, get old, and die; but still this man lived. All through the summer he was young, like a young man; and when fall came, and the grass began to dry up, he began to look older; and about the middle of the winter he was like a very old man, and walked bent over and crooked. In spring he became young again. At last he died.

At last Sweet Medicine said to the people: "I shall not be with you long now. I chose the wrong person; I wanted to be too good-looking. Now I am getting to be old, and have lived as long as I want to; but before I die I have something to tell you. Now, my people, you must not forget what I am telling you this day, and all I have told you and taught you. After I am dead, you must come together often, and talk over these things; and when you do so always call my name. A time is coming when you will meet other people, and you will fight with them, and will kill each other. Each tribe will want the land of each other tribe, and you will be fighting always."

He pointed to the south, and said: "Far away in that direction is another kind of buffalo, with long hair hanging down its neck, and a tail that drags on the ground, an animal with a round hoof, not split like a buffalo's, and with teeth in the upper part of its mouth, as well as below. This animal you shall ride on.

"The buffalo will disappear; and when the buffalo have gone, the next animal you will have to eat will be spotted. When you get toward the end, you people will begin to become gray very young, and will come to marry even your relations. You may reach a point where you will be ashamed of nothing, and will act as if you were crazy.

"Soon you will find among you a people who have hair all over their faces, and whose skin is white; and when that time comes, you will be controlled by them. The white people will be all over the land, and at last you will disappear."

Sweet Medicine died in the summer, when he was a young man. His brother also had lived with the people for a long time. He did not grow old and then young again. He continued to be a middle-aged man for many generations. At last he too died, having lived longer than Sweet Medicine.

WIHIO STORIES

Tales of Wihio

THE Wihio stories of the Cheyennes belong to the widely spread series of Indian tales which deal with the acts and adventures of the trickster, variously known as Nana bosho, Napi, Coyote, and by other names. He possesses supernatural power and is on terms of friendship with the birds and the animals, and in him malice and simplicity are curiously combined. He is always more or less in difficulties.

The Cheyenne term Wihio is used to designate a white man, and has besides the meaning "spider." The individual bearing the name occasionally appears in stories of a more serious character, and is sometimes appealed to for help and may give it. More often, however, he fills the rôle of mischief-maker or villain. Often he seems to possess intelligence greater than that of most of the Indians, as the etymology of his name might seem to suggest.

Most of the stories told about the Blackfoot Napi are recognized by the Cheyennes as being substantially their own stories about Wihio.

HE LOSES HIS HAIR

ONE day Wihio was walking about, when he saw two young women sitting on the ground. He went up to them, saying to himself, "Here are my nieces." He had never seen them before and did not know who they were. Then he said to them: "My nieces, I am glad to see you. I have lice in my hair; I want you both to pick the lice out of my head." He lay down on the ground and one got on each side of him, looking for the lice.

While they were doing this he fell asleep, and when he was asleep the two girls got cockle burrs, as many as they could find, and stuck them all through his hair; then they both left him and went away. After a time Wihio awoke and found his head completely covered with the burrs. He tried to touch his hair, but he kept pricking his fingers.

After feeling his head he started off to go back to his lodge. As he was going along he saw a mouse running in the grass. Wihio said: "Stop, my nephew; I want to see you a minute." The mouse came to him and said, "What is it you want?" Wihio replied, "My head is full of cockle burrs and I want you to gnaw off all my hair." He lay down on the ground and the mouse gnawed his hair all off, leaving his head quite bare. When Wihio got up he saw his hair lying in a bunch before him, full of burrs. He said, "That is good, I feel better now."

He walked on to his lodge, and when his wife came out and saw that he had no hair she said to him, "What have you been doing?" and struck him on the back. Wihio said: "Wait; do not strike me; I have heard a very bad story. Come here, my children," and he embraced them. "I heard you were all dead, so I had my hair cut off. It very nearly killed me when I heard you were all dead."

PLUMS IN THE WATER

AS Wihio was walking along the river bank he looked down into the water and saw there many plums. He said, "Good; there are many plums down there, and I can get all I want to eat." He took off his leggings, jumped into the water, and felt around for the plums as long as he could hold his breath, for the water was deep, but he could feel nothing. He got up on the bank and again looked into the water and saw the plums, and said, "I must have dived in the wrong place."

He dived in again and felt about for the plums, but still could not reach them and came up again.

Then he got a large stone and tied it around his neck so that he could stay longer under water, and again jumped in. That time he was nearly drowned, but at last he managed to get free from the stone and to crawl out.

He lay down on his back on the bank to get his breath and rest, and as he looked up he saw above him the plum bush full of fruit. What he had seen in the water was the reflection of the plums.

A MEDICINE MAN'S ARROWS

A MAN who possessed great power was traveling down the creek by himself. As he came to each big tree, he stopped and looked at it. If it was straight and had not many limbs, he would kick it and knock it over. He only had to kick the tree once. He knocked down all the best trees he came to.

Wihio came to meet him and said, "Why are you knocking down all the best trees, my brother?" The man did not answer him, but went along kicking down the trees. Wihio caught hold of him, saying, "You must stop this."

The man said, "I am getting my arrow sticks; soon I am going out on the warpath and I need good, straight arrows." Wihio said: "You cannot use these big trees for arrows. Stop knocking them down." The medicine man said: "Do not bother me. I told you I was getting my arrow sticks." Wihio said, "If those are your arrow sticks, shoot at me with one of them."

The medicine man said, "Go over yonder and stand." Wihio walked over a little way and stopped, but the medicine man motioned him to go on farther. Wihio stopped four times and each time was told to go farther, till he reached the top of a big hill. The man picked up one of the trees, turned the root end toward Wihio and threw it; he did not use a bow. It flew toward Wihio, and as it came the leaves made a noise like the wind.

He saw it coming, for it came slowly, and he tried to dodge it, first one side and then the other, but the tree followed him. He came to a hole and tried to creep in, but the hole was too small and he could only put in his head. The tree struck him and carried away his body, leaving his head sticking in the hole. The man walked up to where the head lay; the body was some distance away.

Wihio's head said, "Take pity on me and put me back on my body again." The man replied, "I will cure you; I only wanted to show you I could shoot with the trees," so he put the head on the shoulders of Wihio's body and he was cured.

"You are a good shot," said Wihio.

THE WOMAN'S CAMP

WIHIO was traveling up the river when he came to a big camp. All the people were outside, and when he walked up to them he saw they were all women; there was not one man among them. When they saw him, they all ran toward him and began calling out, "Come with me; come to my lodge," and some caught hold of him, but he said, "No; I own another [I see another woman that I like better]," for behind him he saw a very handsome woman. Wihio said to the others, "Keep quiet now; this one first picked me out for her husband." The others let him go, so he walked up to this one and she took him to her lodge; there was only one trail by which to reach it, for the timber was growing close all around it. There were many big plum bushes there. The lodge was painted with stripes all around it and when he went in he saw on each side a nice bed, with white buffalo skins hanging over the head and backrests.

The lodge lining was decorated with porcupine quills. He married this woman.

One day he told his wife he was going on a trip up the river. When he had gone a long distance, he came to another camp, but here, instead of women, all the people were men. Wihio said to them: "Come here, my friends; come around me. I have something to tell you." The men all crowded around him and he said, "Farther down the river I have found a camp in which there are only women; that will be a very good thing for all of us." The men said to one another, "That is good; take us there." Others said, "Let us go with him." They got around him and said, "Wait; you may go off and leave us, for you are a swift runner."

The news was so good they were afraid he would get away before he had showed them the village. So they tied rocks to his feet and put a robe on him and filled it with stones. After they had loaded him with stones, they said, "Where is the camp?" And when he told them, they all started to run there. Wihio's burden of stones was so heavy that he could hardly walk, so he followed behind slowly. He called to them, asking them to come back and wait for him, and when they did not stop he told them to look out for his lodge and said it was painted in stripes and that his wife was a handsome woman; they must not go there. They all answered, "Oh, no, we will not go there."

The Indians all ran to the camp and picked out the best-looking women for their wives; and one of them chose Wihio's wife for his wife. When Wihio arrived he walked up to his lodge, saying to himself, "I think everything is right, in here," but he found a man in the lodge sitting beside his wife. This man said, "I have taken your wife; you will have to go out and get another; be quick now before they are all gone." So Wihio had to go out and stand in the middle of the camp with the rocks still tied all around him. He hunted all over and finally found a little old lodge off to one side. He went in and found a very old woman sitting there. She said, "Come in, my son-in-law." Wihio said, "I am not your son-in-law," but she still said he was, though he said again that he was not. He walked up to her and sat down beside her and said, "I want to marry you; I want you for my wife." So she agreed and he married her. She was the oldest woman in the camp.

WIHIO AND COYOTE

THERE was a stream running through a level country, and Wihio was traveling along its banks. He seemed to have come a long way, for he looked tired. On his back he was carrying a sack.

At length he came to a prairie dog town. The dogs were all standing up about the holes or feeding near them.

One of the dogs called across to Wihio, "Friend, where are you going?"

The man answered, "I am going into the upper country to sing for some people."

"What have you in your pack?" asked the dog.

Wihio said, "I am carrying my songs in this pack."

One of the dogs called out, "Come over here and sing for us."

"No," replied Wihio, "I am in a hurry, you will keep me. I have a long way to go before night."

The dog said to him, "Oh, come on, sing for us."

"Well," answered the man, "I will sing for you a little while, so that you can dance."

Wihio told them all to stand around in a circle. Then he picked out certain ones and put them side by side to dance together. These that he had chosen were all the fattest ones.

He said to the dogs: "Now, while you are dancing you must all keep your eyes shut. Do not open them; do not look."

Then he began to sing, and they to dance. He took off his bundle and unwrapped it, and took from it a club, and as the dogs danced around before him, he knocked the fattest ones on the head, one at a time. One dog was left, still dancing; he was afraid to open his eyes. But as he heard no footsteps of others dancing, he stretched out his paws, and he could feel no one else; and at last he opened his eyes, and saw that all the others were dead. He called out, "Oh, he has killed us all!" and ran away to his hole.

Wihio took the dogs to the stream, and kindled a fire and singed them and roasted them, and had a great feast there. When he had eaten them all, he took up his bundle and started on up the stream.

He followed up the creek, going around the bends, and across sandbars, and at length he came to a place where many ducks were swimming about. He pretended not to see them, and when he had passed them, one of the ducks said to his fellows, "There goes Wihio," and called to him.

Wihio stopped and looked around, and one of the ducks said, "What is it that you are carrying on your back?"

The man answered, "These are my songs." One of the ducks asked him if he would not stop and sing for them.

"No," said Wihio, "I have a long way to go. I have to go and sing for some other people."

"Oh," said the duck, "just sing us a song or two; it won't take you long."

Then he turned back to them and said: "Well, I will sing for you. Come out here where it is level, and you can dance."

The ducks were all glad that he was going to sing, and came out to the level place, at a little distance from the water. Wihio said, "Now, you must all stand in a circle."

He took his bundle from his back and began to open it, and said: "You must all dance here with your eyes shut. If you open them you will have bad eyes; they will be red." Then he sang, and the ducks began to dance, and as they danced by him he tapped one on the head with his club, and pulled it out of the circle, and then another and another. Every little while he would call out to them, "Dance hard, now!"

The little grebe was anxious to see what was going on, and pretty soon he opened his eyes just a little way, and saw what Wihio was doing. He called out, "Oh, he is killing us all!" Then he and all the other ducks ran away to the creek and into the water, and disappeared. Wihio said to himself, "I will teach them to want songs and to dance; I will eat them."

He gathered up the ducks, and took them to a place where there was a good shade, and got them ready for cooking. After they were cleaned, he stuck them up on green sticks about the fire to roast, and one very fat one he put in the ashes to roast, saying, "I will eat that one last."

A long way off there was a coyote, who must have smelled the cooking, and perhaps caused a little wind to blow; just enough to move the trees. Two branches of the two trees Wihio was sitting under were crossed, and as the wind blew they rubbed together and made a screeching noise.

Wihio called out to the trees: "What are you quarreling about? Why don't you stop it?" The noise continued, and Wihio spoke to the trees two or three times; and at last he got up to stop it.

He climbed one of the trees, and went up the crossing branches and again said: "Why do you trees quarrel? Stop it." He put his hand between the two branches and tried to push them apart; but they closed on his hand and he found he could not pull it away. As he sat there, a prisoner, he saw a coyote come over the hill, looking about and smelling.

Wihio said to the trees: "Let me go now; there comes a coyote. He will eat my food." But the trees did not answer or move.

When the coyote got closer, Wihio called out to him: "Do not come smelling about here. I will not give you anything to eat."

The coyote got still closer, and Wihio said to the trees again: "Let me go! Let me get down! He will eat my food, I tell you." The trees still held him.

The coyote came still closer to the fire, and Wihio called out to him again: "Go away, Little Face! I will not give you anything."

When the coyote heard this he came on faster, and when he got to the fire he ate up all the food that was there. Wihio kept pulling and working hard to get his hand loose, but he could not free it. Before the coyote had eaten all the food, Wihio called out to him, "Do not eat all; you have had plenty."

The duck that was roasting in the ashes Wihio had stuffed with meat, cut up fine, and he thought that it would be very good. He called out to the coyote, "You have eaten all the rest, do not eat the one I have in the ashes." When the coyote heard this he took the duck out of the ashes, ate all the meat that it was stuffed with, filled it full of dry ashes, and put it back where it had been. Then he went away.

At last Wihio managed to get his hand free, for now the trees let him go. He climbed down and went to the fire, and saw that all his food was gone. But he said to himself, "That rascal missed the best piece"; and he dug down in the ashes for the duck that was covered up. He took a big bite out of it, and then he began to spit, for he found that he had a mouthful of ashes. He said of the coyote: "He has treated me badly. If ever I find him, I will kill him."

He determined to punish the coyote, and to catch him he followed his tracks. At length he came up with him, and found him asleep on the sunny side of a hill, for the coyote was full, and went to sleep as soon as he lay down. Wihio walked up to the coyote and stood looking at him, and said: "There lies the sharp-nosed thing. I will kill and eat him. Now, how shall I kill him? If I hit him in the ribs it will bruise and spoil the meat. If I hit him on the head, it will spoil that. If I scare him to death, it will not be good either." So he considered.

Now all the time he was talking to himself the coyote was awake, and lying with his eyes partly open, watching him. While Wihio was trying to think how to kill him, the coyote suddenly jumped to his feet and ran off. Wihio said, "You got away from me that time, but next time I catch you I shall kill you."

Again he started on the coyote's trail, and followed him; and at last came up with him and found him asleep under a pile of drift wood. When he found him he called him all kinds of bad names, and then he began to try to decide in what way he should kill him. He kept saying: "I wonder how I can kill him without bruising him. If I were to throw him in the creek and drown him, that would spoil him. I will make a big fire and throw him into it and burn him to death. He will roast at the same time, and then I can eat him."

By this time the coyote had awakened, but he did not move. He lay there as if sound asleep. Wihio took some of the drift wood and built a big fire, and stooped down to take the coyote up by all four legs. He said, "If I throw him in the fire hard, it will bruise him; I will lay him in it gently." He walked up to the fire and held the coyote over it, to lay him down on it, but just as he was placing him there, the coyote gave a spring and jumped out of his hands on the other side of the fire. He jumped into the river and swam across it, and climbed up on the other bank, looking back at Wihio. Wihio saw him no more.

WHERE THE MICE DANCED

ONE day the little mice were having a dance. They were dancing in an elk skull. Wihio came walking along over the prairie, and heard the singing, but could not tell from whence it came. He listened, and for a long time looked everywhere to find the singers. At last he found the place.

When he found the skull where they were dancing, he got down on his knees and looked into it. He said to the mice, "Oh, my little brothers, let me come in; I want to dance too."

"No," said the mice, "you must stay outside. You cannot come in. There is not room for you here."

Wihio kept begging them to let him come in, but they would not consent. Then he made up his mind that he would go in anyhow. It looked nice in there. A white lodge was standing there, food was being cooked, and preparations were being made for a great feast.

Wihio made himself small, so as to go in the hole at the back of the elk's skull. The hole was small, but at last, by twisting and turning, Wihio got his head in. When he did this, the mice all became frightened, and scampered out of the skull and ran away.

When Wihio saw that no one was left in the skull, he tried to get his head out of the hole, but he could not. His head was stuck fast. For a long time he tried to free himself, but he could not get the skull off his head, and at last he started to go home. He could not see where he was going, and for a long time he wandered about on the prairie, stumbling over stones and buffalo bones, and falling down into ravines, all the time crying.

At last he reached the river, and followed it down toward his camp. His children were in swimming near the camp, and when they saw him they did not know what it was they saw and were frightened, and ran home crying. His wife came out of the lodge to see what had scared the children. She saw a person coming with an elk's skull for a head, and she did not know what to think of it. When she heard the person talking she knew her husband's voice. Then she was angry, and got an axe and tried to break the elk skull. While she was trying to break the skull off, she more than once knocked Wihio down; but at last she set him free.

THE BACK SCRAPER

A LONG time ago a man was seen down close by the water, standing on his hands and knees, while a woman was scraping his back with a flesher. When she got through, and the man stood up on his feet, there was a big pile of scrapings —chips shaved off as from a buffalo's hide—and they cooked and ate these.

Wihio came down the stream, and when he saw what was going on, he began to cry, saying, "I wish I could do as my friend does."

The man said to him: "Do not cry, friend; you may do as I do. Whenever you get very hungry, and your children are hungry, you may do this, but do not repeat it more than four times."

Wihio went on his way, and when he reached home he told his wife what he had seen, and got down on all fours and told her to scrape his back.

She was afraid, and said to him: "What are you going to do? Do you not know that this will hurt you?" But he said, "Go ahead and do as I tell you." So she scraped his back, and cut off a quantity of scrapings, as if from a buffalo hide, and they cooked and ate them.

A short time afterward, Wihio's children again were hungry,

and again he got down on all fours and had his back scraped. The children were glad when they saw him do it; they knew that they were now to get something to eat.

Now Wihio forgot that he had done this before, and this time, when he got up, he said, "Now I have done this once." The third time it was done, he said, "This is twice." The fourth time he said, "This is three times."

Then one day he said, "Now I can do this once more"—but it was really the fifth time—and when his wife began to scrape his back, she scraped the skin off, and it hurt; and Wihio began to shout with pain and dodged away.

After this Wihio went back to the man he had seen, and complained that the fourth time he had been hurt. But the man said, "You did this too often, and have made a fool of yourself." He passed his hand over Wihio's back and healed the wounds, so that they no longer hurt.

After he had healed him, the man spoke to his wife and said, "Let me have your dress." The woman took off her dress and handed it to him, and the man took it and cut some pieces from it, and threw them in the kettle with the rest of the dress; and after they had cooked for a while, presently he took them out, for they were pieces of fine back-fat.

Then Wihio began to cry, saying, "I wish I could do what my brother can."

The man said: "Do not cry, brother, you can do this; but you must not do it more than four times. Also, while the food is boiling, you must stir the kettle four times." Then Wihio went home glad.

After he had reached home, he said to his wife: "Now to-day I have learned something. We will no longer be hungry. Let me have your dress."

The woman said to him: "Ah, you have been off somewhere and you have learned something. This time you had better be careful." Nevertheless, she gave him the dress, and he began to cut it up. Then the woman scolded, crying out, "Here, what are you doing with my dress?"

"Wait," said Wihio, "you shall see." He put the pieces in the kettle, and when it was boiled he took out pieces of fine backfat. The children began to jump up and down, and to dance and clap their hands. With the meat in the pot was the dress, as good as ever.

After this, Wihio did this again, and again got food, but he made a mistake in his counting, so that when he had done this the third time, he counted it as twice, and the fourth time as three times.

Now Wihio was about to do this once more, the last time,— as he thought,—and he asked the man to come and eat with him. He put the dress in the pot, stirred it four times, and then began to look for meat in the pot. But there was none there, only the skin dress boiled and all shrunk up to a ball.

The invited man said to Wihio: "You do not do things as I tell you. You always make mistakes." He stirred the kettle four times, took out meat, and they ate. Now the man rose to go, and said to Wihio: "I cannot teach you anything more; you do not do things right. It is useless to teach you." Then he went away.

THE LOST EYES

ONE day as Wihio was going along he saw a man lying on his back on the prairie. As Wihio watched, the man said something, and immediately his eyes flew out of his head, and into the air, and hung in the air far above him. Then the man spoke again, and his eyes flew back into his head. Wihio watched the man for a little while, and then he went up to him, crying, and said to him, "Oh, my brother, I want to do that!"

"Very well," said the man, "I will teach you how to do it; but if I tell you, you must only do it four times. If you do it the fifth time, something bad will happen to you." Then the man explained to Wihio how to do this strange thing, and afterward he went on his way.

Now Wihio was glad, and he thought that he would try at once and see if he could really do it. He tried, and his eyes flew out of his head, and then he spoke again and they came back. Then Wihio started on his way. He had not gone far before he wished to try to do the trick again, and he lay down and sent his eyes up into the air, and then called them back. It made him proud to feel that he could do so strange a thing, and he did it over and over again. The second time that he did it he forgot that he had done it once before, and said to himself, "This is once"; but when he called to his eyes to come back the fifth time, they did not come, and then he knew that he had made a mistake. He crept all over the prairie, feeling for his eyes, but could not find them. At last, weary and in pain, he lay down to rest. While he was lying there, a mouse from the grass ran over his chest. He put up his hand and caught it, and said, "O Mouse! I have lost my eyes; lend me yours, so that I may see where to go." The mouse said, "Brother, I cannot lend you both mine, for then I could see nothing, but I will lend you one of them." So Wihio took one of the mouse's eyes, and put it in his own socket. It was so small he could see only a little, but it was better than no eye at all. Wihio went on very slowly, for he could hardly see. At last he met with a buffalo bull, and said to him, "Little brother, I am almost blind; lend me one of your eyes, so that I may see where to go." The bull lent him one, and he went on his way. In one of his eye-sockets was the big bull's eye, and in the other the little mouse's eye.

HE CATCHES FISH

ONCE there was a man who wished to go fishing, but he had no fishing line and no bait. So he cut a strip of his skin from each side of his body, beginning at his feet and running up his leg and side, and the side of his face, until the strips almost met on his forehead, just over his nose. He threw the strips of skin down into the water, and bent down his head and waited. After a little while he felt something pulling at the strips of skin, and jerked his head back and tightened the strips, and they flew out of the water and threw the fish that had been biting at them out onto the bank. Thus he caught many fish—a big pile. He kept on down the river, fishing wherever the water looked right for it.

After a time, Wihio came along, and when he saw the man catching fish, he began to cry, and say, "O my friend, I want that power."

For a little while the man did not answer him, but at last he said, "Very well, I will give you this power; but you must not do this more than four times at each bend of the creek." The man took out his knife and said to Wihio, "Lie down." Wihio did so, and he began to cut the strips from his skin. "O friend," said Wihio, "that tickles, that hurts"; but he lay still until the man had cut the strips on both sides up to his forehead, and left them hanging. Then Wihio got up. "Now," said the man, "I have told you that you must not do this more than four times at each bend of the river." Then the man went on his way, carrying his load of fish.

Wihio was longing to try this, to see whether he could catch fish. He went down below where his friend had been, and began to fish, and when the fish took hold of the strips of skin, he threw his head back and threw the fish out, until he had a big pile. He was glad, and said, "Ah, this is the way I am going to support my wife and children." He put the fish in a sack, and started on down the river. He had gone only a little way when he began to fish again, and again caught a great many, and then went on. He said to himself, "That is once that I have done this"; he did not remember the first trial. He went a little farther, and again caught many fish. Then again he was pleased, and said, "This is good; this is twice." His sack was now nearly full.

Again he tried it, and caught many. "That is three times," he said; but really it was four times.

The next time he began to fish, something caught hold of the strips of skin, and when he threw back his head, he could not pull this thing out of the water. Instead, it began to pull him in. He caught hold of the grass and weeds and brush, to hold himself, but they all pulled up. Finally, this great fish dragged him into the water and swallowed him. Now Wihio was so large that when the fish swallowed him it choked and died, and then floated down the stream.

Wihio's camp was down the stream from where he had been fishing, and his wife and his children were there. Early the next morning his wife went down to the stream for water, and there lying on a sandbar she saw a great big fish. The woman dropped her bucket and ran back to the camp, and called out: "Oh, children, down on the sandbar is the biggest fish I ever saw! Hurry and come down!" She ran and got her knife, and they all went down to the fish. They dragged it out on the sandbar, and the woman began to cut it up.

Wihio had heard her talking, and recognized her voice, and called out: "Hold on, my wife! Be careful! Do not cut me!" When the fish was cut open, and he got out, he said to his wife, "I wish to have the choice pieces of this fish saved for me, for I caught it." Then his wife was angry, and she began to beat him, and she knocked him about on the sandbar, while the strips of skin on his forehead flew about. At last Wihio begged his wife to cut off the strips, and she did so.

A SCABBY BULL

ONE time in the spring a herd of scabby bulls were lying together on the prairie. Presently one of them rose to his feet and went up on the hill. He stood there for a time, looking about, and then turned and ran down toward the other bulls. Just before he reached them, he stopped and shook himself, and all the old hair came off his body, so that he stood there naked. Then the bull went to the herd, and lay down among them.

After a little while he rose again and went up on the hill, as before. Again he ran down to the other bulls, stopped and shook himself, and short new hairs came out all over him. Once more he lay down.

Again he got up and went to the top of the hill, and again ran down, and stopped and shook himself, and he turned into an old scabby bull again. He went over and lay down.

A fourth time he went up on the hill, and came down running as hard as he could, and shook himself, and at once he was covered with new long hair, and looked round and smooth.

Wihio came out from behind the hill, where he had been watching, and went up to the bulls, crying; "Oh," he said, "I want to be able to do that; I want to be a bull."

The bull said, "You saw what I did, and where I stopped; you do the same; do just as I did."

Wihio went up on the hill and did as the bull had done, and when he shook himself he turned into a scabby bull. He did not wait long; he went up, and then ran down again and shook himself, and was covered with new hair. The third time he turned into a scabby bull when he shook himself. The fourth time he did it he had fine long new hair. He liked this; so soon he went up again, and again ran down and shook himself, and turned into a scabby bull again.

"Ah," said his bull friend, "you are now really a bull, and you must look out for people, because they kill us. We can smell them if we get to leeward of them, and if we see or smell them we must run hard." Soon all the bulls got up and went on, and Wihio with them.

Before they had gone far, Wihio called out, "Look out! I can smell them; they are coming." The other bulls turned up their noses, but could smell nothing; but Wihio was frightened, and kept thinking he could smell something.

The bulls traveled a long way, and at last were tired and lay down. Wihio was very tired and went to sleep. After a time the other bulls got up and went on, leaving Wihio sleeping there, and when he awoke he was alone. When he saw that he was alone, he thought that the people had chased the other bulls away, and he was frightened almost to death. He ran this way and that way, and fell down steep places, and into ravines, and bruised himself badly. Sometimes he would call out, "I am not a bull, I am Wihio." It sounded just like the grunting of a bull. The more he ran, the more frightened he was, and he ran until he could run no longer.

HOW HE GOT TONGUE

WIHIO was living in his home, and not far away was a camp of people. One day he had nothing to eat, and no way to kill anything; so he paid a visit to one of his neighbors, hoping that he would be asked to eat with him.

When Wihio stepped into the lodge he saw that there was plenty of food there—dried meat and back-fat and tongues.

Every time the man went out he killed an elk, and when he did so he took the tongue out and saved it, and tongues hung all about his lodge. Wihio longed for the tongues, but the man did not offer him any; he just gave him some dried meat. As Wihio was returning to his lodge, he saw a coyote not far off, and called to him, asking him to come in.

When the coyote had sat down, Wihio told him about what he had seen in the man's lodge, and he asked the coyote to go there with him again, so they might eat there.

The coyote thought the man would not let him come in, because everyone knows that coyotes always steal meat.

"Well," said Wihio, "let us arrange some plan by which you can come. What can we do? How can we get in?" The coyote thought for a long time, and at last he told Wihio how they might do what they wished to. The coyote said: "Do you dress up like a woman, and tie me up like a baby, and carry me there. Give me good things to eat when you get the meat."

"Ah," said Wihio, "it is good; I will give you a part of everything that is given to me." Then he began to tie up the coyote like a baby, so that he could carry him. After he had done so he took up the coyote on his arm like a baby, and went back to the lodge and said to the man, "My child is crying for food." Wihio whispered to the coyote to cry for tongue, and he did so. The man asked Wihio what the baby wanted, and Wihio said, "He is crying for tongue." The man took a tongue and put it in the water and boiled it.

After the tongue was cooked the man gave it to Wihio, who began to eat, and gave the coyote only just a taste of it. Wihio ate all he could, for he was hungry. The coyote kept whispering to him, "Give me some too; I am hungry"; but Wihio continued to eat, and just dipped his fingers in the soup and let the coyote lick them. At last the coyote grew angry and said, "I am going to tell him about you, that you have dressed me up like a baby in order to get some tongue."

Wihio kept on eating very fast, and gave the coyote none of the tongue, and at last went out of the lodge, carrying the baby. He went to the river, and said to the coyote: "You were going to tell of me, were you? You ought to keep quiet when I am eating; you trouble me too much." Then he threw the coyote, all tied up, into the river, and he floated down the stream.

THE TURNING STONES

ONE day Wihio was walking along over the prairie when he saw a man going about commanding stones to turn over, and at once they turned over without being touched.

Wihio watched the man until he had done this several times, and then he walked up to him crying, and spoke to him, saying, "My brother, I am poor; take pity on me; I want to do this."

The man said, "Do not cry, friend; this is easy. I will tell you how to do it; but if I tell you, you must do just as I say; otherwise trouble will come to you."

The man gave him his power, and told him to exercise it only four times, and Wihio said he would do so. He was glad to have this power, and he turned over one rock after another; but after he had done this two or three times he could not remember how many times he had done it, and when he turned over the fourth stone he said, "This is three times."

When he tried it the fifth time, the great stone, instead of turning over away from him, as all the others had, turned over toward him, and began to roll at him. Wihio ran back to get out of the way, but the stone rolled after him, and he ran away from it. The rock kept rolling after him, and chased him far until he was very tired and could just stagger along ahead of the rock, which was hitting his heels at every step. Presently Wihio fell down, tired out, and the rock rolled over him, and held him to the ground, lying on his chest. Wihio struggled and squirmed, but he could not move the stone. After he was caught he called for help. The buffalo came, and ran at the stone, hitting it with their heads, and trying to push it away, but they only broke their horns; they could not move it. Other animals tried, but they could not do it. Wihio kept looking about for help, but there was none.

At last he saw a bird in the sky—a nighthawk flying—and called to it, saying: "Ah, little brother, this stone has been saying bad things about you; it said you had a round head and big eyes, a pinched-up beak and a wide mouth, and that you were a very ugly bird. I told him not to speak so, but when I said this to him he jumped on me, and holds me down."

When the nighthawk heard this he flew far up in the sky, and then darted straight down and struck the stone squarely in the middle, and it broke into many pieces, which flew in different directions. Then Wihio was able to get up and walk away.

THE WONDERFUL SACK

A LONG time ago a man was living in a lodge by himself. He had no wife nor family, but about his lodge much meat was hanging on the branches and the drying scaffolds, and he had many hides and robes.

One day Wihio came that way, and entered the lodge and spoke to the man, saying: "I am glad that I have found you, my brother; I have been looking for you for a long time, and have asked everyone where you were. At last I got sure news about you, and learned where your lodge was; so I came straight to you."

After Wihio had said this the man began to cook food for him; and while he was cooking, Wihio was sitting there looking about the lodge. Tied up to a lodge pole at the back of the lodge was a great sack. Wihio could not think what might be in this sack, and kept wondering what it contained. The longer he looked at it the more curious he grew.

After he had eaten, Wihio said to the man, "My brother, may I sleep here tonight with you?" The man said, "Yes, yes; stay if you wish."

When night came they made up the beds to sleep. The man had been watching Wihio, and had seen him looking at the sack, and thought that Wihio wished to take it; so he took a cupful of water and put it on the ground at the back side of the fire, in front of the sack.

Soon they went to bed, and the man fell asleep; but Wihio did not sleep; he lay there watching and listening.

When the man was sleeping, Wihio arose, and reached up and untied the sack from the lodge pole, and put it on his back and started out of the lodge, carrying it.

Before he had gone far he suddenly came to the shores of a big lake, and started to go around it, running fast so that the man should not overtake him. He ran until nearly morning along the shores of this lake, which seemed to have no end. By this time he was very tired and sleepy; so he lay down to rest a little, the sack being still on his back so that he could start again just as soon as he awoke.

In the morning when the man awoke, he saw Wihio lying there with his head on the sack, and said to him, "My brother, what are you doing with my sack?" Wihio awoke, and was very much astonished to find himself still in the lodge. He did not know how to answer the man, but at last he said, "My brother, you have treated me so nicely that I was going to offer to carry your sack for you when you moved." The man took the sack and tied it to the lodge pole, where it belonged.

After they had eaten, they sat there talking, and Wihio said to the man, "My brother, what are you afraid of?" The man replied, "My brother, I am afraid of nothing except a goose."

Wihio said, "I also am afraid of that; a goose is a very dangerous bird." After a little while Wihio said to the man, "My brother, I am going," and he went out.

When night came, Wihio came back to the camp in the shape of a goose, and went behind the lodge and called loudly. The man was frightened and took his sack on his back, and rushed out of the lodge and ran away; and Wihio was glad, and went back to where he had left his wife and family. When he got to them he said: "My children, I am glad; now I have got what I have long wished for. I have driven from his lodge a person who has a good home and plenty of food. We will go there and live."

After they reached the lodge, Wihio told his wife about the sack, saying to her, "I want to find out what is in that sack, and I shall follow that man until I do so."

When they had eaten, Wihio set out to follow the tracks of the man, to see where he had gone. He followed him for a long time, but at last he found him, and again called out like a goose, and frightened the man. But when the man ran away he carried the sack with him. Twice more Wihio frightened him, and each time when the man ran away he took the sack; but the fourth time he left it behind him, and Wihio took it. But when the man dropped the sack he called out, saying, "I can open that sack only four times." Now Wihio put the sack on his back, and went back to the lodge, and said to his wife, "Well, I have got the thing I wished for."

After he had reached the lodge, Wihio untied the sack and opened the mouth, for he wished to see what was in it. As soon as he opened the mouth, a buffalo ran out, and the heads of other cows were seen crowding toward the mouth of the sack. Then Wihio quickly tied it up again.

"Aha," he said, "that is the way I shall do." He killed the buffalo, and they had plenty of food. When all the meat was gone he opened the sack again, and another cow ran out, and he tied up the sack and killed the cow.

When this meat was gone he let out another buffalo, and then again; but he had forgotten to keep count of the buffalo he had killed, and when he had opened the sack the fourth time he said, "That is three times."

A fifth time he opened the sack, and the moment it was opened many buffalo rushed out, and he could not close the sack. They came out in such numbers that they trampled on and killed him and all his family. Not one was left alive.

The buffalo started north and south and west and east, and spread all over the world. This is where the buffalo came from; and this is the last of Wihio.